NEPANTLA²

Expanding Frontiers:
Interdisciplinary
Approaches to Studies
of Women, Gender, and
Sexuality

SERIES EDITORS:

Karen J. Leong
Andrea Smith

NEPANTLA SQUARED

Transgender Mestiz@ Histories
in Times of Global Shift

LINDA HEIDENREICH

University of Nebraska Press / Lincoln

Library of Congress Cataloging-in-Publication Data
Names: Heidenreich, Linda, 1964– author.
Title: Nepantla squared: transgender mestiz@ histories in times of global shift / Linda Heidenreich.
Description: Lincoln: University of Nebraska Press, [2020] | Series: Expanding frontiers: interdisciplinary approaches to studies of women, gender, and sexuality | Includes bibliographical references and index.
Identifiers: LCCN 2020010787
ISBN 9781496213402 (hardback)
ISBN 9781496221964 (paperback)
ISBN 9781496222398 (epub)
ISBN 9781496222404 (mobi)
ISBN 9781496222411 (pdf)
Subjects: LCSH: Transgender people—History. | Mestizos—History. | Mestizaje—History. | Feminist theory. | Queer theory.
Classification: LCC HQ77.9 .H438 2020
DDC 306.76/809—dc23
LC record available at https://lccn.loc.gov/2020010787

Set in Chaparral Pro by Laura Buis.

With gratitude to
Dolores del Carmen Heidenreich
Karen Gallaghar
Guadalupe Tonantzín

CONTENTS

ILLUSTRATIONS

ACKNOWLEDGMENTS

For most scholars the research and crafting of a monograph can take years, weaving in and out of the many challenges of their lives. So it was for *Nepantla²*. This journey began with research into the life of a young transgender woman, Gwen Amber Rose Araujo, whose life was cut short due to the fear and hate of peers, also young, who had learned to perform their masculinity through violence. In trying to make sense of a world that could produce so much violence, by and against young people, the project grew and evolved, as did the questions driving it. The vectors critical to understanding our violent world multiplied and wove themselves into the text that you hold in your hands: one about economic shifts, about gender, about the ancient philosophers of Anahuac who gifted us the philosophy of nepantla, about labor activists and Zapatistas, and about a fierce Chicana feminist by the name of Gloria E. Anzaldúa.

And so I wrote, and as I wrote my perspectives on life, gender, and the universe shifted and fluxed. Friends died, elders aged, sobrinos birthed babies, presidential elections came and went, and the earth continued to warm. As someone who identifies as queer, mestiz@, materialist, and Catholic, I believe that my history and all my selves play a critical role in shaping my lens—my ability to understand our past and to dream and shape both the present and the future. This work, then, emerged from a world and life of motion-change, and is very much about change: California's economic and cultural shifts with the emergence of monopoly capitalism, and the more recent economic and cultural shifts bringing us into the epoch of global capitalism.

Earlier versions of chapters 2 and 4 were published as journal articles. Thus, I thank the *Journal of Chicana/Latina Studies* for allowing me to use material from "Learning from the Death of Gwen Araujo?—Transphobic Racial Subordination and Queer Latina Survival in the Twenty-First Century" (vol. 6, no. 1 [Fall 2006]: 50–86), and its editorial staff and readers for their incredible insights and editing of that earlier work. Similarly, an earlier iteration of chapter 4 appeared as "Jack Mugarrieta Garland: A Queer Mestiz@ in the 'American West,'" in *Lilith: A Feminist History Journal* 21 (August 2015): 65–77, with generous support and insights from their staff and readers. The editors of these two journals continue to promote gendered, scholarly work that not only allows but also encourages historians and other humanities scholars to think outside the box.

As much as writing a monograph is a journey, it is not one that we take alone. For the historian, archives are the water of life, and several of them were critical to the making of *Nepantla²*. The GLBT Historical Society, in San Francisco, California, is a treasure trove for anyone researching our histories. The welcoming and supportive staff there made the early research of this project joyful. Similarly, the staff at the San Francisco History Center, in the main branch of the San Francisco Public Library, consistently went beyond the standard commitment to helping patrons find sources. At the San Francisco History Center it was refreshing to see archivists who treated everyone who came through their doors with the utmost respect, valuing everyone's project—not just those who seemed to be more important. Later in the project it was the staff at the Nettie Lee Benson Latin American Collection who created an atmosphere welcoming to scholars of all ages. There were, of course, many other sites critical to making this work a reality, and while I cannot list them all here, I can express my gratefulness that so many of the places where I conducted the research for this work were welcoming. To have a world in which all of us can shape our narratives, we must have archivists, such as those at the places listed above, who welcome all who come searching for answers.

I live and work at a university on the Washington-Idaho border, amid fields of wheat, lentils, and chickpeas on land that if not for colonizing wars would still be in the hands of the Palus and the Nimiipuu people. Grants from Washington State University, my home institution, in the form of an initiation grant at the beginning of the project and a block grant when I needed to go back to California to hit up one last archive, made this work possible. Noel Sturgeon was, in the early years of the project, absolutely the most supportive chair a scholar could ever hope for. My colegas in the Department of Women's Studies made our space a productive and supportive one: Judy Meuth, Marian Sciachitano, Pam Thoma, and Nishant Shahani—they all rock. I thank them for their collaboration on the important stuff, especially movies and birthdays and bowling. Thanks to Nishant Shahani for input on many of these chapters and for keeping me honest with our weekly writing time. And our manuscripts collection staff, especially Trevor Bond, again made time to help me with images.

While archives may be the water of life, public libraries are in close competition for that title. Most of the newspaper research for the chapter on Babe Bean was completed at the Chavez branch of the Stockton Public Library, home to fabulous librarians and old-school microfilm machines. The San Joaquin historical society was generous with its resources, and a gentleman by the name of Mike Fitzgerald from the *Stockton Daily News* helped me to chase down images of McLeod Lake. Mike's love and enthusiasm for Stockton history is absolutely contagious. While he may be retired by the time this goes to print I do hope that his column will remain available online for years to come. Finally, in Stockton as well, it was the Haggin Museum that generously provided me with images of McLeod Lake, the home of Babe Bean in the late 1890s.

Over the years I presented various versions of book chapters at the annual conferences of the National Association for Chicana and Chicano Studies (NACCS), the summer institute for Mujeres Activas en Letras y Cambio Social (MALCS), and Mundo Zurdo, the conference of the Society for the Study of Gloria Anzaldúa. It was in these vibrant spaces that I received invaluable input, critiques, and consejos on the project. Antonia Castañeda, who always makes time to read our stuff, of course provided input at these gatherings. I am grateful for her faith in our work and in our generation. Thanks to las mujeres of MALCS for their years of support and mentorship and for creating spaces where we can share our work and refuel for the year ahead. And thanks to Rita Urquijo Ruiz, Démian Pritchard, and Irene Mata for being there during the many ups and downs of the manuscript, sitting in on paper presentations at NACCS, MALCS, and Mundo Zurdo, but most of all for their hermandad.

Karen Leong, whom I met at the annual conference of the Western History Association, persuaded me to send this work to the University of Nebraska Press for its Expanding Frontiers series. She is an amazing scholar who is invested in the work of colleagues old and new, and is committed to making the Western History Association a place where innovative work can happen. Karen and Andrea Smith read the early chapters and provided critical input on moving the manuscript forward. When it was nearly completed, graduate students Verónica Sandoval and Leigh Gaskin labored over the bibliography and inspired me with their own work.

Interviews are at the heart of much of this work. Researching survival in violent times means asking people to take risks and to be vulnerable. Several people generously gave time to speak with me about difficult but critical histories: Connie Champagne, of Community United against Violence, and Christopher Daley, of the Transgender Law Center, spoke with me when this project was still very much in its inception. Isa Noyola, of the Transgender Law Center (TLC), took time from her busy schedule for an interview toward the close of the project. Thanks also go to the staff of TLC, especially Adrian Martínez and Ola Osaze, for allowing me to hang out and volunteer for a couple of weeks in 2016. The work done by TLC continues to inspire me and remains a beacon to those of us who work among the wheat fields. Finally, I can never say thank you enough to Sylvia Guerrero, Gwen's mom, who talked with me following the violent passing of her daughter. Sylvia's activism continues to inspire me. In writing and excavating the histories of those of us whom the dominant institutions of our society would marginalize, interviews and voices are critical. The written word is not enough.

The support of multiple communities was necessary to make this work possible, and I know that I am missing many of them here. But I close with a final note of thanks. To my family at Sacred Heart, especially the Sacred Heart walkers and Beth Buyserie; to my brother George and his family for welcoming me into their Stockton home so that I could make full use of the resources in their city; to George, to my mother, Dolores Heidenreich, and to my spouse, Karen Gallaghar, for their love and patience digo gracias de todo corazón.

As mestiz@s and as Chican@ people, we understand *nepantla*, in-between spaces, as shaping our world and our lives, and as you will read in the following chapters, it is this philosophy that clearly shapes this work. Yet it is also strongly shaped by the world of science fiction and my belief that we must think outside the box if we are to change our communities and our larger society for the good. Thus, as the labor for this text came to a close, I realized that in addition to the philosophy of nepantla, the world of science fiction also influenced how I read the past—specifically the prophetic work of Octavia Butler. It was her work, *The Parable of the Sower*, where the idea that *we* shape the world and shape the deity was introduced to readers of science fiction. Butler's fictive religion of Earthseed—that "All that you touch you Change. All that you Change Changes you. The only lasting truth is Change"—resonates and weaves through our nepantlan times. The faith echoes that of the sixteenth-century mystic Teresa of Ávila, with one significant difference: Ávila wrote, "All is change, God alone is constant." In writing and researching histories of socioeconomic shifts, gendered lives, and people's resistance, I have become convinced that "all is change" and we do shape it.

INTRODUCTION

History as Nepantla[2]

> Is this in fact what we are bearing witness to: the end of one epoch and the painful birthing of another?
> —Cherríe Moraga, preface to *This Bridge Called My Back*

Nepantla is an ancient philosophy that views the world through motion-change, insisting that rather than a great chain of being, or survival of the fittest, the world is a great cloth—woven through with energy. The creative energy is made manifest in both positive and negative ways—energy, events, and happenings pushing and pulling in and out of each other like the warp and weft of a great loom.[1] It is a philosophy that dominated Anahuac prior to the arrival of the Spaniards, perhaps prior to the founding of Tenochtitlan. We know it was developed most fully by the poets and philosophers of central Mexico during the time of the Aztec empire. For many, including myself, it continues to influence our worldview today. I am determined that nepantla is key to understanding our past and our present—that unless we can understand the time of motion-change in which we live, we risk total subjugation by global capital. That this philosophy intersects with the more recent work of trans scholars of color is not coincidental; as will be discussed below, it is scholars such as C. Riley Snorton and Kale Bantigue Fajardo who are mapping the trans-ness of space and time—drawing our attention to the multiple ways that gender, space, and time are indeed part of a great weave.[2] As Snorton's *Black on Both Sides* was and is "an effort to think expansively about . . . blackness and black studies, and transness and trans studies," so this work is an attempt to think expansively about Chicanx-ness, Chicanx history and Chicanx studies, and transness, trans history, and trans studies.[3] It is about political economy, space, history, gender, globalization, and resistance in motion.

I came to the philosophy of nepantla through the work of Gloria Anzaldúa, the Chicana theorist who wrote of nepantla as "lugar de medio" and a space "where you are changing."[4] During the summer of 2015 I was able to spend time in her archive at the University of Texas, Austin, and there discovered that her connection to nepantla, like mine, was also very tied to political economy. As I write in chapter 1, it was she who noted the connection between nepantla as motion-change and the late twentieth-century emergence of the Ejército Zapatista de Liberación Nacional (EZLN), slowly mapping out, in her notes, how they are connected.[5]

Yet I am a mestiza very different from Gloria Anzaldúa. I am a Euro-Chican@ mix, with siblings and cousins from around the color wheel, some assimilated, some not, some deciding that Mexico is still home, some so far from home that the first colonial language is long lost.[6] My maternal grandparents hailed from Mexico and Costa Rica. Yet having an amateur genealogist in the family, I learned as a young adult that our roots, on the Alcazar side of the family, were Arab—a family of Moriscos moving away from the metropol back in the age of colonization, when things were looking bad for anyone who lacked *limpieza de sangre*.[7] This heritage is different from that of friends and colleagues who trace their own histories to the resistance of Yaqui peoples—or who spent their summers under admonitions to stay out of the sun so as not to look Indigenous. It is this mixing, the marrying back and forth (marry whom you love), and moving back and forth until the border became too heavily militarized, the cartel violence too visible, and the cost of plane tickets too outrageous, that shaped and shape my lens. Perhaps it is the movement and fluidity of my own family or perhaps it is the influence of Chicanx studies— the first classroom where I heard my own family histories reflected in any dominant narrative—that birthed this deep resonance within me. What I can tell you is that for this gender queer, Euro-Chican@, who traces their mestiz@ roots back to Catholic converts fleeing an increasingly hostile metropol, nepantla helps me to make sense of our past and our world.

As a scholar-activist who believes that our subject positions matter, that, as Alicia Gaspar de Alba explains, "we do not see irrespective of our bodies, nor can we see the subjects of our study . . . outside of the bodies that have produced them or of the historical political, or cultural context in which they have been produced," my social location is important for you, the reader, to understand as framing, at least in part, this work.[8] Nepantla, through the lens of my own body and history, helps me to understand how it is that those of us who live in between genders are so visible in times of economic motion-change; and it helps me to understand how we—those of us who live in the interstices of Western culture—might hold the key to engaging the epochal shift in which we now find ourselves.

While the early chapters of this volume focus on periods when the label transgender did not exist, I choose to employ the term in a manner similar to that of Susan Stryker and C. Riley Snorton. Historian and queer theorist Stryker notes: "Some people move away from their birth-assigned gender because they feel strongly that they properly belong to another gender in which it would be better for them to live; others want to strike out toward some new location, some space not yet clearly defined or concretely occupied. . . . [Transgender] is the movement across a socially imposed boundary away from an unchosen starting place."[9] Throughout this book I use *transgender* for nineteenth-century people who moved away from their birth-assigned gender as well as for twentieth- and twenty-first-century people who overtly claim/ed the term.

Yet as C. Riley Snorton and Kale Bantigue Fajardo have noted, transgender can also move us beyond Western binaries and labels of containment. Transgender can call attention to relationships and movement. Challenging binaries, Snorton engages the term *trans* as a way to speak "more about movement with no clear origin and no point of arrival."[10] Fajardo, likewise, mobilized and engaged the concept of transgender to "emphasize the transnational, trans-Pacific, and transport connections between the Philippines and regional and diasporic geographies."[11] While our contemporary politics sometimes push us to use neat and discrete labels such as transgender to fight for basic human rights, trans and transgender can signify a rejection of binaries and encompass movement across and through gender, history, space, and time. Trans is nepantlan. Throughout this text trans is engaged as an identity label, as a political label, and as movement and resistance.

Trans mestiz@, then, calls attention to the trans-ness of my subjects, while also engaging the @, as does Frank Galarte, to refuse the binary implied by *mestiza/o*. In this text *trans* and *transgender* function as umbrella terms to draw attention to the many ways that all of our struggles are connected—even while the privilege that we bring from our specific social locations is very different in terms of racial, spatial, and class privilege as well as in terms of gender privilege. Poor and working-class transgender women of color receive the brunt of violence throughout the western hemisphere, and as will be discussed in chapters 4 and 5, we all need to mobilize resources to end the reign of terror that so many trans people are not surviving.[12] One key to ending that terror, I argue, is to map the role of global capital in shaping our gendered lives, and to use multiple visions and strategies to transform the current epoch. While at times I am threatened by male persons who become angry when they cannot assign me a comfortable gender, the quantity and quality of the violence I negotiate pales in comparison to that of transgender women, especially transgender women of color. I am convinced that it is only by creating a safer world for transgender women of color that I will ever be safe. In part, my work is very selfish.

And so I offer you a map. Sitting in an office on land taken from the Palus and the Nimiipuu, I work in a region of motion-change where many of us have yet to fully grapple with the change around us. History is motion; it will stop only when life stops.[13] The map I offer here is strongly shaped by my embodied experience of motion-change. I am Euro-Chican@ and gender-queer. Binaries erase my existence. Because I see all history as genealogy in the Foucauldian sense of the word—messy and incomplete and heavy with possibilities—this project rejects binaries and pulls the bodies of labor organizers into the broad and expansive umbrella of trans and queer. Using nepantla as my tool, I map the weave of nineteenth-century economic shifts and I map the weave of the economic shift of our current era. Looking at visible transgender lives during these epochal shifts in capital, we can gain deep and useful understandings both of how gender is constructed and contained, and of how capital functions to create the social structures within which we live. In this, our epochal shift to totalizing global capital, whether we are able to resist and envision a different future or must succumb to a totalizing system of exploitation, where our bodies are valued primarily as machines that produce surplus value, will depend on our ability to map and challenge the dispersed power that is weaving our era. This book on nepantla is my "granito de arena" toward the dream and realization of revolutionary resistance.

Tools for Mapping

This is a queer Chicanx history project. Those of us who engage in queer Chicanx history know that the field is, of necessity, interdisciplinary. Rodolfo Acuña, in mapping the status of Chicanx history at the dawn of the twenty-first century, pointed out that the field pulls/pools tools from a number of disciplines; it is rooted in the liberation movements of the 1960s and '70s. At its best it makes use of theoretical tools, such as neo-Marxism, that offer "useful paradigms" for understanding structural inequalities—it is eclectic.[14] Similarly, Roderick Ferguson, in developing a queer of color analysis, noted that such analysis is necessarily "a heterogeneous enterprise, made up of woman of color feminism, materialist analysis, post structuralist theory, and queer critique."[15] Thus queer Chicanx methodologies are plural—and they are overtly oppositional—making strategic use of multiple and shifting methodologies to meet the multiple and shifting challenges of our lives.[16] The requisite tools for mapping the motion-change of the last epochal shift in capital, as well as the present shift, weave together to make this study possible: Chicanx history, Chicana feminism, LGBTQ studies, globalization studies, and of course the queen of them all—queer Chicanx studies. Below find my mapping of the tools that make *Nepantla²* possible. Those of you who read the volume from cover to cover will notice that I also pull from critical race studies (especially LatCrit) and materialist economic theories, and so I offer a note regarding specific works from both fields at the close of this genealogy.

To(o) Queer the Chican@

The queer Chicanx methodology engaged throughout this text finds its deepest roots in the groundbreaking work of Chicana feminist scholars and activists of the late twentieth century. The subheading itself is taken from Anzaldúa's influential "To(o) Queer the Chicana," in which she argued for the role of subject position in writing and reading queer Chicana work, called for a more diversified body of queer scholarship, and reminded readers that lesbian and queer are not, substantially, the same thing.[17] Looking at the intersections of race, class, and gender would tell us as much. These lessons, passed onto us from her generation, a generation of scholar-activists, continue to influence Chicanx scholarship, especially queer Chicanx scholarship.

Of course counterhegemonic work prior to the renaissance in Chicana feminisms in part created the foundation for that change, with George I. Sánchez, Jovita González, Américo Paredes, and Ernesto Galarza speaking back to the producers of knowledge and common sense early in the twentieth century. Like these early works, *Nepantla²* rejects all claims to American exceptionalism, acknowledging that trans mestiz@ lives, in the United States and throughout the Americas, struggled within a context of empire and capitalist exploitation.[18] When, in chapter 2, I address Jack's involvement in the Spanish-American War, it is in this painful context where even trans forefathers, in striving for survival, became complicit in the larger destructive forces of motion-change in their own time.

One of the strongest influences on this text, and perhaps on the broader field of queer Chicanx studies, is Chicana feminist scholarship. Like early Chicano studies Chicana feminist scholarship challenged, and continues to challenge, disciplinary boundaries; it insisted on scholarship that is useful, and it sexed and gendered the curriculum. Chicana feminist periodicals such as *Encuentro Feminil*, founded in 1973, took the lead in centering Chicana experiences and challenging patriarchy.[19] *Encuentro* mapped the ways in which Chicana struggles were and are "racial as well as sexual."[20] *Encuentro Feminíl, Regeneración,* and *El Grito Del Norte* were rooted in the intersections of race and gender, activism and scholarship.[21] As in Ferguson's work, the interdisciplinarity and intersectionality of this text are not new tools but ones rooted in women of color feminisms, specifically Chicana feminism.

It was this generation of Chicana feminists who also looked to the past to understand the present and to imagine a different future. Nowhere is this use of the past to create the future more apparent than in Chicana reclamations and retrofittings of the archetypes that were too often used to contain Chicanas: La Llorona, Our Lady of Guadalupe, and Malintzín Tenepal.[22] In a climate where the men in the movement often labeled Chicana activists "Malinches," the women struck back with their activism and with their pens. The result was a queering of Malinche and other archetypes once used to contain and constrain Chicanas.[23] As noted by Esquivel, Chicana lesbians were central not only to the reclamation of cultural symbols and historical figures but also to the development of Chicana feminist analysis.[24] That is to say, from its beginnings Chicana feminist scholarship was very queer and, in relation, today's queer Chicanx scholarship is very feminista. It is my hope that throughout *Nepantla²* the voices of Anzaldúa, Castañeda, Apodaca, and other foundational Chicana feminist voices will ring clearly and that *Nepantla²* will contribute to the fabric and legacy of this work.

While the foundational Chicana feminist texts of the late twentieth century strongly influence this text in its intersectionality and insistence on racing and classing gendered histories, the decade of the 1970s also saw the publication of María Linda Apodaca's "The Chicana Woman: An Historical Materialist Perspective," with its foundational critique of capitalism. Apodaca's work, like that of Rosaura Sánchez among Chicana literary scholars, insisted on the importance of a materialist analysis to all Chicana scholarship. Through her mapping of socioeconomic systems prior to both 1846 and 1521, Apodaca argued that a gendered and materialist analysis is the key to challenging structural inequalities today. And equally important, she articulated a theme that continued and continues to influence and drive Chicana scholars to do the work at hand: "We must have histories that can be the basis for future social action."[25] It is the work of Apodaca as well as historians such as Vicki L. Ruiz, Antonia Castañeda, and Deena González that allows those of us who produce queer Chicanx histories to insist on work that is materialist and intersectional.[26] Jack Garland was a trans mestiz@ who came of age in the time of motion-change when the United States was expanding its empire, one driven by a racialized monopoly capitalism that would force one of Garland's siblings to seek survival through extralegal means. It would also push Garland himself to the spatial margins of Stockton, California, and, later, San Francisco. Likewise, the access of Gwen Araujo's family to resources following her death would pale in contrast to those accessed by the family of Matthew Shepard because of the specific ways that gendered and raced capital shaped the lives of both families.

As will be discussed in chapter 2, it is *Borderlands: La Nueva Mestiza*, as well as Gloria Anzaldúa's earlier work addressing "un Mundo Zurdo," that remains among the strongest influences for this volume.[27] While some scholars, such as Sheila Marie Contreras, critique *Borderlands* for its broad use of anthropological texts and use of the mythic over the historical, it is often Anzaldúa's hybrid use of such sources that continues to speak to so many Chican@s and mestiz@s today. For Chicanx historians, reflecting on and noting the relationships between Chicanx and Indigenous histories will remain critical as Indigenous communities continue to strive for land sovereignty. Thus, like Morgensen, I approach Anzaldúa as a scholar who worked on the borderlands of indigeneity.[28] Part of the power of Anzaldúa's work is that she claimed and constructed a mestiza identity not as a denial of her Indigenous roots but as an embracing thereof.[29] Perhaps her most famous line, "This land was Mexican once, is Indian always," best describes the overlap and tensions between our communities. Even while Mexico claimed this land, it was, in fact, "Indian always." We do our best work when we can see that history. As a Chicanx historian whose work is rooted, in part, in that of Anzaldúa, this work is necessarily one of hybridity and borderlands.

To be Chicana and feminist in the 1970s and '80s, when Anzaldúa wrote, was a very queer thing indeed; to write queer Chicanx history in the twenty-first century is possible only because of the Chicana feminists of the seventies and eighties. This work remains faithful to the liberatory values taught to us by that generation even while incorporating new tools from related communities and disciplines.[30]

New Threads

While Chicanx studies, especially that devoted to feminist and queer topics, provides many of the tools necessary for constructing a text such as *Nepantla²*, queer Chicanx scholarship, like the world in which we live, is woven from multiple overlapping threads, themes, textiles. Thus LGBTQ studies, as an interdiscipline that overlaps with queer Chicanx studies, provided multiple and diverse tools for the construction of this work. To a large extent, this study builds on the work of Leslie Feinberg.[31] Like *Transgender Warriors*, it is a work of excavation, mapping the lives of two transgender warriors who struggled to survive in the heteropatriarchal world of their times.[32] Like *Trans Liberation*, it attempts to theorize lives, to learn something from their struggles that might aid other queer Chicanxs who do not fit into the dominant gender categories of the early twenty-first century.

While Feinberg's work is central to this text, other authors addressing Euro-American transgender experiences also produced critical work that make possible much of the emerging transgender scholarship, including that by Patrick Califia, Susan Stryker, and J. Halberstam in their critical theorizing of the functions of transgender lives and realities in the larger, dominant U.S. society.[33] For example, it was Califia in 1997 who, highlighting the legacy of Louis Sullivan, boldly challenged lesbian historians for appropriating the life of Jack Garland.[34] The work of these scholars continues to challenge gendered violence in the United States, making critical contributions to everyday survival. Peter Boag's sweeping history of cross-dressing in the U.S. national West stands as a reminder of the importance of intersectional analysis, as does the work of Clare Sears and Emily Skidmore.[35]

As this work builds on the foundations established by queer and feminist Chicanx scholars, the recent innovations of trans scholars of color from other racialized communities both provide critical tools for understanding our trans Chicanx past and demonstrate the varied and historically grounded roots of our work. Again the words of Alicia Gaspar de Alba come to mind: "We do not see irrespective of our bodies, nor can we see the subjects of our study . . . outside of the bodies that have produced them or of the historical political, or cultural context in which they have been produced."[36] Thus Kale Bantigue Fajardo's expansive use of *trans*, "evoking movement across and inbetween spaces" and "movement between and across culturally constructed and racialized and classed masculinities and femininities, as well as movement in/through/between spaces," helps make intelligible not only the nepantlan movement of trans historical figures such as Jack Garland, a trans man who constructed his masculine self through movement, but also the movement and movements of the EZLN as its adherents moved from and into the communities of southern Chiapas, challenging women's roles and insisting that resistance to global capital is not futile.[37] As Fajardo deployed transgender to "emphasize the transnational, trans-pacific, and transport connections and cultural flows between the Philippines, and regional and diasporic geographies," so *Nepantla²* deploys transgender to emphasize the movement of Mexican and Honduran immigrants and refugees north, in a space which, like the Pacific Ocean, has become a site of intense motion-change of goods and people and capital.[38]

While Fajardo's work is strongly rooted in his Filipino history and heritage, Snorton's work, while providing critical tools for trans history and for trans studies in general, emerges from a space of blackness, where blackness is a "condition of possibility."[39] As trans intersects with blackness, then it becomes a vital tool for mapping and analyzing not only sex and sexuality but also ways of being. Building directly on the work of Kai M. Green and Treva Ellison, Snorton mobilizes trans as "a politic and epistemic operation that attempts to bring forth 'forms of collective life that can enliven and sustain us in a future worth living.'"[40] *Nepantla²* moves beyond static historical excavation to engage trans as a fierce Chicanx tool, intersecting with our Chican@ histories, lives, politics, and migrations. Trans, in the expansive and powerful sense of the word mobilized by Fajardo and Snorton, as well as Green and Ellison, helps to expose the multiple connections that weave and connect transgender men and women,

Zapatistas, refugees, and capital throughout history but especially in times of global shift.

Critically Queer

Critical race theory (CRT) and critical queer studies, fields that emerged out of the critical race scholarship of the 1980s, are a third key element influencing this project. CRT scholars such as Kimberlé Crenshaw, Daren Richard Hutchinson, and Francisco Valdes shaped and shape this work.[41] It was queer crit scholar Dean Spade who mapped how hate crimes legislation, while valuing our communities through symbolic justice, bolsters the carceral system that today flourishes in U.S. society, making more vulnerable the most vulnerable among LGBTQ communities. The Matthew Shepard and James Byrd Jr. Hate Crimes Prevention Act, for example, "provides millions of dollars to enhance police and prosecutorial resources."[42] While, after the murder of Gwen Amber Araujo, I initially embraced hate crimes legislation, wanting through any means to say our lives matter, the lives of our young people matter, the work of Dean Spade made me see that legislation such as hate crimes bills often cause more harm than good to most of our interwoven communities.[43] *Normal Life* pushed my analysis of Gwen's life and death, and the activism that flowed from her loss, to expand and critique the possibilities of trans activism. All of the above fields and vibrant interdisciplines produce texts that are useful to nepantler@ scholars and activists. Chicana feminist Tey Diana Rebolledo called us to accountability almost two decades ago, when in "The Politics of Poetics" she reminded us of Sor Juana's now classic critique of Aristotle: "He would have been a better philosopher had he studied cooking." Queer Chicanx history is necessarily interdisciplinary. It is rooted in and must continue to be grounded in our histories and experiences. Equally important, it must be useful.[44]

The Work at Hand

I have organized this work into five chapters, moving back and forth between macro mappings of nepantla and socioeconomic shifts at the state and, at times, global levels, and chapters that focus on the lives of specific transgender mestiz@s—specifically Jack Garland and Gwen

Amber Rose Araujo. Chapter 1, "A World Created through Motion," maps not only the early concept of nepantla as utilized by the Mexica peoples of central Mexico, who understood it as the motion-change that creates the world, but also the theory as utilized by twentieth-century Chicanx scholars. The chapter engages the theories of Gloria Anzaldúa, Paula Moya, and Chela Sandoval to argue that queer mestiz@s are especially equipped to see and navigate time-spaces of nepantla; it also focuses on the life and work of Gloria Anzaldúa as an example of this concept. Particular attention is paid to the reclamation of the concept by Gloria Anzaldúa and the manner in which she studied and deployed it at multiple levels. The chapter closes with an argument that post-1848 California was a time and space of nepantla, where shifts in capital created a violent time-space of motion-change where pockets of resistance formed but were ultimately contained by monopoly capital.

Drawing on nineteenth- and early twentieth-century newspapers, as well as other archival sources, chapter 2, "Motion-Change in the Life and Times of Jack Mugarrieta Garland," excavates the life of Jack Garland, named at birth Elvira Mugarrieta, who lived in California at the end of the nineteenth century and the beginning of the twentieth. The chapter excavates Jack's family history, his father's love of Mexico, commitment to family, and to his community. It maps the family's socioeconomic status and then the life that Jack lived as he moved from surviving as Elvira to Babe Bean to Jack Garland. Doing so demonstrates the importance of recognizing nepantla in space and time in order to expose the ways in which gender structures labor systems and the ability to access material resources in specific epochs of capitalism. At the close of the nineteenth century, as gender binaries and national capitalism became entrenched in California, there was no longer space for mestiz@s who lived between genders.

While Jack Garland lived through an epochal shift in capital, so did Gwen Amber Araujo, whom the text addresses in chapter 4. Thus, chapter 3, "NAFTA and Generative Movement in the Sixth Sun," paints a context for the visibility of transgender mestiz@s in the late twentieth and early twenty-first centuries. The chapter briefly maps global shifts beginning in the 1960s, which culminated in trade agreements at the close of the century. The focus, however, is on the North American Free Trade Agreement (NAFTA) as a destructive force, which was and is met by creative resistance, such as that found in EZLN, a movement having its roots, in part, in the 1974 massacre that took place in the town of Nepantla, Mexico.[45] The chapter also addresses creative resistance on the part of city workers such as the Duro Bag workers of Tamaulipas. Communities such as these, I argue, can help us move into a new sun.

Chapter 4, "Motion-Change in the Life and Times of Gwen Amber Rose Araujo," addresses the life and death of a young transgender teen murdered in 2002. In the context of the economic shifts of the late twentieth century, specifically in Northern California, this chapter provides a brief biography of Gwen and an accounting of her violent death. But it also maps the discrepancy between the media coverage of cisgender white gay males and transgender people of color, thus engaging the concept of "shades of queer" and drawing attention to nepantler@s whose lives are located within a rupture where race, sex, and gender inequality seek to stabilize Western economies. The chapter closes on a positive note, utilizing interviews from local community groups such as the Transgender Law Center and Community United against Violence, as well as Gwen's mother, to demonstrate how, within this specific time of motion-change, one community was able to unite to demand justice and respect for young queer lives.

Chapter 5, "Nepantler@s of the Sixth Sun," engages a hemispheric lens as I map shifts in global capital during the first decade of the twenty-first century, and the related shifts in immigration and the safety, or lack thereof, of transgender mestiz@s. For Chicanxs, the twenty-first century brought with it the hope of a new way of life, or a Sixth Sun. Yet as we moved into the twenty-first century, the hope of a more just society remained contested. Thus I place the immigration of transgender mestiz@s in our time in a larger context of movement and displacement of people due to the current epochal shift in capital. A quick survey of legal newsletters might bring one hope, as organizations such as the Transgender Law Center have been able to successfully win asylum for some transgender women fleeing their homelands.[46] Yet recent history has also demonstrated that in this age of global capital, transgender mestiz@s are still not safe. Indeed, "transgender and gender-nonconforming people of color living in poverty are disproportionately profiled by the police, subjected to police misconduct and charged with survival-related crimes." And those held in detention centers are subjected to harassment and violence.[47] So, while highlighting the critical work of organizations such the Transgender Law Center, I also map the work that remains to be done.

In this, our present nepantlan time, it is critical that we learn from the past and utilize tools both old and new to carve out spaces of resistance. Thus, in closing I make an intentional callout to the Mexican and Chicanx dream of a Sixth Sun that must absolutely include transgender mestiz@s. I map how, even as I was drafting the closing chapters of this work, a violent weaving continued to construct our present. We saw positive motion-change as the U.S. Ninth Circuit Court, in *Avendano Hernández v. Lynch*, distinguished between the status of transgender and gay refugees, a critical turn in the struggle for transgender safety. Yet just one year later we saw destructive motion-change, as almost half the American voting public cast their ballot for a man who publicly and boldly dehumanized women, immigrants, and other minorities. And so I call attention to the fact that according to precolonial calendars, we are now entering the Sixth Sun—not coincidentally at the same time that we are in yet another epochal shift of capital. In mapping the intensive weaving of motion-change during the time in which this text saw its completion, I ask you to imagine a different future, and to strive to create it.

NEPANTLA²

CHAPTER ONE

A World Created through Motion

I suggest that while Chicana and other women-of-color feminists
acknowledge the conflicts they experience, they attempt to work
through them to create a qualitatively new and better social order.
Furthermore, they do so in ways that require them to stake out political
positions—positions that are generally justified with reference to a
substantive conception of the human good.
   —Paula Moya, "Chicana Feminism and Postmodernist Theory"

We must act in the everyday world. Words are not enough. We must
perform visible and public acts that may make us more vulnerable to the
very oppressions that we are fighting against. But, our vulnerability can
be the source of our power—*if we use it.*
   —Gloria Anzaldúa, "El Mundo Zurdo"

This chapter focuses on the concept of nepantla, not as an abstract
philosophy but as one which, from its earliest uses, appears to have
been a pragmatic tool for understanding and moving in our world.
Thus I begin with a brief discussion of nepantlan philosophy in the
lives of precolonial Americans within the context of the culture from
which it emerged; I then map the queerly consistent ways in which the
philosophy was reclaimed and then mobilized by Chicana feminists;
and finally I utilize the philosophy as a tool for understanding economic motion-change at the end of the nineteenth century and the
beginning of the twentieth. In doing so, I honor the legacy of Gloria
Anzaldúa, who called us all to honor and engage difficult times and
places of nepantla and who saw a connection between economic strife
and nepantlan struggles.

Nepantla, in the precolonial world, referred to an in-between space and, equally important, an in-between motion, what Maffie calls "motion-change"—"middling, intermixing, and mutually reciprocating motion-change."[1] Such motion-change was critical to self-generation and generation, the creation of society and the world itself. Yet who were these people—our philosophical and intellectual ancestors who created a social world that refused dualistic binaries?

The Aztecs are not the only Indigenous ancestors of Chicanxs, yet culturally they remain prominent, because as with most empires, their influence spread beyond the metropol. At the time of the conquest, the Aztec empire was the most powerful on the North American continent, with pyramids as tall as 197 feet and territory that stretched from just north of modern-day Mexico City to the Guatemalan border. By 1521, the year the Spanish arrived in the capital, Tenochtitlan, over two hundred thousand people lived in the city.[2] If we look beyond stereotypes, both good and bad, of the Aztecs, we see that their world was gendered, hierarchical, and much like ours, full of contradictions. Like us, they produced ways of knowing and of understanding the world around them. And key to these ways of knowing was the philosophy of nepantla.

The Gendered World That Birthed a Philosophy of Balance

We only fill an earthly ministry, O friend:
We have to leave the lovely songs we give,
Alas, we have to leave the flowers in the end . . .

The flowers open their crowns, grow, germinate and bloom:
From in you, poet, flower songs bloom and descend
As rain and scatter over those destined to doom.
Nahuatl poem, translated by Rafael Jesús González

The Aztec world was one of poetry and philosophy. Poet-philosophers wove songs about this world and the next, scattered them over the people of the empire, and watched them rain down.[3] While those who received them were "destined to doom," the ideas and the poems were immortalized, passed down from generation to generation through the school systems and through public ceremony.[4] At the time of conquest, some poems would be transcribed and translated for the colonizers—ideas, cosmovisions, philosophies that had deep roots in the soil of the Americas. In that world poetry was the language of truth—*in xochitl in cuicatl*—flower and song. The very language of the people, Nahuatl, was conducive to philosophy, with inflective grammar and disfrasismos. The poet-philosophers, *tlamatinime*, sought truth. Like philosophers from other cultures, they were concerned with knowledge, the nature of knowledge, and the meaning of life.[5]

The empire built on the many cultures that preceded it, and so while we received the philosophy of nepantla from the Aztecs, it is possible that the philosophy flourished in Mesoamerica long before the rise of the empire, perhaps with the mother culture of the Americas, the Olmecas, whose culture spanned the centuries from 1500 BCE to 300 BCE, with their stratified society of housing complexes, agriculture, organized religion, and professional artists; or perhaps the concept originated with the Toltecs, who flourished from 950 CE to 1150 CE and from whom the Aztec empire borrowed so much culture. It was over the Toltecs that the great philosopher king Topiltzin Ce Acatle Queztalcoatl ruled, overseeing yet another era of cultural flourishing and innovation.[6] León Portilla, citing the Códice Matritense de la Real Academica, notes, "The development of Nahuatl philosophy from Toltec times must be credited to whole generations of wise men, known by ancient tradition as 'those who carried with them the black and red ink, the manuscripts and the pictures, wisdom.'"[7]

It was the poet-philosopher Nezahualcoyotl of Texcoco (1402–72) who promulgated many of the songs and poems that carried unifying values and philosophies throughout the empire. He built gardens and parks, codified the various laws of the region into the *Code of Eighty Laws*, and founded a self-governing academy for scholars and poets, and a school system where all citizen-children were expected to study.[8] By 1440 Nezahualcoyotl's songs were sung throughout the Nahuatl-speaking world.[9] The poet-philosophers of Texcoco were so prolific and their work so influential that the fires of the Grand Inquisitor Juan de Zumaraga were not able to annihilate their truths.[10] While much excavating and creating genealogies of Aztec philosophy and culture remain to be done, today, thanks to the work of Miguel León-Portilla in the middle of the twentieth century, the flourishing of Chicanx knowledge production later in the century, and the work of more contemporary scholars such as Davíd Carrasco and James Maffie today, we know much of this cosmovision and philosophy, including the rich and useful philosophy of nepantla.

The Mexican people lived in the fifth age, or Fifth Sun. According to their cosmology, four ages had preceded theirs: earth, wind, fire, and water. The Fifth Sun was an age of motion or weaving; inamic pairs of energy, all flowing from Teotl, wove their world.[11] Together the weaving of the inamic partners—creative and destructive—were and are nepantla. For the Mexica people "nepantla motion-change has always already existed . . . is mutually middling, betwixt-and-betweening, and reciprocating. It unifies inamic partners in a balance of agonistic tension. . . . It joins, mixes, fuses, and weaves things together, and it does so in a manner that is abundant with mutuality and reciprocity. It is middle and middling."[12] Nepantla was a middle space but also generative motion. It wove the world, the physical-spiritual world of the Mexica people. Theirs, like ours, was a world in motion.

The society within which the philosophy flourished was, like ours, constructed through gender, and like ours men held more institutional power than women. Yet there were significant differences between their world and ours and in fact between their world and that of their European counterparts. Understanding that gendered world is central to understanding the world that birthed the philosophy that structures this text; it can also help us to see how other philosophies and cosmovisions, including Judeo-Christian traditions, are influenced by the gendered worlds that birthed and nurtured them.

Many argue that Mexica women held more status in their society than did the European women of their time. As Louise Burkhart notes, Mexica women worked as "marketers, doctors, artisans, priests, and perhaps, occasionally, rulers."[13] Unlike European women, upon marriage, Mexica women did not lose their property rights, and if a couple divorced, she took her property with her. Kinship was traced through male or female lines, or both.[14] While women were respected and held power, in Mexica society, as in so many other cultures, women's roles were tied to the home.[15] But it was not a world divided between public and private spheres any more than it was a world divided between the spiritual and the physical; instead, all was connected and infused with the sacred, and women's and men's spaces were spiritually connected. Thus a house was a microcosm of the city, and the city was a microcosm of the universe; a home was cosmically connected to the world around it.[16] It was women's responsibility to sweep their homes, and their skill at sweeping could affect the performance of their spouses on the battlefield. Likewise deities swept. While usually it was female deities who swept, such as Coatlicue, who conceived Huitzilophochtli while sweeping, or Chimalman, who conceived Quetzalcoatl while doing the same, Quetzalcoatl himself also swept, clearing the roads for the rain god.[17]

In this warrior society, men earned status through bravery in battle, and women could not join the warrior societies of the Eagle or the Jaguar. Instead, women gained status through childbirth.[18] Women gave birth not only to children but also to weavings, which they bartered for other goods. The role of women in the economy was critical: men worked in the fields, women bartered in the marketplace—thus a woman's marketing skills could improve or ruin her family's finances. In addition to buying and selling, women also held public positions as *tianquizpan tlayacanqui*, market administrators.[19] A woman who gave birth, was successful in the marketplace, and lived a long life was venerated in her old age.

The birthing of cloth was spiritually charged and powerful; spinning and weaving "empower[ed] weavers to join together inamic partners into a middle, mutually reciprocating, agonistically tensed unity. They also enable[d] humans to participate and contribute to the ongoing weaving of the Fifth Age and sacred nepantla processing of teotl."[20] Women wove the cloth to be bartered in the marketplace, and the Mexica peoples lived in a world woven together—a "grand weaving-in-progress."[21] To complicate matters further, it was women who wielded the batten, a male-gendered tool. According to Maffie, "In the hands of a woman, a batten attested to her ability to successfully wield, temporarily dominate, and incorporate a preeminently male-gendered instrument and male power symbol, and therefore attested to her command of creative transformation."[22] In fact, Cihuacoatl, a powerful creation goddess, was sometimes depicted as holding a shield and batten, and "women's . . . brooms and spinning implements were spoken of as weapons in the ongoing social and political battle with chaos."[23] This cosmic connection between male and female, public and private, may explain in part the rights that women retained within marriage.

It was this gendered world that brought us the philosophy of nepantla—a patriarchal world where women also held power, where men held most public positions, but where there was no linguistic equivalent for "whore."[24] While this warrior society insisted on blood sacrifice, poets and philosophers were celebrated, the spiritual and physical refused to split, and the philosophy flourished, to be reseeded in the Chicanx Renaissance of the late twentieth century. As the twentieth century was ending, Chicanx communities, especially farm worker and student communities, rejected the assimilationist rhetoric of the dominant society. They looked to the nationalist symbols claimed and mobilized by Mexico in the War for Independence and the Revolution. Engaging in what historian Maylei Blackwell calls retrofitting, they used symbols such as Our Lady of Guadalupe, Malinche, and Aztec warriors to create community pride.[25] That is to say, they mobilized old symbols and historical figures, envisioning them anew through the lens of their own struggles and embodied experiences. With the late twentieth-century renaissance in Chicana feminisms, Chicanas took these symbols once again and mobilized them, at times, as Contreras notes, erasing the Indigenous histories from which they sprang. At its best, feminist retrofitting highlighted the histories from which those symbols emerged as well the hybridity and borderlands from which the activists struggled.

Toward a Nepantlan Life: Gloria Evangelina Anzaldúa

Being tricultural, monolingual, bilingual, or multilingual . . . in a state of perpetual transition, the mestiza faces the dilemma of the mixed breed. . . . At some point on our way to a new consciousness, we will have to leave the . . . split between the two mortal combatants somehow healed so that we are on both shores at once and, at once, see through serpent and eagle eyes. Or perhaps we will decide to disengage from the dominant culture all together . . . cross the border into a wholly new and separate territory. . . . The possibilities are numerous once we decide to act and not react.

—Gloria Anzaldúa, *Borderlands*

Centuries after the Spanish invaded Anahuac, nepantla would become central to the work of Gloria Anzaldúa, Pat Mora, and those of us who, today, see a unity in the movement and change that creates our world and who are drawn to those places and place-times when change and motion are most visible. Drawing on and building on Mexica philosophy and poetry (and philosophy in poetry) Anzaldúa came to articulate nepantla as "a limited space where you are neither this nor that but where you are changing" and, equally important, as "a way of seeing the world."[26] As Chicanxs we run with this philosophy—because we do see the world through a lens of nepantla, "that ambiguous, tentative, ever-changing space we inhabit."[27] For queer Chicanxs, nepantla is the cultural space that we, as queer mestiz@s, inhabit; we are multicultural, multiracial, we live outside of traditional gender roles, *we embody change.*

During the Chicano movement of the 1960s and '70s, Chicanxs from the West Coast to Chicago challenged "Western" ways of knowing. For the poets, scholars, and activists of the time, philosophies such as nepantla opened doors to mobilizing their own mestizaje to join in the shaping of their society and world.[28] Yet the path back to nepantla was a difficult one; initial reclamations of Aztec and Mexica knowledges did not move beyond the patriarchal boundaries of the ancient past. Instead they applied a broad and romantic brush to the past, limiting its liberatory potential.[29]

It was Chicana feminists who challenged the broad strokes of male writers, historians, and activists. From María Linda Apodaca's critique of Aztec patriarchy and call for a Chicana materialist interpretation of the past, to the many reclamations and reenvisionings of iconic figures such as La Malinche, Aztec and Mexica history and ways of knowing would slowly emerge as tools with which we might continue to shape our world.[30] Chicanas constructed a distinctly feminista lens that rejected unquestioning ethnic nationalist fundamentalism, emphasized a refusal of a mind/body split, and insisted that we make use of our own mestizaje. Mobilizing philosophies of nepantla was central to this movement, and the work of Gloria Anzaldúa was central to this ongoing project. Read through a lens of Chicana materialism, as noted by Sonia Saldívar-Hull, "Anzaldúa's claim of indigeneity in Texas, with its legacy of genocidal Texas Ranger Militias, is much more complex than the romanticized Aztec warriors of the Chicano movement imagination; hers was a dangerous, radical move."[31]

Gloria Evangelina Anzaldúa was a daughter of the borderlands and of nepantla. Born into a sharecropping and field-worker family in South Texas, she lived, for the first six years of her life, on the ranch settlement of Jesus María, a place without indoor plumbing but rich in stories and narrative.[32] The elders in her family, especially her grandparents, told her stories, family histories, and tales of survival; and so the young Gloria learned to hear stories and to tell stories, at times working the images into the tactile medium of leather.[33]

As an adult Anzaldúa recalled having been an outsider, even as a toddler. When, at the age of three months, she began menstruating, her mother saw it as punishment for having conceived her before marriage, and so she treated the young Gloria's different body as something shameful—to be hidden.[34] And so the young outsider learned to hide her body, worked in the fields during the day, and escaped into reading whenever she could. Her father, who was unable to finish high school, worried about his own children missing school and so stopped taking them through migrant circuits while they were still in grammar school; thus the young Gloria still worked the fields locally but was able to experience a segregated yet stable grammar school education. Anzaldúa's experiences in the fields, first as a migrant child laborer and then as a young field-worker, would later allow her to labor as a bridge between migrant families and teachers in the Texas public school system.[35]

When Anzaldúa was twelve, her father died in a horrible car accident. He had not only provided for the family but also nurtured his daughter's curiosity and encouraged her to strive for a university education.[36] Without him the family had to struggle harder against poverty. Anzaldúa qualified for advanced-placement classes in high school and attended Texas Women's University for her freshman year of college—she had a creative essay published in the school literary journal—but then left because the tuition was untenable. After two years of working a day job, she returned to school, this time at Pan American University.[37]

It was at Pan American University (now the University of Texas, Rio Grande Valley) that she forged the Chicana feminist mestiza consciousness that would infuse her later writings—reflecting on the intersections of her daily life: struggle, place, in-betweenness, race, roots, gender, and class. This identity, of course, would continue to grow and shift and redefine itself.[38] But it was to this time, while she was still working in the fields and going to school, that she attributed her emerging mestiza consciousness. In her own words, "I was a senior at Pan American University and I was still working in the fields. That struggle led me to consciousness-raising with feminists. When César Chávez and the farmworkers in Texas were having talks, I would go to their meetings. La Raza Unida was growing strong in the sixties, and I participated in some of their conferences. At one point, the feminist movement and the farmworker's struggle and the Raza Unida struggle all came together for me."[39]

The lens she brought to her experiences, and that would later be articulated in her public writings, was revolutionary. It became foundational to the powerful and transformative work of later Chicana feminists and scholar activists, of theorists as diverse as Paula Moya and Chela Sandoval, Irene Lara, and Emma Pérez.[40]

Mestizas, Anzaldúa argued, possess an intersectional lens; we write from the violent spaces of borderlands, and, when we embrace our identities, we can lead the world in negotiating postmodernity. It is the mestiza who "reinterprets history and, using new symbols . . . shapes new myths . . . adopts new perspectives toward the dark-skinned, women and queers . . . strengthens her tolerance (and intolerance) for ambiguity."[41] As noted by Chela Sandoval, Anzaldúa's theories of mestiza consciousness allowed for the strategic alliances of women of color in the 1970s—sometimes named "outsider/within (Patricia Hill Collins)," sometimes named "house of difference (Trin Minh-ha)";

third-world feminist theories of in-betweeness allowed for an oppositional movement to flourish.[42] Such knowledge was and is a critical
tool for survival and resistance in the postmodern era.[43] It is a critical
tool for mapping nepantlan change.

It was in the 1970s, after moving to California, that Anzaldúa began
working on *This Bridge Called My Back: Writings by Radical Women of
Color*. In it she introduced concepts about movement, change, and
revolution.[44] In fact, it is here that we can clearly see the seeds of her
later theories regarding spaces of nepantla. In "La Prieta," first printed
in that volume—she wrote of El Mundo Zurdo as space where, as out-
siders, "Third World women, lesbians, feminists, and feminist-oriented
men of all colors" might band together and change the world: "I believe
by changing ourselves we change the world, that traveling El Mundo
Zurdo path is the path of a two-way movement—a going deep into
the self and expanding out into the world, a simultaneous recreation
of the self and a reconstruction of society."[45] Similarly, in the essay
"Mundo Zurdo," she drew attention to the left-handed world of "the
colored, the queer, the poor, the female, the physically challenged."[46]
She drew connections between and among those of us who live and
move in El Mundo Zurdo, calling us to self-love, coalition, and revolution. There is power in El Mundo Zurdo, she reminded us—if we
do not flee our world but mobilize within it.

Five years after coediting *This Bridge*, Anzaldúa published *Borderlands: La Nueva Mestiza*, the first bilingual crossover text that made its
way into white classrooms and reading spaces throughout the United
States. In it she more fully developed her concepts of borderlands and
mestiza consciousness, and introduced the concept of the Coatlicue
state. It was and is a text about new ways of knowing, "beyond the
hegemonic, a multiply queer way of knowing."[47]

It was in *Borderlands* that "la conciencia de la mestiza" was explicitly addressed in a chapter with the same name; using both prose and
poetry she enfleshed the theory. For Anzaldúa, once again, it was this
embracing of our mestizaje that enabled us to envision a new world.
And in this work, ways of knowing were and are rooted in movement.
Central to her later mobilization of nepantla, mestiza consciousness
was and is about in-betweeness and about movement: lo molido is

being worked in the metate, the comal is sizzling hot, the tortilla consumed, the pestle, like the batten, destroys and creates.[48]

In *Borderlands* Anzaldúa also reclaimed Coatlicue and wrote of both physical and affective spaces of movement. In reclaiming Coatlicue, a goddess of creation and destruction, Anzaldúa was among the first Chicanas to reclaim or retrofit Mexica female deities and to mobilize them for liberatory purposes. For this labor, Irene Lara would later name her a "daughter of Coatlicue."[49] For Anzaldúa, the Coatlicue state was an in-between state—between cultures but also between life and death, sanity and insanity—a breaking point where, if we do not break, we can see different futures. The Coatlicue state, as one of many transition spaces on the way to conocimiento, new knowledge, was a place of nepantla.[50] In reclaiming Coatlicue, Anzaldúa rejected the idea not only of racial purity but also of a static world and a static identity. Differences do not melt into one another and disappear; they create friction. If you embrace the friction, you can use it. For mestizas, if we own it we also "invoke the unconquered spirit of Aztlán," that place and vision of a just world beyond colonialism.[51]

Anzaldúa's work on nepantla became more explicit as she continued to explore connections between activism and spirituality. In her last published essay she wrote of the power of nepantlan spaces in times of crisis—because nepantla itself is a transition space, movement space, and site of conflict. In response to the attack on the U.S. World Trade Center towers and the rise of twenty-first-century violence, Clara Lomas and Claire Joysmith solicited testimonios from scholars and activists and artists from Mexico and the United States.[52] Anzaldúa's would be the lengthiest of these essays, drawing connections between the violence of the attacks and the colonial and imperialist violence that continues to shape our world. Amid her critique she once again suggested remedies: "Nepantla is the space in-between the locus and sign of transition. In nepantla we realize that realities clash, authority figures of the various groups demand contradictory commitment. . . . We're caught in remolinos, each with different[,] often contradictory forms of cognition, perspectives, worldviews, belief systems—all occupying the transitional nepantla space."[53] Anzaldúa sought to awaken us to the fact that we live in nepantlan times. Our world weaves itself into existence through struggle, and we live in the midst of that struggle. We are the porous rock, the rolling pin, the comal, *and* the hungry mouth. As in the time of the Fifth Sun, and in the shift to monopoly capitalism, we live in a world of motion-change—within this motion, we must "shift." Anzaldúa's engagement with the philosophy of nepantla spanned three decades: from the movement of El Mundo Zurdo to the nepantlan space of 9-11. This understanding of the world as neither this nor that but both—of movement and change—came from her embodied experience in "the historical political, [and] cultural context in which" she grew and from which she developed ways of knowing that continue to influence us today.[54]

Monopoly Capital and Labor Organizing: Inamic Partners of the Late Nineteenth Century

Bringing a nepantlan lens to place and space, as did Anzaldúa, marks late nineteenth-century California as *space* of movement and in-betweeness: a space where feudal economies met monopoly capitalism, and where Indigenous, mestiza/o, and Euro-American cultures violently clashed. Yet marking this space as a space of nepantla also sheds light on its potential for productive generation—the creation of new life, and new possibilities. Could it be that monopoly capitalism did not need to triumph—that it was not the inevitable outcome of the U.S. Invasion? If we let go of a Western insistence on binaries, then the answer is yes.

So let us return to that time. For while the ultimate outcome was monopoly capitalism and a violently entrenched dual gender system, the latter part of the nineteenth century and the early part of the twentieth were a time of intense movement and change, with multiple ethnicities, classes, peoples, and economic systems shifting and moving. This upheaval was especially true of the state of California, and while in a time-place of nepantla, California was a generative space of gender plurality. Thus Jack Mugarrieta Garland, the focus of chapter 2, was born in San Francisco in 1869, worked as a news reporter in Stockton, California, while living as a masculine woman until the turn of the century, and then served as a translator during the U.S. war in the Philippines, returning to California to live as a man until his death in 1936. Studies by historians such as Jonathan Ned Katz and Peter Boag demonstrate that it is during this time that other people were able to live between genders in California and beyond.[55]

Indeed, early twentieth-century California was *Nueva Nepantla*. And today, in the twenty-first century, California, once again, is Nueva Nepantla, as more than one hundred first people's tribes and nations continue to grow and rebuild and we once again have opportunities for liberatory motion-change.[56] In the 1990s, for example, Advocates for Indigenous California Language Survival established projects such as the Master-Apprentice Programs, teaming elders with younger tribal members to pass on language skills.[57] The program thrived, and the apprentices went on to found language programs in public schools and community summer camps. Likewise, some California schools reached out to elders to consult with them on California history curriculum.[58] Yet it appears the battle will be, once again, one of creative and destructive forces. In 2007, when the United Nations passed the Declaration on the Rights of Indigenous Peoples, four nations voted against it. The United States was one of those four.[59]

And so we return to the economic space of late nineteenth-century greater Mexico. The texts of the Californios depict this time and space as a violent one, and indeed it was. To a large extent the violence was driven by a global shift toward capitalist imperialism—that is, the trans-ing of an entire economic system giving rise to violent motion-change. In the nation-state, corporations played a growing role in influencing public policy. U.S. capitalists invested in weaker countries to extract labor and raw materials, and the United States expanded its lands and influence of power through the acquisition of colonies and territories.[60] Desirous of northern Mexico for its "minerals and markets" and for railroad expansion (that is, extension of markets), the United States launched its invasion of the land in 1846.[61] Historians as diverse as Rodolfo Acuña and Raymund Paredes, and more recently, Stephen Pitti and Laura E. Gómez, mapped the violence of the Invasion; throughout the northern territories and specifically in California, women were assaulted, and unarmed men as well as soldiers were killed.[62]

Euro-Americans used lynch law to establish white rule and economic dominance throughout the territory. Of the 597 Mexicanos lynched between 1848 and 1928, only sixty-four were murdered outside of any juridico-legal system of the U.S. national West. The rest of the victims were lynched after arrest, when mobs refused to allow them access to a legal trial, or rejected the verdict of the jury.[63] As noted by Carrigan and Webb, a lack of courts in the U.S. national West alone cannot account for the number of Mexicanos killed during this time; only by taking into consideration ideologies of manifest destiny, Euro-American racism, and economic interests can the disproportionate number of killings of Mexicans and those perceived to be Mexican be explained.[64] Also critical to gender history, the construction of womanhood as white meant that Mexicanas and Latinas were not safe from such violence, as demonstrated by the lynching of Juana Loaiza, sometimes called Josefa, by white men in Downieville in 1851.[65] In the words of Miroslava Chávez-García, "The American conquest in 1846 brought legal, economic, political, cultural, demographic, and social transformations that undermined Mexican society and culture and that left its people impoverished and landless."[66]

The treaty that ended the war included a promise that those in the newly acquired territories would be eligible to become U.S. citizens with their rights respected, but the rise of scientific racism and emerging discourses of Anglo-Saxonism precluded this outcome.[67] As Molina notes, the incoming Euro-Americans, in part, used the language of capitalism and economic progress to justify the subordination of the Mexican population of the Southwest, arguing that the primarily feudal economy of the region was a sign of racial inferiority.[68] When, two months after the war, gold was discovered in Northern California, a white Protestant culture and capitalist economy exacerbated the violent clash of conflict and created an extended period of in-betweeness.

Mining, railroads, and agriculture transformed the landscape, economic system, and culture of California. As Tomás Almaguer mapped in his now classic *Racial Fault Lines*, the initial industry, the mining of precious metals, brought rapid changes and upheaval to the state. Speculators brought quartz and hydraulic mining technology with them and "for nearly two decades mining was both the single largest source of employment and the largest capital investment sector in the state." In 1859 gold mining brought $50 million into the state, but when its profits declined thereafter, it was replaced in the top tier by agribusiness and, by extension, the railroads.[69]

And it would be railroads, in large part, that tied the United States, including California, to the larger global economy. The era was one of a shift to national capitalism, global in scope but regulated by national powers with the nation-state subsidizing the ruling class in its endeavors and, in doing so, spreading a new technology throughout the state and the nation.[70] Indeed, as argued by scholars as diverse as John H. White and Karl Polanyi, in the modern and postmodern eras, culture and technology were and are inseparable; technology is an integral part of a peoples' culture.[71] In nepantlan terms, technology and economy are integral to the weave of any given time. Thus as the railroads moved to California they brought with them the *culture* of monopoly capitalism. Wealth and accumulation became values and virtues. Between 1862 and 1872 the railroads built over one thousand miles of railroad across the state. From the 1870s to the turn of the century, railroads dominated Nueva Nepantla.[72] They contributed to the race-stratified labor market of California, and to the rise of yet another powerful strand in the weave of late nineteenth-century capitalism—U.S. agribusiness.[73]

California, in its chaos and movement, was a microcosm and simultaneously a product of larger global shifts. Global displacement of working people, as a result of empire and capitalist accumulation, fueled and fed movement into California. In this second wave of global colonial disruption, colonial and capitalist greed dovetailed, pushing Chinese laborers from their homelands. As a result of the British Opium Wars, China was required to pay the British 21 million silver dollars and open its ports to foreign trade. Peasants no longer had a market for piece goods, and dockworkers and those in related fields lost their jobs as the provincial capital of Guangdong faltered, labor recruiters from abroad were no longer policed, and poverty and chaos pushed Chinese laborers west to Hawaii, Latin America, and California.[74]

Likewise, similar colonial-capitalist practices pushed Irish and Mexican laborers into California's labor pool. Throughout the Irish famine of the 1840s and 1850s, English settlers continued to export grain and cattle to English markets. Already impoverished due to displacement through enclosure of once commonly held lands and the growth of the settlers' cattle industry in Ireland, where "between 1820 and 1840, livestock increased at a faster rate than the population, and cattle exports more than quadrupled," Irish women and men fled to the United States to escape famine and colonialism.[75] Added to this labor pool were Mexicanas/os and Chicanas/os pushed from their land following the U.S. Invasion.

The movement, weaving, and violent clashes in Nueva Nepantla were constructed through the unnatural forces of empire, of monopoly capitalism with its technologies of the railroad and the telegraph, and the cultures embedded and flowing from these powerful systems and technologies. Creating chaos within the chaos, empire and monopoly capitalism pulled and pushed those driven from their own homelands into the labor pools of California, where Mexicana/o laborers were pulled not from their homeland abroad but from their homeland within, constructing a world of movement in which bodies and persons were pulled into the space from other nations, at the same time that peoples, Indigenous and mestiza/o, were displaced through the invasion of their nations.

The Irish labored on railroads, often with high mortality rates, and distanced themselves from Black laborers and then Chinese laborers as they moved west.[76] Between 1866 and 1869 the Central Pacific Railroad employed over ten thousand Chinese immigrants.[77] Indigenous peoples were moved onto reservations, subjected to genocidal practices, and forced into indentured servitude.[78] Mestizas/os were pushed off their land and out of the professions into day labor and agricultural jobs. By the close of the century, with rabid anti-Chinese activism on the part of white laborers, Mexican and Mexican American workers came to labor as section hands on railroads throughout California.[79]

The move of the Irish to identify as white labor, in opposition to Black and Asian labor, gestures toward the ability of monopoly capitalism to triumph at the turn of the century. As British and U.S. imperialism together created a world of displacement and movement in California and globally, Chicanas/os and displaced immigrants competed for survival in California. The Irish, surviving the racialization of one empire, found that in their new empire, they could, and so did, claim whiteness—whiteness in opposition to their fellow laborers.[80] Whiteness became a destructive force in the service of capitalism, stabilizing economic systems even while dividing labor against itself, constructing racialized class and gender systems. Even in the U.S. South, following a devastating civil war in which 750,000 lives were lost, poor whites, holding onto their whiteness as property, failed to make a coalition with poor African Americans, thus ensuring the exploitation and subjugation of themselves by monopoly capital.[81] The new world of monopoly capitalism, it would seem, was one where resistance was indeed futile, where the triumph of the new order was inevitable.

We can see how Euro-American settlers, in their blindness to the people they met on their arrival, left themselves vulnerable to loss and defeat. In the California of 1879 the vast majority of farms were small enterprises, where farmers had control of their labor. Only 3.9 percent of California's crops were produced by large agribusinesses. By 1899 that percentage had risen to 43.3. Small farmers found it increasingly difficult to survive.[82] Having established themselves in opposition to first peoples and the mestizas/os who preceded them to the area, they could not imagine alliances with those groups against monopoly capitalism. Throughout California and the larger Southwest, labor-intensive and capital-intensive crops, requiring ever-evolving technologies, came to dominate.[83] Out of a violent chaos, order emerged, and the order was violently suffocating.

Yet when we shift our gaze to agriculture we can see that the triumph of monopoly capitalism in California might not have been as encompassing as it came to be. Pockets of resistance, as much as monopoly capitalism, comprised the weave of the time. In fact it is laborers such as the Mexicans and Japanese of Oxnard, California, who stand out as challenging and disrupting the rise of turn-of-the-century agribusiness. In Southern California, Mexican and Japanese laborers formed alliances in the now infamous Oxnard strike of 1903. By then, in Oxnard, the Irish were living on the west side of town with other Euro-Americans and enjoying the fruits of limited upward mobility given to those who allied themselves with capital. Japanese and Mexican contractors and workers joined together across class, racial, and linguistic lines and formed a successful union, busting a white-contractor monopoly on farm labor and raising the minimum wage to between five and six dollars per acre.[84] Oxnard stands out as exceptional, because it is one of the few examples, in this time of violent motion-change, of workers' wages and rights being protected. The union was short-lived, in part because of the overt and rabid racism of Samuel Gompers.[85] Yet while this particular instance of worker resistance was contained, it remains an example of the unity of people despite differences and of how shifts in capital are not destined to triumph but are only part of the great weave of any given time.

Throughout this period, mutual aid societies, labor strikes, and the Spanish-language press created pockets of resistance throughout the state.[86] For most fractures, however, the pockets of resistance remained small. And perhaps in seeing it was not enough to challenge the machine structurally, we can learn to or be reminded of what we need to do to generate a different future. We can realize Polanyi's argument, from another century, in an earlier epoch of capital, that while resistance has not stopped the march of capital, it has, at times slowed it.[87]

And so here I shift to a more focused examination of Nueva Nepantla, to a life within Nepantla²: that of Jack Garland, who was born into a mixed ethnic family in this land of motion-change, and who in the course of his life trans-ed gender. Jack moved through a world in motion, one marked with pockets of resistance, and survived. By the time he died at sixty-seven, the youth with whom he worked saw him as an elder, calling him simply "Uncle Jack."

CHAPTER TWO

Motion-Change in the Life and Times of Jack Mugarrieta Garland

Sexual hierarchies . . . are always at the service of a project of
domination that can sustain itself only by dividing, on a continuously
renewed basis, those it intends to rule. . . . We can see . . . that the
human body and not the steam engine, and not even the clock, was the
first machine developed by capitalism.

—Silvia Federici, *Caliban and the Witch*

Our task as Chicanos and as historians is to present the history of the
Chicana and the Chicano in light of the capitalist development that
permeated the United States and the world. To present a different
history will mask the already hidden histories and perpetuate the
existence of exploitation and subjugation.

—María Linda Apodaca, "The Chicana Woman: An Historical
     Materialist Perspective"

Jack Garland was born in 1869 in San Francisco, California—a world
of motion-change. He was given the name Elvira Mugarrieta by his
parents, and raised in a struggling middle-class family in the rapidly
changing Golden State. His father, José Mugarrieta, was the Mexican
consul to California. Jack lived his childhood as a tomboy, his young
adult life socially as a masculine woman, and his middle age and final
years as a man.[1] What can we learn from the life of this person who
crossed gender boundaries at the dawn of the twentieth century, when
capitalism was expanding throughout greater Mexico? To begin to
understand the lives of those who live in nepantlan times, we must
engage in an interdisciplinary analysis, addressing how race, gender,

and capital intersect to construct identity in U.S. society. Failure to do so erases the specificity of the queer mestiz@ past; it also limits our ability to understand the role of capital and capitalist shifts in shaping our lives today.

I am not the first historian to turn my gaze to Jack Mugarrieta Garland. Yet the first substantial work to acknowledge his life was primarily an excavation and explored neither the role of ethnicity in his life nor the deep historical context of his time.[2] Louis Sullivan's 1990 monograph, though, did the groundbreaking job of introducing a larger reading public to a history of a transgender person of Mexican descent.[3] Several years later historian Nan Alamilla Boyd, in her overview of nineteenth-century transgender and lesbian histories, briefly addressed Jack's life. There she asserted that "one cannot overlook Garland's racial, class, and national passings."[4] More recently Emily Skidmore addressed Jack's life within the context of U.S. imperialism, yet even she did not explore those moments in his life when he seemed to move between ethnicities.[5] I am not convinced that Garland did pass—not through all phases of his life. Furthermore, on reading these three fine works I am still not sure how the socioeconomic context of his time intersected with Jack's ethnicity and gender. As Molina notes, while white supremacy was foundational in shaping the racial hierarchy of the United States, capitalist expansion was also central to shaping how such hierarchies took shape.[6] In times of nepantla upheavals create shifting and sometimes visible synergies between capital, race, and gender. Studies of race and gender that ignore the role of capitalism in the United States also ignore the critical tools given to us by Chicana historians such as Maria Linda Apodaca and Antonia Castañeda.[7]

Bringing a nepantlan lens to the life and history of Jack Mugarrieta Garland, we can see his ethnicity in relation to capital; rooting his life in the context of the U.S. Invasion and its aftermath makes it possible to see his raced and gendered life as a weaving that was part of the great motion-change of California—Nueva Nepantla. In this chapter I take tools developed and applied by Chicana historians who placed the histories of women in the economic systems of their times, and utilize them through a lens of nepantla, recognizing the time of Jack

Garland as one of epochal economic shift. Placing Jack in the historical and economic context of his time demonstrates the importance of historical tools to interdisciplines such as Chicanx studies, gender studies, and queer theory and reminds us of the salience of precolonial philosophies in our own time.

Nepantla[2]

Jack was born on December 9, 1869, to José Marcos Mugarrieta and Eliza Garland in a San Francisco hospital. The world he entered was one of change, a place that had once been Mexico. To paraphrase Gloria Anzaldúa, San Francisco had been Mexico once, was Indian always.[8] The shift to national and monopoly capitalism was inherently patriarchal and would demand static raced-gender roles, producing a gendered labor system that was necessarily raced. The appropriation of land and resources from nonwhite nations fueled white discourses of racial purity in the United States—discourses in which white women were to protect the purity of their race by preserving their homes and producing and rearing young white citizens. They were to nurture and to pass on civilized values from one generation to the next.[9] White men were to protect women and children and to earn wages in the public sphere. The integration of an ideology of white domesticity into California culture did not exclude women from the workplace; instead, as in other regions of greater Mexico, it created a cheap labor pool where women from a variety of communities—immigrant and racialized—could be utilized as hyperexploited workers.[10]

The gendered labor systems of pre-Invasion California briefly disrupted the new gendered political economy, but soon the commonalities of the systems outweighed their differences. Mexican ideologies of domesticity and maternalism dovetailed with those of monopoly capitalism in such a manner that gender roles and gendered labor were reinscribed and bolstered. In the semifeudal society of early nineteenth-century California, most women had labored. Like other rural areas of Mexico, the productive labor of women was necessary for the survival of the community. Women ground corn, made soap, laundered clothing by hand, gathered herbs for healing, tended gardens, guarded ranchos while their spouses were away, and more.[11]

Yet this labor did not preclude ideologies of subservience and, in relation, domesticity. Instead, to receive the protection of the larger community, women were to be obedient to God, the clergy, their fathers, and their husbands.[12] As noted by Evelyn Nakano Glenn, after the invasion, within their own communities, "Mexican women were placed in the difficult position of being expected to maintain men's pride, demonstrate loyalty and support, and uphold standards of respectability and purity."[13] Once institutions such as English-language newspapers and Protestant public schools were in place, the critical role that subservience played for women under the old rule was reinscribed onto the new.[14]

For Mexicana and Chicana women the merging of two gendered labor systems, one of which was hyperracialized, meant that they were hyperexploitable as workers. White women were worthy of protection because they were *white* women. They maintained their status and protections through what Amy Kaplan has termed "manifest domesticity," in opposition to women of color. Women of color, belonging to communities that were hyperexploited economically, were forced into wage labor to support their families, thus reinscribing their position outside white womanhood.[15] Castañeda notes that a construction of white women throughout greater Mexico as "gentle tamers" garnered them status, privileges, and protections explicitly at the expense of other women.[16] She also argues that while propertyless mestizas were stereotyped as loose and valueless, some landed women were stereotyped as desirable in marriage; the socioeconomic status of women prior to the Invasion, in part, determined their status following the Invasion.[17]

By the 1880s, when Jack was a teen, a majority of Mexicans in the United States were laborers.[18] Displaced Californios, Mexican immigrants, and Chileans were quickly becoming "the first Latino industrial workers in the United States."[19] Displaced Mexican women were pushed into domestic industries.[20] Railroads and agribusiness were in the process of revolutionizing the California economy. And white Protestant culture had established itself in most major cities, with white women constructing themselves as the civilizers of the region.[21] The construction of white Protestant women as civilizers of urban cities such as San Francisco would also be used to justify the policing of public space and eventually confine those who did not conform to gender roles or domesticity to private spaces.[22]

Family Affairs

Jack's family was bicultural and interracial—with José Marcos making sure the children learned both English and Spanish and could function in both cultures. Jack would be raised in both cultures, fluent in Spanish and in English, baptized and raised Catholic, as were both of his parents, and sent to parochial schools run by women religious.[23] The in-betweenness of his childhood would most likely be complicated by that of the women religious who taught him and who themselves lived lives of contradiction.

At a time when most California Mexicanos and Chicanos were laborers, Jack was born into a professional family. And, as noted by Borunda, class status would have mattered both in José Marcos Mugarrieta's native Mexico and in the United States. Workers leaving Mexico to find labor in the latter part of the nineteenth century were most often pushed into the fields and barrios of greater Mexico; landed families and middle-class families who had access to formal education in Mexico sometimes found work as middle-class professionals or white-collar workers. While eventually some of these families lost status, initially, they held an advantage working-class laborers lacked.[24]

Jack's father, José Marcos Mugarrieta, was the first Mexican consul to California, known among Mexicanos as "the great patriot." José Marcos was a soldier, a poet, and a man of letters. During the U.S. Invasion, he fought to protect his beloved Mexico. After the war he served first as secretary of war, then as an aide to President Mariano Arista. Yet this was a time of unrest in Mexico; many citizens craved social reforms to benefit the poor as well as struggling artisans, yet others, yearning for social and economic stability, had begun to talk of benign monarchies. Liberals and conservatives struggled for power, and the threat of civil war resurfaced with each new election. Arista and Mugarrieta were liberals—liberals who did not stay in power for long. Arista was elected on a reform platform but was soon pushed from office by conservatives who ultimately gave the presidency to General Santa Anna.[25] And so José Marcos Mugarrieta accompanied his president into exile. When in 1853 Arista died, Mugarrieta brought his heart back to Mexico to be laid to rest. By that time Mugarrieta had established a reputation as a patriot, a man who loved his country dearly. When the liberals returned to power, Mugarrieta again sought to serve his country.

It was, in part, Mugarrieta's love for his country that brought him to California. When he offered to establish the first Mexican consulate in California, the Mexican government appointed him to the post. Two years later he was north of Mexico, working in a land that was once Mexico, trying to support Mexicans who had decided to stay in their homes post-Invasion. He also strove to support newer Mexican immigrants who sometimes traveled north, seeking work and opportunity. Like consuls from other countries, he organized patriotic events to remind Mexicans living in California of their homeland.[26]

Jack's mother was the daughter of Rice Garland, who served three terms as a representative from Louisiana in the U.S. Congress.[27] In 1846 he left Louisiana and established a law practice in Brownsville, Texas, where he conducted activity that accounts for probable tensions between the Garland and Mugarrieta families. For Rice Garland was a land speculator, a Euro-American who bought up land during and after the U.S. Invasion—land already claimed by Tejanas/os. Garland went so far to place notices in Texas newspapers, in both English and Spanish, reminding the inhabitants of Texas that Mexican laws no longer applied in Texas and the Southwest. U.S. law now reigned supreme and "by the laws of Texas no alien can hold real estate within its limits."[28] His statements were meant to threaten and intimidate. Yet by 1861, when Rice Garland died, José Marcos Mugarrieta and Eliza Garland were already married.[29]

While tensions may have existed between Mugarrieta and his father-in-law, correspondence with his wife and his mother-in-law stressed only his love of family. In his personal letters, he repeated time and again that his great loves were his country, God, and family. His letters were sometimes effusive, assuring his mother-in-law, for example, that love, not money, was the most important thing in life, and that he and his "querida rubia" lived better on bread and water than "many other people with their riches."[30]

Perhaps the love for his family that José Marcos professed is why Jack does not mention family tensions in his remembrances. Instead he paints a portrait of an ideal childhood struck by tragedy. His father represented all things noble, and his mother was a perfect lady—a woman who was devastated by her husband's death, who struggled to keep the family together, and to keep her young, somewhat unruly tomboy in good schools.[31]

From the time Eliza Garland and José Mugarrieta married until Mugarrieta's untimely death in 1886, the family was often short of funds. Mexico's government was devastated by the U.S. Invasion and the civil strife that followed; its civil servants received irregular paychecks. After Mugarrieta left his post as consul he patched together various skilled jobs to support his family. He worked for a while at a local bank, taught Spanish, and worked as a translator. The family continued to struggle economically; poverty was a constant threat.[32]

Early Years

While throughout the nineteenth century there was a stigma attached to masculine women—whether by Church or later by the medical profession, Jack, still called Elvira, was welcomed and loved by his family. He preferred to play with boys, refusing dolls and getting into trouble generally. His parents' response to his gender-disruptive behavior was to send him to a convent school, where he would be forced to socialize with young middle-class ladies.[33] And so while the family did not have money to set aside for savings, they did find money for parochial schools. This middle-class education would later make it possible for Garland to support himself, first as a cross-dressing woman and later as a man.

In convent school Mugarrieta Garland was taught by strong women who themselves lived lives of contradiction. Though they vowed to be obedient to a patriarchal Church, their communities contained seeds of democracy, with the women electing their own leadership, responsible for the formation of each new generation.[34] We do not have the name of the convent school to which Mugarrieta Garland was sent, but we do know quite a bit about the Catholic schools in the San Francisco Bay area. During Mugarrieta Garland's adolescence, many were run by Dominican sisters or women religious with roots in Europe—France to be specific. The presence of these women throughout California (and the entire hemisphere), would strongly weave and shape the culture in which nineteenth-century Catholic women were raised.

That a disproportionate number of San Francisco's Catholic institutions were founded by French women religious was not unique to the city. Throughout the nineteenth century, France saw a "phenomenal increase in the number of religious sisters," so that by 1880, two hundred thousand women had entered the vowed life. According to Susan O'Brien the increase was part of a structural shift in the life of women religious that would have a strong effect on women throughout Europe and the Americas. The majority of women entering religious life lived in active, not cloistered communities. They worked as nurses, teachers, teacher educators, and social workers.[35] Important to understanding women's roles within the Catholic Church is that also at this time the structure of Catholic women's communities changed so that their organizations were now headed by one superior, from their own communities, who answered directly to Rome, effectively removing local clergy as middlemen between them and their metropol. With the late nineteenth century as a world in motion, women religious made structural shifts to shape their own lives and the world around them.[36]

From the bursting women's communities of France, women religious went out to Ireland, Great Britain, India, Latin America, Africa, and the United States. Not ironically, the shift to national capitalism in France, with the rise of a middle class and the association of clericalism with monarchism, also spurred the spread of a particular brand of independent womanhood throughout Europe and the Americas. It was not just numbers and zeal but also concerns of anticlericalism that moved the women religious beyond France. In the late nineteenth century, for example, the Jesuits were expelled from France. French women's general superiors made strategic moves to ensure their communities would survive regardless of the political climate in their home country.[37] Such radical shifts in structure at the same time that women traveled across oceans and dispersed throughout five continents calls to mind a dynamic image of motion-change as well as trans-ing in the Kale Bantigue Fajardo sense of the word—where transgender encompasses diasporic geographies and cultural flows.[38] Mugarrieta Garland was taught by women who crossed oceans and claimed power, who lived lives of contradiction and in-betweeness, whose way of life was one of transition.

Santa Catarina's, later renamed St. Catherine's, was the first Catholic girls' school to be founded in California. It preceded the U.S. Invasion and, as an institution, it would be shaped by the cultural and economic shifts that followed. Its location was in Monterey, the capital of Alta California before the U.S. Invasion.[39] Not surprisingly, its founder was a French Dominican, Mother Mary Goemaere, who set out from France with a handful of sisters and a missionary priest to found her school in what was then Mexico. Later biographers would write of her as both "orderly, gracious, precise" and "strong and forceful."[40]

After Mother Mary's arrival in California in 1850, the order quickly became a multiethnic organization. The founding sisters were French, but soon two Californianas joined them: Concepción Argüello and Jacinta Castro. The fact that the convent was home to five sisters speaking three different languages (French, Spanish, and English) was reflective of the philosophy of many women religious communities of the time. For example, Mother Mary of St. Euphrasia of the Congregation of Our Lady of Charity is noted as exhorting her missionary sisters, "You will go forth and pitch your tents from one end of the earth to the other. . . . Your zeal must not be contented with one town, one foundation; it must comprise all lands and all people. . . . Since we are all of us pastors, or if you will, shepherdesses, we must not confine ourselves to one narrow spot. As for me, I do not wish any longer to be called French: I am Italian, English, German, Spanish; I am American, African, Indian."[41] Mother Mary's exhortation to her sisters as "pastors" gestures toward the contradictions lived by Catholic women religious of her time. They were strong, often adventurous women, who worshipped a colonial God in the context of a patriarchal Church where they could neither serve as priests nor hold office outside their own women's communities. In the words of Sarah Mulhall Adelman, their institutions demonstrated "a dynamic political culture of female self-governance . . . simultaneously empowering for the women involved and constrained within limits imposed by their religion and contemporary society."[42]

Students at the order's first school, Santa Catarina, could study a number of subjects, including reading, writing, religion, history, math, French, Spanish, English, music, and sewing. Then, in 1872, the school was renamed St. Catherine's and, according to Sister Patricia Dougherty, "became anglicized in name and personnel."[43] The shifts in women's roles throughout the state seems to have been repeated in Catholic schools, where the Euro-American standard of womanhood came to dominate. This white middle-class standard would be shaped by the demands of industrial capitalism, which required middle-class women to be "circumscribed within the home," their education a "disciplinary technology" to shape them into skilled, disciplined, domestic bodies.[44] The Catholic Church in California, like the larger state, was becoming a Euro-American space.

And so, whether the convent school Mugarrieta Garland attended was founded by French missionaries or by an American order, by the time he entered the school the curriculum would have been influenced by the dominant culture. This is not to say that the curriculum was not rigorous. By the close of the century, most of the Catholic girl's schools still taught botany as well as natural philosophy and mythology.[45] We do not know how Mugarrieta Garland did in sewing classes, or if he was required to take them. But we know that he learned all that he could from his writing courses and that the skills he obtained at school not only would allow him to work in the news profession later in life but would bring comment from those who observed him at work.[46] Mugarrieta Garland, had access to a formal education, but it was in the context of an ideology of domesticity, in an institution where Euro-American values were in the ascendancy.

While Mugarrieta Garland shifted from student to news reporter, and the Catholic schools of California shifted from a Mexican or multicultural environment to a Euro-American one, the medical profession throughout Europe and the United States was also undergoing a transition. The field of mental health, in fact, was flourishing, and the medical profession, as an emerging professional class, played a critical role in moving to stabilize the nation and the state of California. This stabilization required the policing and incarceration or hospitalization of bodies that did not fit into the gender roles assumed by the dominant culture, which was becoming increasingly pronounced in Nueva Nepantla.[47] Thus as Europe and the United States embraced monopoly capital, late nineteenth-century sexologists wrote about *homo-sexuals* and *inverts* who were attracted to members of the same sex or did not fit into socially accepted gender roles, or both. For some, like Richard von Krafft-Ebing, the two identities were one and the same: a person attracted to members of their own sex had mild cases of "homosexuality"; those with severe cases believed they were persons of the opposite sex.[48] Both were sick and could be reintegrated into society only if their psychological gender could be brought into line with their biological sex. While, for much of the late nineteenth century, many who challenged gender roles avoided the asylum, even in Nueva Nepantla not all were so fortunate. In San Francisco in 1890, Dick/Mamie Ruble was sent to the Stockton Insane Asylum for dressing as a man and insisting they were neither male nor female. After being subjected to a medical exam and declared female, they were committed to the Stockton insane asylum where they remained until their death.[49]

Two years prior to Ruble's incarceration, in May 1888, when Mugarrieta Garland was nineteen years old, he too was an inmate at the Stockton insane asylum. To date we know little about this time in his life; because of state records, however, we do know more about the context. In 1851 the state legislature had selected the institution to house California's mental patients, and in 1853 it was renamed the Insane Asylum of the State of California.[50] That the population of the institution grew so dramatically is indicative of a desire to bring stability to the region. Californians were admitted for causes as diverse as "religion" and "reading trashy novels."[51] Magennis and Lacy, in their study of asylum records for the State of Colorado during this time, found that immigrants and low-income residents were incarcerated at higher rates than native-born people and middle-class persons.[52] While a full-scale study of the records of California's asylum has yet to be completed, it appears that Mugarrieta Garland may have been swept up in a larger national attempt to stabilize regions recently acquired from Mexico while they were incorporated into the nation-state's larger project of industrialization and drive toward monopoly capitalism.

At the time of his incarceration the state asylum was grossly overcrowded. Its superintendent complained that they were housing five hundred more patients than the buildings were intended to hold. In the women's wing, patients overflowed into the attic, and the building itself had poor plumbing and poor ventilation.[53] In contrast to the close supervision and policing of his time in the nepantlan spaces of his convent school, the state asylum would have been one of chaos. With women sleeping in hallways and one hundred women crowded into the attic, only one female matron patrolled their population.[54] The lead physician reported women "danc[ing] around," "quarrelsome," and "noisy."[55] Yet it would be to Stockton that Mugarrieta Garland, having taken the name of Babe Bean, would travel twelve years later. Could it be that he, in this space of chaos and motion change, met other persons striving to move beyond the gender assigned them by the dominant society?

Causes of insanity

CAUSE	MEN	WOMEN
Injury to head	16	2
Intemperance	32	7
Love affairs	3	2
Masturbation	39	0
Opium or morphine habit	4	1
Reading trashy novels	0	1
Religion	10	3
Uterine troubles	0	4

Adapted from "Director's Report," *Appendix to the Journals of the Senate and Assembly* 6 (1889): 27–28, California State Archives.

For Mugarrieta Garland, cryptic notes in the hospitals' admissions logs list under "Evidence of Insanity" the reason "addicted to the habit of using opium," yet the attending physician had him discharged one month later, stating he was "in good health, rational and quite intelligent—not insane."[56] Was he admitted because he had used opium? Or was he admitted because he had begun to challenge gender norms? Had he already discovered that in working-class neighborhoods he could evade matrons determined to police the gender of the next generation? Mugarrieta Garland spent one month in the chaos of the State Asylum of California, in an overcrowded space with over one hundred women who did not meet the expectations of the communities from which they came. Upon his release into the custody of his mother, he returned to San Francisco, where he lived until 1897, when he returned Stockton as a person actively and overtly trans-ing gender.

The childhood of Mugarrieta Garland, who would grow to be Jack Garland, tells of a world in flux—a space and place of nepantla—where middle-class status, especially for ethnic Mexicans in the United States, was tenuous, and where socioeconomic shifts in the United States were so rapid that in mixed-race families, some members could benefit at the expense of others. Amid all this turmoil and motion-change, Jack, as a youth, was sent first to one nepantlan institution and then to another. Both institutions were established to shape women into Christian wives and mothers. The first, as a convent school, was a place of relative privilege and equipped Bean with the skills to live independently as a young adult. The second, a place that also policed gender roles, was a space of chaos incarcerating people from a variety of backgrounds who failed to live up to California's newly industrialized expectations. In the San Francisco to which Mugarrieta Garland returned, his family would struggle to cling to their middle-class status, at times failing to do so.

Becoming Babe Bean

When Mugarrieta Garland was in his teens, his father died. His mother took in sewing in an attempt to support the family, but wages for women's work in the late nineteenth century were not enough to support a family. As explained by Roslyn Feldberg, "sex segregation, male domination, and lower wages for women [became] an integral part of industrial capitalism in the United States. If men's work was to be both part of the definition of manliness and something that only men could do (at higher wages), sex segregation was crucial."[57]

While Eliza Mugarrieta took in sewing, one of her sons, William Mugarrieta, found work as a porter. We learn of his fate because while working as a porter he resorted to petty theft and was arrested for stealing a purse.[58] Ill with tuberculosis, he was sentenced to five years in San Quentin for his crime. Yet here, once again, the in-between status of the family, as Mexican and American, and tenuously middle class, becomes apparent—for the family wrote letters to California governor James H. Budd asking that William be released. The petitions of the family moved the governor, in part, because of the family's status, as he noted, "He belongs to a most excellent family, who are very desirous that he should not die and be buried a convict."[59] William was released from prison in March 1896 but was so ill he had a coughing attack while still on the ferry carrying him home, and according to the *San Francisco Call*, "a violent hemorrhage followed, and for a time it seemed as though he would die on the wharf."[60] Had the family shared the status of other Chicanx and ethnic Mexican families of their time, their requests might not have been granted; had they possessed a stable white middle-class status, William might not have been sentenced to five years in San Quentin. He died at the age of twenty-five while in the custody of his family.[61]

Sometime in 1897 Mugarrieta Garland made the transition to living as Babe Bean, or at times Beebe Bean. And he began to wear men's clothing, yet did not necessarily live as a man. When we look to late nineteenth-century and early twentieth-century newspapers, it becomes clear that Bean was not alone in his decision to live in a man's world.[62] As will be discussed below, among trans men of color there was William Cathay, a freed slave who joined the 38th U.S. Infantry Regiment during the Civil War, lived as a man, and went on to become a buffalo soldier.[63] And then there is Ralph Kerwineo who, it appears, chose women as his intimate partners. [64] Bean and Cathay and Kerwineo all crossed gender lines at a time when doing so put them at risk for harassment and, at times, incarceration, for capital was moving to stabilize itself.

In this climate of economic and gender flux, Mugarrieta Garland became Babe Bean. Socially he lived as a masculine woman, dressed like a man, and lived in a man's neighborhood. While we do not know about the early childhood of Cathay or Kerwineo, we do know something of Jack's childhood. If we return to local newspaper articles addressing his childhood, we meet a masculine child rebelling against their assigned gender. According to one of his childhood neighbors, he "was always a most peculiar, original child, and a regular tomboy, never caring anything at all for the many little trifles which usually interest and delight youthful femininity. The finest doll in the world had no attraction for her if a top or a kite were handy."[65] Into this mix, however, we must also add race and ethnicity, for Mugarrieta Garland was also of Mexican descent, living in a land that "was Mexican once." And so we come to know Babe Bean, a young masculine person, who had behaved in a masculine manner from his earliest childhood, and who, as a young adult, chose to dress as a man and labor in a man's world, in a space where Euro-Americans continued to use the language of empire in describing mestiza women.

The Life and Times of Babe Bean

By 1897, when Bean returned to Stockton, California, he was twenty-eight years old and had developed a new persona—Babe Bean. Babe Bean was bold. But having outgrown the rough-and-tumble of his childhood days, Bean now adopted the ways not of tomboys but of men. In fact, it may be that Bean's initial intention, in Stockton, was to live as a man. Dressed as a man, Bean did not speak but responded to any questions with pencil and paper. During Bean's initial appearance as Bean, the people of Stockton seemed unsure regarding his sex and noted, "The mystery is still out as to whether "Babe" Bean is a boy or a girl, a man or a woman. It is true that this peculiar personage could be taken for a male or female."[66] The "mystery" was solved for the readers of the *Stockton Daily Record* three days later when the paper reported on Bean running to catch a late-night streetcar. "She was thrown on her head to the pavement, turned two or three somersaults and lay limp as a rag."[67] Bean was taken to the local drugstore for treatment, and thereafter debate regarding his sex did not appear in the local press; instead the press assumed Bean was female.

For the remainder of Bean's stay in Stockton, he dressed as a man, secured work as a man, and lived in a man's neighborhood. He traveled in male environments, and eventually left Stockton to go work as a reporter covering a man's war. Yet he did not publicly identify as a man; in the semiurban town of Stockton, his in-between gender identity sometimes caused him problems, attracting the attention of police officers as well as of civilians who wished to police gender. He lived in between genders, and it would appear, in between ethnicities.

The Stockton of Babe Bean's time was both Euro-dominant and multiethnic.[68] Yokoch peoples of the region had been joined by Californianas/os and Mexican immigrants, people referred to as "Spanish" by the local Euro-Americans.[69] Most of the ethnic Mexican residents were not very wealthy; their dance hall was located along McLeod's Lake, a low-income area of town.[70] Not surprisingly, it is here that Bean chose to make his home. As in his childhood, did he continue to move back and forth between cultures? We cannot be certain, but his decision to live on McLeod's Lake may have, in part, been because it was a hybrid space.

And it may have been his biracial status that also allowed him to dress and work as a man in a world where capital was moving to stabilize gender, for Bean was living not just in the U.S. national West, but in California, where Euro-Americans continued to struggle to justify their possession of the land. Amid this conflict, a new body of popular culture emerged, one that racialized elite Californiana and ethnic Mexican women, especially those with one white parent, as sexually desirable. As argued by Shelley Streeby, from the time of the U.S. Invasion, well into the 1870s, newspaper stories and dime novels addressed the U.S. Invasion with tales of Yankee heroism. Critical to Bean's history is that many of these stories featured cross-dressing heroines: Mexican women who dressed as men to defend their country against Yankee invaders, but who ultimately fell in love with a U.S. soldier and resumed feminine attire and social roles.[71]

Initially as Bean adopted masculine attire and a masculine life, he did not do anything resembling the mythologized cross-dressing maidens of post-Invasion dime novels. Instead, Bean lived on an ark on McLeod Lake, a masculine, working-class, multiethnic neighborhood.[72] Rather than places that celebrated empire, such neighborhoods were unglamorous spaces where people struggled to get along.

1. McLeod's Lake and ark dwellers. Courtesy of the Haggin Museum, Stockton, California.

Arks provided a stable dwelling for their owners and renters: simple houseboats, they had no utilities and were eventually declared a public nuisance and done away with.[73] But in the 1890s their owners and renters hung on. An ark could be purchased for twenty-five dollars, or rented for four to six dollars a month—there was no docking fee. Many men were able to support themselves by fishing from their arks.[74]

Throughout Bean's early weeks in Stockton the public's response was mixed but often hostile. Bean was looking for work and living in a working-class area of town. It was clear he was not invested in finding a Yankee soldier to sweep him off his feet. In Stockton, in September of 1897, Bean was arrested for wearing men's clothing but was soon released, according to the press, because "in as much as it is merely a whim on her part to dress as she does, and is not for the purpose of disguise, there is said to be no legal reason why she should not wear pants instead of a skirt."[75] Bean was also released, in part, because he knew his rights under the law. When questioned, Bean pointed out that he had been careful "not to infringe against the law, which is that the wearing of apparel belonging to the other sex is punish-

THE NEAT AND TASTY INTERIOR OF BABE BEAN'S ARK.
[Reproduced From a Photograph by the Mail Artist.]

2. Babe Bean at home in his ark. From the *Stockton Evening Mail*,
October 9, 1987.

able only when it is done for the purpose of committing an offense
against the law."[76] With the rise of industrialization throughout the
United States, gender roles had been reinscribed in terms of public and
private spheres, yet in Stockton, there was not yet a law prohibiting
women from crossing the line into the public world of men, dressing
themselves in men's clothing, and doing a man's job.[77]

While Bean had allies, he was also treated as a freak—at times with
outright hostility. Thus while his gender expression and identity as a
person in between gender binaries was not yet illegal, it did make him
the object of public ridicule. The local press published several stories
referring to Bean as a "woman or girl or what not," a "bright faced
girl-boy," a "What-is-it," and a "freak."[78] Women in Stockton threatened to "stand her up"—to expose Bean and make him stand trial,
as did the police.[79] The women also threatened to "dunk [Bean] in
McLeod's lake," bringing to mind the work of Federici and the specter

of the witch, the need to humiliate and attack bodies that disrupt the function of capital in Western societies.[80] Yet in the late nineteenth century, before monopoly capitalism had completed its domination of greater Mexico, Bean was able to move from being treated as a freak to being just another resident of McLeod's Lake.

Despite hostility Bean continued to dress as a man and through diligent labor won himself the respect of local newspaper editors. At first he earned money writing about himself, or as one uncharitable neighbor described the situation, "she earns some money herself . . . by being such a freak that newspapers pay her for telling them about it."[81] The initial news articles printed in the *Stockton Evening Mail* were about his life as a local spectacle. Yet within a year of his arrival, this situation changed. The *Mail* hired him on as a regular correspondent.[82] Bean was sent out to report on everything from baby shows to the conditions at the state asylum both within and beyond the city limits; it appears that he earned the respect of the editor of the *Mail* as well as its readership.[83]

While living as a person in between genders Bean also lived as a person in between cultures. As historian Nan Alamilla Boyd noted, the fact that Bean sometimes passed as a man raises the question of passing ethnically.[84] While Boyd suggests that Bean did pass in Stockton, newspaper evidence suggests that during the time Bean lived as a cross-dressing woman—a masculine woman—he may not have passed as Euro-American. As Bean did in his childhood, he continued to live between cultures. Thus, when, in September 1897, Bean was accused of being Clara Garcia and "half Spanish," he denied his name was Clara but not that he was mixed race. As discussed below, this is when the press also objectified him with language similar to that with which they objectified women of Mexican descent. Bean, according to the press, was "indignant" at being confused with Clara Garcia, but the article also noted that Bean's indignation was at being associated with "immoral behavior."[85]

Just two months following the Clara Garcia incident, Bean made use of his bicultural skills in a public setting. He returned to the state asylum not as an inmate but as an observer. Did he fear encounters with staff who might recognize him from his month-long stay the

"I'll write it for to-morrow's Mail," was the response jotted down yesterday by Babe Bean, the mute ark-dweller of McLeod's lake when asked by a Mail representative for her opinion of men and women, as she has seen them in Stockton.

[Sketched by the Mail Artist.]

3. Working for the *Stockton Evening Mail*. From the *Stockton Evening Mail*, September 28, 1897.

decade prior? We have only Bean's published account of the visit and so do not know if any staff or inmates remained from the time of his incarceration. What we do know is that Bean reports going to the "Latin quarter" of the hospital and visiting, in Spanish, with a Mexican patient.[86] Whether or not Bean chose to pass at this point in his life, it seems doubtful that he would seek out assignments and spaces such as this, and perhaps make public use of his bilingual skills, were he passing as non-Hispanic. Later, in Manila, he would work as a translator. Bean's gender and cultural identity, then, seemed to coincide. While living as a masculine woman, he did not necessarily pass as white and was read as a bicultural person, as was apparent when at least one Spanish-speaking person approached Bean at the asylum and presumed that he spoke Spanish. Likewise, while in Manila, Bean moved easily between cultures, translating for the troops and then staying with a community of Jesuits, playing their organ, and offering to write the community's history.[87]

It appears that while living as a masculine woman, Bean either did not attempt to pass as white or could not pass as white. Once again, popular culture can teach us something about race, economy, and empire. While Bean lived in Stockton, newspapers wrote of his "dark hair and full mouth that tell of love of music, adventure and pleasure," much as the press earlier wrote objectifying descriptions of Californianas, and pulp novelists wrote of desirable cross-dressing mixed-race Mexican women.[88] While Bean adopted male attire and engaged in male labor, the press attempted to use the language of empire to claim Bean as a racialized feminine body who, like the heroines of their dime novels, might wear pants but also had the desirable features of dark hair and a "full mouth" that would justify conquest and containment.

Yet Bean refused to be contained. Instead he remained single and on McLeod's Lake, an in-between space where could support himself writing for local papers. He was able to secure labor as a news reporter and earn a living, not enough to afford an apartment but enough to pay rent on a houseboat. Bean was objectified, yet not relegated to the secondary labor market as were so many ethnic Mexicans of his time. In the late nineteenth century, as a mestiz@ violating gender boundaries, he was still allowed to exist outside of asylums and outside of the penal system.

At the close of the nineteenth century, Bean lived about five years of his life as a bicultural gender-nonconforming person in a town that continued to grow, shift, and not quite stabilize. Bean's neighbors identified him as female, yet he wore men's clothing. Bean did not go by his family name of Mugarrieta, but made no secret of his fluency in Spanish. He lived on an ark, or houseboat, in Stockton, California, in the working-class multiethnic area of town, where the "Spanish" dance hall was located. Yet in Stockton even the multiethnic space of

McLeod's Lake was fading and stabilizing. In June of 1900 the arks of the lake were declared a public nuisance, and little over a decade later the last of the arks were removed from the lake.[89] At the same time the railroads that were transforming the culture and economy of the continent gained dominance in Stockton, with its first depot having been constructed in 1898, agribusiness came to dominate the region and multistory buildings such as the Bank of Stockton began to populate downtown. Monopoly capital had come to Stockton, California.[90]

From Babe Bean to Uncle Jack: Circumstances Not of Our Choosing

When we weave gender into the cloth of late nineteenth-century Nueva Nepantla, the historical record does not necessarily become one of hope. As discussed in chapter 1, this was the era of the railroad and of Manifest Destiny. At the turn of the century the ideology of Manifest Destiny was expanded to the Caribbean and the Pacific basin.[91] Yet of the very few mestiz@ and trans people of color during this era, those who challenged the shift to empire or monopoly capitalism have not been located. Those we have found went along to get along; survival amid upheaval and, at times, violent change appears to have been the goal. Babe Bean, as addressed below, stowed away on a steamer to go see the action in the U.S. war in the Philippines.[92] There he acquired a military tattoo while serving as a volunteer with the 24th Regiment working as a translator.[93] Similarly William Cathay joined the 38th Infantry, a segregated African American regiment, and was sent to Kansas and New Mexico in part to put down Indigenous uprisings.[94] Neither Garland nor Cathay challenged monopoly capitalism—it appears that both served empire.

From early in the twentieth century we do have a record of the spouse of a transgender man of color speaking back to the dominant white public and challenging the racism of her time. Her defense of their family, following their exposure, gestures toward the challenges that women of color and trans people of color faced at the beginning of the last century. Here I am referring to Marie White, the spouse of Ralph Kerwineo, who, when exposed by the media of her time, challenged the racism against which she and Ralph struggled, pointing out, "You of the Caucasian race know nothing of the obstacles that are set in the way of people of dark skins, whatever their nationality. You know nothing of the trials, hardships, insults, sneers and jeers that we have to endure. You know nothing of the struggle that any dark-skinned person who rises to the top must make."[95] Yet while White spoke out in 1916, it appears that even this couple attempted to pass in order to survive. As noted by Emily Skidmore, White and Kerwineo had initially claimed Indigenous and South American heritages. At one point in time Kerwineo managed to secure housing in a predominantly white neighborhood.[96] To date we lack records from this time-space of nepantla of transgender heroes who refused empire. We have the voice of White, who loved a trans man, speaking out against the racism of the time, yet her voice appears anomalous within a larger context where survival as people who trans-ed was tenuous. Perhaps this is why Bean, who was soon to embrace an identity as Jack, did not challenge the empire of his time.

With the entrance of the United States into the Spanish-American War, Bean left California for the Philippines. By 1899 the people of the Philippines had already made clear their desire for independence, yet Bean and thousands of others left the continent for the islands. Initially Bean secured passage as a mess boy on an army transport ship to Hawaii, then stowed away on the same ship when it left dock for Manila.[97] Upon landing he worked as a translator for the troops.[98] While Bean had sometimes gone by the names of Jean or Jack while living in Stockton, he came to use the name more regularly among the troops, at times living as a male correspondent and translator and at times as female.[99] And, while in the Philippines, Jack continued to move between cultures. When mugged and injured in Manila, he stayed at a Jesuit house. The Jesuits in the Philippines were Spanish, and in the Philippine War for Independence were "not the object of hatred on the part of the native population" as were some of the other religious orders.[100] Whether he lived with the Jesuits as a man or a woman is not clear. He later wrote of playing the organ for them and offering to return and write their history.[101]

For Bean, this was a time of transition, for as Bean increasingly used the name of Jack, monopoly capitalism expanded and then stabilized throughout greater Mexico, demanding a stable gender binary. The war in the Philippines contributed to the new order, with the United States expanding its markets. As noted by Schoonover, following the wars in Cuba and the Philippines, "the U.S. economy experienced a boost in Asian and Caribbean trade. . . . In one year, U.S. imports from Asia rose forty million dollars and exports rose fifteen million."[102] Yet despite the increased movement of goods, monopoly capitalism did not adjust to accommodate a third gender; instead it categorized it as diseased and in need of correction so that it could be reintegrated into a larger productive society.[103] Like the witch of primitive accumulation, the deviant body had to be reformed or destroyed. Men produced, women secured the home; there was no place within monopoly capitalism for a third sex.

Upon his return from the Philippines, Babe Bean, now Jack, discovered that the California to which he returned was not the same place he had left. With each passing year, the West Coast moved to stabilize itself, its class structure, its race taxonomy, and in relation, its gender categories. In 1903 the local government approved San Francisco's Police Ordinance 819, which increased the penalties for cross-dressing. While as early as 1863 cross-dressing, along with several other behaviors labeled as "immoral," were listed as misdemeanors and subject to fines, at the turn of the century the law became even more severe and now read: "Prohibiting the Wearing of Apparel of Opposite Sex: Be it ordained by the People of the City and County of San Francisco as follows: It shall be unlawful for any person to appear, upon any public highway, in the dress, clothing or apparel not belonging to or usually worn by persons of his or her sex." The punishment for cross-dressing was now five hundred dollars in fines or six months' incarceration.[104]

It is at this time, Louis Sullivan argues, that Bean began to live full-time as a man. He took his mother's last name, and the person who had been Babe Bean became Jack Garland, a white male. It was turn-of-the-century California, monopoly capitalism was king, and a body had to claim either a male or a female identity to survive under its reign. And so Jack lived the life of a man on the margins and disappeared into the working-class masses of San Francisco's urban landscape. Following the San Francisco earthquake of 1906 Garland served as an accredited male nurse with the Red Cross.[105] But then he falls from the records, not appearing in any census data, with only scant references to his later life in the obituaries and sensationalist news articles that followed his death.

In those newspaper reports, it appears that his race, unlike that while he lived as Babe Bean, was unmarked. Absent from any accounts are objectifying descriptions of his "dark hair and full mouth"; neither are there stereotypes employed by the press when writing of ethnic-Mexican men. Looking at the function of unmarked race and what López refers to as the *transparency phenomenon*—that when race is unmarked in U.S. society the subject is considered white—it may be that Bean, in becoming Jack, also whitened.[106] Yet as both Peter Boag and Nan Alamilla Boyd point out, while gender and racial categories became more rigid following the turn of the century, in the poor and working-class neighborhoods of San Francisco, residents created pockets of resistance, where the rigid binaries of the newly emergent middle class did not necessarily apply.[107] While we do not know much of Jack's life after he took up residence in San Francisco, we do know that he roamed the streets at night, visiting with homeless men and giving away the little bit of money that he managed to earn for himself. When he collapsed on a San Francisco street in 1936 he was wearing a worn blue suit. Homeless youth had come to refer to him as "Uncle Jack."[108] Jack's decision to blend in with the poor and destitute of the city was one way to survive outside the rigid lines of the now entrenched gender binaries of white, capitalist America. It was a place of few resources, and thus less scrutiny.

Looking at the life of Jack Mugarrieta Garland through lenses of gender and political economy, we are able to gain insight into how gender, race, and class functioned in late nineteenth-century and early twentieth-century California. We find the lives of transgender people, including one transgender mestiz@, buried in newspaper archives, their genders challenged and contained upon their deaths. Thus, before the passage of legislation outlawing transvestism, while gender and capital remained in flux in Nueva Nepantla, Bean was able to support himself in the masculine world of newspapers. Bean was often treated as a freak, but police were not able to detain him for anything beyond questioning. In a time when women seldom earned a living wage, Bean supported himself reporting for local newspapers. As America moved into the twentieth century, there were fewer places, outside medical and correctional institutions, for transgender people to exist; labor was directed into one gendered sphere or the other. Unlike so many mestizas and mestizos who were pushed into the secondary labor market, Bean's "dark hair and full mouth" meant that he was sometimes objectified by the press but not excluded from collecting a paycheck from them.

In late nineteenth- and early twentieth-century California, gender and race were critical tools in constructing monopoly capitalism, and monopoly capitalism played a critical role in restricting and eventually erasing transgender mestiz@s. We know of Garland because his father was a well-known person in his own time, because of the historical excavation of Louis Sullivan, and because Jack's gender was disciplined upon his death. We know little of his life as a man living in San Francisco, it appears, because as capitalism stabilized itself throughout California, transgender bodies, including those of transgender mestiz@s, needed to hide in the cracks and fissures of the new economy. Looking at his life we can begin to see how the flux and stabilization of capitalism played a significant role in our queer mestiz@ past. It gives us cause to pause and think about how, in our present time of nepantla, its flux and stabilization might also influence our queer mestiz@ present and our queer mestiz@ futures.

CHAPTER THREE

NAFTA and Generative Movement in the Sixth Sun

Reality is a nepantla-process in progress.
—James Maffie, *Aztec Philosophy: Understanding a World in Motion*

The air that comes from above smells like fear. Not the air below. The air below smells nice, like things that are changing, like everything is getting better and more beautiful. Like hope, that's what the air below smells like to me.
—Subcomandante Insurgente Marcos in Ramírez, *The Fire and the Word*

As discussed in the opening chapters, nepantla is not only a middle space but also motion. The motion is generative, allowing for structural change, in fact driving and shaping it. While Mexica philosophers, from their gendered world, promulgated poems and songs of change and balance, in the late twentieth century, Chicanx scholars and activists revived some of the early teachings. Chicana feminists such as Gloria Anzaldúa brought nuance and depth to the work, and today scholars such as Lara Medina, Alicia Gaspar de Alba, and James Maffie apply the generative philosophy to the world around us.[1] It was Anzaldúa who argued that it is also the place from which those who challenge the status quo and who struggle for justice, labor.[2] Even in her early works, she argued that people of El Mundo Zurdo, "Third World women, lesbians, feminists, and feminist-oriented men of all colors," can embody such change.[3] And so in this chapter I focus on movement and change: destructive and creative. While, like Maffie, I hold that reality itself is process, I also hold that some time-spaces are more prone to movement than others, producing extraordinary generative change; our early twenty-first century is, like the beginning of the last century, a time of accelerated generative change. Thus in this chapter I move into the late twentieth century, to the socioeconomic shifts that gave rise to the world in which we continue to struggle today.

At first glance, this, our time, appears to be an unqueer time—a time of capitalist exploitation where bodies are of value only in their productivity. Yet a closer look reveals a weaving—albeit at present an unbalanced weaving—of economic consolidation and exploitation met by peoples' networked resistance. It is here that we must direct our queer gaze—to the world of globalization and the worlds of people's resistance. Engaging the work of Kale Bantigue Fajardo as it intersects with philosophies of nepantla, we can also see that the present, like the earlier turn-of-the-century shift to monopoly capitalism, is a time of trans-ing. Trade agreements tear down barriers, generating a movement of goods across borders, capital into third-world countries, and peoples from their homelands into export processing zones, or to the countries whose capital gave rise to the movement tearing at their homelands. Such movement intersects with the elimination of social programs that once served the common good—causing devastation to the people on the ground—driving people of El Mundo Zurdo, already the most vulnerable of their countries, to either despair or action. In the words of Claire Joysmith, these are "nepantlan times."[4]

This chapter addresses the function of today's global capital, returning to the theme of globalization, with a focus on trans-ing in relation to neoliberalism. Doing so, of course, means looking at the North American Free Trade Agreement (NAFTA), its function in the displacement and movement of people, and thus its role as a destructive force in today's generative change.[5] NAFTA *embodies* the inamic destructive force of economic globalization in our region. Yet it does not exist in isolation, and so I also briefly address the neoliberal shifts out of which NAFTA emerged, and sociopolitical and economic vacuums created by draconian trade agreements such as NAFTA that further fueled the violence pushing so many queer and nonqueer gente to flee to the North.[6] I also address both rural and urban resistance as it weaves and confronts such destructive movement. I provide a genealogy of the rise of the Zapatistas, including their roots in both the Fuerzas de Liberación Nacional (FLN) and the Indigenous movements of Chiapas—movements that preceded the arrival of the Ejército Zapatista de Liberación Nacional (EZLN) in the forests of the Lacandón jungle. I also look to workers in factories who have risen to fight the heightened exploitation driven by NAFTA and similar agreements, gesturing toward the varied and contentious weave that is our time. It is this movement—this weaving—that marks our sun as nepantlan and trans-ing.

Raices: On Mexico's Dirty War(s), Neoliberalism, and the Rise of Indigenous Democracies

We Indigenous women have begun to reflect on our rights and the rights of our people. . . . About fifty women from Tzotzil, Tzeltal, Tojola'bal, and Mam ethnic groups came together in the city of San Cristóbal. . . . We came from communities in the municipalities of San Juan Chamula, San Cristóbal de las Casas, Motozintla, La Independencia, Oxchuc, Teopisca, Ocosingo, Chenalhó, Chanal, and Pantelhó. We talked about poverty, discrimination, and injustice suffered by the Indigenous peoples, and we talked about violence and the mistreatment of women.
—Grupo de Mujeres de San Cristóbal de las Casas, 1994

In her later years, as Anzaldúa wrote of nepantla as place and motion, she turned to the town of San Miguel Nepantla, the home of Sor Juana Inés de la Cruz, as a generative space of nepantla. And so it is here, in the home of Sor Juana, that our opening scene for this discussion of globalization as nepantlan is placed. In her notebooks Anzaldúa wrote of nepantla as space and a site of origin for the Zapatista movement. Building on the work of Julie Reynolds, who had interviewed her in 1994, she wrote of the town as the birthplace of Sor Juana and of the site where the Mexican government massacred members of the FLN, the movement born in the cities of Mexico, that would be born again in the rural communities of Chiapas and the Lacandón jungle.[7] On February 14, 1974, as part of Operation Nepantla, federal troops invaded the general headquarters of the FLN, killing five members and arresting two others. They proceeded to El Chilar, the FLN ranch in the Lacandón jungle, executing and disappearing much of the leadership. While the violence of the raids is frightening, it was not unusual for the time, for in its efforts to modernize the nation-state, the federal government was in the midst of Mexico's Dirty War.[8]

The late twentieth century was a time of hope, repression, and revolution throughout the Americas; with the Cuban revolution of 1959 and the Sandinista revolution of 1979, a loud and clear message reverberated throughout the hemisphere: resistance is not futile.[9] In Mexico, even as this message was heard among multiple and diverse-dispersed communities, the federal and many state governments implemented neoliberal policies that reduced social programs and privatized communal landholdings. Rural and urban resistance groups, most advocating some form of socialism, emerged, as did government repression of these same movements. Even while welcoming refugees from Chile, Argentina, Guatemala, Nicaragua, and El Salvador, the federal government of Mexico waged war against political dissent within its own borders. While the Tlatelolco massacre was the most public exhibition of state-sponsored violence, it did not stand alone.[10] Federal troops and government-sponsored militias engaged in strikebreaking, raids on universities, and attacks on demonstrations in urban areas throughout Mexico. Activists, including those who were not involved in any guerilla movements, were jailed or disappeared. In rural areas the government engaged in "low-level bombing, scorched-earth tactics, and starvation." The war lasted from 1964 to 1982, during which an estimated three thousand citizens were disappeared, another three thousand executed, and seven thousand tortured.[11] It was a time of nepantlan violence, and the revolutionary communities of the late twentieth century, including the EZLN, were born from it.

Violence against the rural and Indigenous peoples of Mexico escalated in the 1960s and '70s on the part of both federally sponsored militias and large landowners in the southern state of Chiapas. While the Mexican Revolution, as well as the later government of Lázaro Cárdenas, had promised land reform and distribution among the rural peoples of Mexico, cattle ranches were exempt from land redistribution projects. By 1960, 22 percent of the arable land in Chiapas was used for livestock. Then in 1961 the state government passed a law to promote the livestock industry: taxes on livestock production were reduced, and ranchers were permitted to graze their cattle on ejido lands they claimed were unused. Equally important, the law made it legal for ranchers to hire or raise private militias to protect their property. By 1976, 49 percent of the land in Chiapas was used by cattle ranchers. One percent of the population had come to control half the land of the state.[12] Between 1982 and 1987 meat production increased by over 400 percent in the region.[13] And private armies and militias continued to push Indigenous peoples off communally held ejidos.[14]

While large landowners successfully fought to maintain and at times expand their holdings in the state of Chiapas, throughout the nation Indigenous and other rural peoples continued to struggle to hold onto and claim or reclaim communal property. By 1991, twenty million people, or a quarter of the population of Mexico, according to Neil Harvey, lived on or labored on ejidos—a total of 29,951 documented ejidos throughout the nation. And while land reform failed to free the prime land of Chiapas, the state did award ejidos to some rural and Indigenous communities. Some, such as many of those in southern Chiapas, had been fought for by Indigenous communities and campesinos throughout the time of Mexico's Dirty War.[15] Others were formed on forested lands not claimed by ranchers or agribusiness because the soil was poor; ranchers and coffee plantations maintained a hold on prime lands.[16] By the close of the century Chiapas remained "a region of large cattle ranches and coffee plantations alongside tiny family plots . . . [with] notoriously unequal distribution of land."[17] The people continued to fight for land throughout the region, all the while the federal government increasingly moved to bring the country into global markets, engaging in neoliberal policies that refused to coexist with communal properties such as ejidos.

While the state government introduced its cattle law, increasing economic inequality and displacing Indigenous peoples throughout the region, the federal government sought to acculturate Indigenous communities into mainstream Mexican culture, sponsoring the Summer Institute of Linguistics in the region—a U.S.-based organization, staffed by Protestant missionaries. In many ways the project was successful: by the twenty-first century a third of the population of Chiapas would be Protestant. This move also brought about a counter move/movement sponsored by the Diocese of San Cristóbal. In the early 1960s, influenced by the Second Vatican Council and by liberation theology, the bishop of San Cristóbal, Samuel Ruiz García, began working with the Indigenous communities of the region, leaning away from paternalistic, assimilationist politics and programs. Ruiz García promoted the education of Indigenous catechists, who then worked with faith communities to apply Christian messages of liberation to problem solving. Community assemblies became common in the Catholic lowlands.[18] And while liberation theology did not directly address issues of gender inequality, small-group Bible discussions allowed for women's voices to emerge, and at times gave rise to literacy workshops that included women. In relation, workshops and discussions on social inequality at times included gender in the mix. Gender as well as class exploitation was becoming part of the shifting weave of southern rural Mexico.[19]

At the same time, international attempts to develop the region, like the state cattle law, exacerbated inequality and exploitation. In 1972 the federal government, funded by the United Nations, implemented the Programa de Desarollo de Chiapas. While its stated goals included improved public health and education, it was the "integrated development for strategic zones" that took priority. The program included building the Chicoasen dam, flooding the Grijalva valley and displacing local campesinos, and building two thousand kilometers of roads. In neither project did the state or federal government consult local communities. The roads resulted in draconian price-fixing by middlemen such as commercial freight carriers; once again rapid growth of the livestock (as well as timber) industry pushed maize farms off arable land. Within this mix of movement and displacement a small number of Indigenous leaders were able to make economic and social gains from the investments, forming an Indigenous middle class, most of whom allied themselves with the ladino middle classes of the region's urban areas.[20]

It was during this time that the FLN began to build in the major cities of Mexico. Through movement and struggle it would become one of several points of origin for late twentieth-century Zapatismo. In its early iterations it embraced a strategy and philosophy of Guevarism—that guerilla leadership and dispersed organizing were critical to revolution—yet from its roots the FLN was eclectic and open to weaving various strategies and philosophies together. From 1969 to 1973 the FLN built an extensive network throughout the states of Nuevo León, Puebla, Veracruz, Tabasco, and Mexico City. They established cells: Estudiantes y Obreros en Lucha, and safe houses.[21] They even established an armed base in the Lacandón jungle—though at this point in time, they were not yet "listening," and sought to use the base more for its strategic location than for forming alliances with the Indigenous communities of the region.[22] While the FLN built its numbers in the urban cities of Mexico and struggled in the Lacandón jungle, the government of Mexico continued to hunt down guerilla leaders and political dissenters throughout the nation.

In February 1974 disaster struck; while investigating the murder of Eugenio Garza Sada, the police discovered an FLN safe house in Monterrey. There they found, interrogated, and tortured two FLN members, who gave them the location of the FLN's general headquarters in Nepantla, Mexico. Naming their action Operation Nepantla, federal troops raided the headquarters, killing five members and uncovering key documents, including the location of the military camp in the Lacandón jungle. The raid on the camp, like the raid on the headquarters, was merciless; federal troops disappeared three of the members and executed another three, burying them in unmarked graves. In the end, only two of the original leaders survived: Mario Sáenz and FernandoYáñez.[23] When the FLN rebuilt and once again relocated in the Lacandón jungle, it would not be to find a strategic military position alone but to listen. Equally important, by the time they returned to the jungle many of the communities they encountered were also radicalized.

The state of Chiapas in 1974 held multiple and dramatic seeds of resistance. Rural cooperatives began to flourish, and gender roles continued to shift, with the women of southern Chiapas gaining tools toward individual and community empowerment. A focal point of many of these strands of change was the First Indigenous Congress of Chiapas, hosted by the diocese of San Cristóbal de las Casas. The governor of Chiapas, Manuel Velasco Suarez, called for an Indigenous congress to celebrate the five hundredth anniversary of the birth of Bartolomé de las Casas. Bishop Samuel Ruiz García accepted his invitation to help with the organization of the congress with the qualification that the government not dictate its structure or agenda. Thus, while government support came from a hope of incorporation and acculturation, the result of the conference was bottom-up organizing.[24] While not part of the official decision-making process, Indigenous women took part in the meetings as well as the marches associated with the congress.[25] Twelve thousand three hundred representatives from Tzotzil, Tzeltal, Chola, and Tojolabal communities came together and addressed health, housing, education, and land concerns. At the close of the congress the communities made several demands, including land rights, health care, and education in their own languages. Prior to, during, and following the congress the diocese supported networking between the communities and regional leftist communities such as the Unión del Pueblo and Línea Proletaria. Thus throughout the late 1970s in southern Chiapas, there were increases in Indigenous networking and Indigenous cooperatives.[26] In relation, Catholic Church–supported cooperatives such as Las Abejas and La Selva would later emerge as ideological allies of EZLN, working toward Indigenous rights.[27]

While women attended the Indigenous Congress and participated in women's groups throughout the 1970s, it would be in the 1980s that, listening to the collaborative voices of women religious and Indigenous women, the diocese established the Coordinadora Diocesana de Mujeres (Diocesan Council of Women, CODIMUJ). Looking back, we see clearly that CODIMUJ was a critical strand in the weaves of Indigenous and gender realities in late twentieth-century Chiapas. CODIMUJ sponsored workshops and facilitated the formation of cooperative bakeries, artisan centers, chicken farms, and, in relation, small markets where women pooled their funds to purchase goods in bulk and thus cut out exploitive middlemen.[28] Some CODIMUJ women went on to become Zapatistas; others tried to remain active in both groups. As noted by Klein, "The EZLN and the diocese employed similar strategies in their work with women: creating spaces for women to have a voice, advocating for women's right to participate, teaching women to read and write, forming women's cooperatives, and organizing women's regional gatherings."[29]

In 1982, amid such organizing, repression, and struggle, economic crisis rocked Mexico once more; the government again looked to devastating neoliberal policies as remedies. Outside influences such as the United States and the International Monetary Fund used the crisis to pressure the government to embrace their neoliberal agenda: elimination of social programs, privatization of state-owned utilities, reductions in trade barriers, industrial deregulation, and foreign investment. As noted by Luisa Paré, the austerity programs imposed by the International Monetary Fund "disproportionately affected peasants and industrial workers, lowering 1988 wages to 1960s levels and significantly reducing living standards, particularly in terms of health and nutrition."[30] While the austerity programs took their toll on the people of Chiapas, General Absalón Castellanos Domínguez was elected governor of the state. This member of the landed elite escalated paramilitary violence against Indigenous communities and political activists.[31] It is not surprising that the 1980s saw the birth of the EZLN.

In November 1982 a remnant of the FLN, now reborn as a mestizo-Indigenous organization, returned to the Lacandón jungle. It was a small group, composed of three mestiza/o and three Indigenous insurgents.[32] For much of the 1980s there was some crossover between the FLN and the EZLN. Comandanta Elisa, for example, who was the commander of EZLN's forces for many years in the 1980s, eventually returned to Mexico City and to her work there in the FLN.[33] While the new group differed from the earlier FLN in its ethnic composition, it also differed from it in its approach to revolution. The EZLN now stressed listening and spent its first year getting to know its small corner of the jungle, sending back to the city for supplies, and then traveling to villages to talk to individuals, and again listening. For Comandante Marcos, who joined the group in its second year, it was the arrival of this small band in the Lacandón jungle that would mark the birth of EZLN.[34]

As the group traveled from village to village, recruiting one member at a time, they found a population that had survived and continued to survive the violence of the dirty war and the Salinas government's commitment to neoliberalism and global capital. As Comandante Abraham would later note, "When the Zapatista Army first came to our village, around 1984, 1985, we had already taken part in peaceful struggles. . . . Since the repression that the compañeros told us about already existed, when the message of the EZLN arrived we were glad, and we felt happy that there was another struggle to defend the security of the small farmers and the poor."[35]

Throughout the 1980s, the work of the EZLN was necessarily clandestine. While some historians mark 1984 as the end of Mexico's Dirty War, for Indigenous peoples of Mexico, as well as mestizas/os working small farms in the south, the war continued into the 1990s.[36] In the course of the decade the government would be tied to the deaths of 814 campesinos, with the leadership of independent peasant and Indigenous organizations as primary targets.[37] Yet the organizing continued. Once enough insurgents were recruited to protect a village, the founding of a clinic would begin. As explained by Comandanta Sandra, during these years "our struggle was clandestine. . . . We organized family by family, village by village, neighborhood by neighborhood—depending on the geography of each region . . . but we were not afraid."[38]

Within the context of accelerated repression and accelerated resistance, gender roles continued to shift. The work of organizations such as CODIMUJ served as watersheds, as did the early FLN commitment to gender equality that the original six brought with them from their training and activism. Yet on the ground, recognizing the equality of women continued to be a fierce struggle, pushing against traditions born of five hundred years of colonization.[39] In its failure to fully integrate women into its leadership and infrastructure the EZLN had much in common with other activist organizations of the time, for in the 1970s and into the 1980s many revolutionary groups, including those in Mexico, failed to question gender roles, at times treating gender struggles as secondary to "people's" liberation.[40] Yet the power of the movement in generating life-giving motion-change was tied to their own struggle to do just this. As Esmerelda, one of the women active in EZLN prior to 1994, explained, the early movement insisted on the right of women to fully participate, but it lacked a gender analysis necessary to fully incorporate women.[41]

An explicit gender analysis, rooted in listening to women throughout the communities of southern Mexico, had to happen for full participation of women to be a possibility—and so women such as Esmerelda pushed the leadership to do just that. Comandanta Susana, head of the women's commission of the Clandestine Revolutionary Indigenous Committee (CCRI) of the EZLN, was commissioned to travel throughout rural communities listening to women and asking them about their wants, needs, and visions.[42] As they engaged in dialogue they asked the communities in each region to draft a revolutionary law for women; these drafts would form the base of the Women's Revolutionary Law.[43]

In 1993 the CCRI voted on the law. Comandante Marcos would later recall,

> Susana had to read the proposals that she had gathered. . . . As she read on, the assembly of the CCRI became more and more restless. You could hear murmurs and comments. Susana, undisturbed, kept charging forward. . . . "We don't want to be forced into marriage with someone we don't want. We want to have the number of children we want and can care for. We want the right to hold positions of authority in the community." At the end there was a weighty silence, the Women's Laws that Susana had just read meant a true revolution for the Indigenous communities. The women authorities were still receiving the translation, in their Indigenous languages. . . . The men looked at each other nervous, restless. All of a sudden, almost at the same time, the translators finished, and in a single movement the women authorities began to applaud and talk among themselves. Needless to say, the Women's Laws were approved unanimously.[44]

In 1993 the Zapatista army also engaged in its first public action, one that scholars such as Neil Harvey and Alex Khasnabish would later write of as EZLN "testing the waters." ANCIEZ (Alianza Nacional

Campesina Independiente Emiliano Zapata), the public face of EZLN, along with other Indigenous organizations such as the Organización Campesina Emilano Zapata, organized a march of thousands on the capital of San Cristóbal.[45] They marched under the banner of "500 years of Indigenous, Black, and Popular Resistance in Chiapas." The protestors tore down the capital's statue of conquistador Diego de Mazariegos, smashing the colonial symbol to pieces.[46] Then ANCIEZ went underground. The Zapatistas returned to their home communities and voted to go to war.[47]

Focusing on the country of Mexico as a crucible of late twentieth-century neoliberalism and global capital, we can see that the forces of neoliberalism had and have multiple manifestations: the extension of agribusiness into the rural areas of Mexico, privatization of communal lands, violent suppression of resistance movements, and the forced movement of people from their home communities to places north—in Mexico and greater Mexico.[48] We can also see that when NAFTA became the governing trade agreement of the North American continent, it did so as part of a larger project of neoliberalism—one which the people of Mexico had resisted for decades. The EZLN comprised several strands of resistance yet did not weave in isolation. Indigenous organizations, the EZLN, and Catholic base communities (comunidades eclesiales de base) such as those in the Diocese of San Cristóbal wove a resistance that would eventually capture the imagination of all of the Americas and beyond. In their resistance and movement, these communities also shifted gender roles, allowing for women leaders in all walks of life.[49] In the context of this nepantlan struggle in Mexico it would be Indigenous peoples who took the lead in challenging the destructive forces of totalizing capital.

NAFTA as Inamic Destructive Force

The discussion that led to the creation of the North American Free Trade Area was—arguably—the most important negotiation between the United States and Mexico since the Treaty of Guadalupe Hidalgo of 1848.

—Sidney Weintraub, *Negotiating NAFTA*

While proponents of NAFTA, such as Sidney Weintraub and Hermann von Bertrab, argued and argue that NAFTA would benefit Mexico, improving a balance of power, restoring trust, and moving Mexico into a position as a competitive player in the world of global capital, to date others point to the trade agreement's destructive force in the lives of workers, small farmers, and Indigenous peoples. The trade agreement, signed by the prime minister of Canada and the presidents of Mexico and the United States in 1992, and passed by the U.S. Congress in 1993, eliminated most trade barriers between the three largest countries of the North American continent, creating incentives for U.S. manufacturers to move south; it priced hundreds of thousands of small farmers in Mexico out of their markets, and established probusiness tribunals to address labor and environmental concerns.[50] While Weintraub did not acknowledge NAFTA as destructive, he was apt in pointing to it as "the most important negotiation between the United States and Mexico since the Treaty of Guadalupe Hidalgo of 1848." In January 1994, NAFTA emerged as a destructive force in the lives of millions, including the people of el Mundo Zurdo living in North America.

NAFTA, according to Hermann von Bertrab, was born on a winter's evening in Davos, Switzerland. The World Economic Forum was meeting, and on one sleepless night President Salinas came into the room of Jaime Serra-Puche, his secretary of commerce, and asked his opinions regarding a possible free trade agreement with the United States. The next day Serra-Puche broached the topic with U.S. trade representative Carla Hills, and machinery was quickly set into motion. The presidents of the two countries, both champions of neoliberalism, exchanged correspondence; Salinas de Gortari made a formal request to the U.S. Congress for George H. W. Bush to be able to negotiate the agreement as a fast-track piece of legislation, and the struggle began.[51]

Proponents of the trade agreement ultimately signed by the governments of Canada, the United States, and Mexico argued that the countries needed such an agreement to remain competitive in a global market. The fact that the idea emerged at the World Economic Forum indicates that economic competitiveness was very likely at the heart of the motivation for the agreement, yet even as proponents began to lobby for fast-track negotiations, labor organizations, environmental groups, and other nongovernmental organizations voiced concerns. Organizations as diverse as the Maryknoll Fathers and Friends of the Earth insisted that labor and environmental protections be included in negotiations, while proponents such as Bertrab treated their demands as "impossible dreams."[52] Amid the back-and-forth of lobbyists and interest groups, on May 24, 2001, less than a year after Mexico first requested fast-track negotiations, Congress agreed to give President Bush the power to negotiate a free trade agreement with Mexico and Canada.[53]

Labor unions, environmentalists, and progressive scholars in Mexico and the United States continued to voice concerns regarding the impact of NAFTA on workers, infrastructure, and economic inequality—all factors of society that influence human rights, stability, and movement. While they did not succeed in their demands to include environmental and labor protections in the initial agreement signed by Presidents Salinas and Bush in December 1992, their persistence did result in the inclusion of two side agreements passed by the U.S. Congress one year later. The side agreements established a Commission on Environmental Cooperation to improve collaboration throughout the region; equally important for workers and the environment, it established panels to which parties could appeal regarding environmental and labor violations.[54] While conservatives applauded the narrow application of protections—only "recognized entities" would have access to the panels and only NAFTA's signatories could "request the dispute settlement procedures be put in motion"—labor and environment proponents saw those same safeguards as red flags.[55] They would continue to argue for stronger protections through to the day of the U.S. Congressional vote.

In Mexico, coalitions such as the Red Mexicana de Acción Frente al Libre Comercio pointed out that the tribunals NAFTA would establish lacked the transparency of national judicial proceedings. The closed doors behind which proceedings would take place could easily allow them to rule that labor and environmental protections were barriers to free trade. They further argued that because NAFTA did not require businesses to invest in the infrastructure around them, the trade agreement would widen the gap between the wealthy and the poor and place unmitigated strain on the infrastructures of export processing zones. For activists in Mexico the fate of rural communities was also critical. Throughout the latter half of the twentieth century the move to cash crops had already displaced many small subsistence farmers. It appeared NAFTA would further disrupt the stability of rural Mexico. Not surprisingly, organizations such as the U.S. Citizens' Task Force on NAFTA shared similar concerns, especially in relation to infrastructure and opaque, extragovernmental tribunals.[56]

Yet by 1993 the U.S.-NAFTA Coalition, the largest pro-NAFTA coalition advocating for the agreement, had grown to twenty-three hundred corporations and lobbying groups; in October of the same year former presidents Ford, Carter, and Bush made a public statement in favor of it. The National Council of La Raza, headed by Raúl Izaguire, also promoted the agreement.[57] And supporters spent over $25 million in an effort to bring members of Congress and their constituents on board. Not surprisingly, on November 17, 1993, the House approved NAFTA with its side agreements; three days later the Senate did the same, and on December 8, 1993, President Bill Clinton signed the agreement into law.[58]

Following the 1993 signing of NAFTA, the concerns of activists in both Mexico and the United States were realized in the factories of export processing zones (EPZs), in the rural countryside, and in the forced movement of people both within and from Mexico. Related to these changes and equally devastating, the vacuum left by displaced persons helped to fuel the rise of drug cartels throughout the country.[59] Fortunately, for each destructive force in the twenty-first century, we can find its inamic, justice-producing counterforce, and so the violent movement wrought by NAFTA and similar trade agreements of our time have been and continue to be met by equally revolutionary movement.

Generative Resistance I: The Fields

From the time he went to the Lacandón jungle until his death in battle on January 1, 1994, Subcomandante Pedro was known for his commitment to the people, his commitment to discipline, and his joy—including the joy with which he would break into poetry, reciting "Tecún Umán," the rhythmic and magical recounting of the Mayan warrior Tecún Umán's brilliant and fatal struggle against the Spanish invaders of his land.[60] It is said that when the people voted to march on San Cristóbal with arms, Subcomandante Pedro danced, because he knew it was time; he knew the action was needed.[61]

For the Zapatistas NAFTA was the last straw—a government action demonstrating that the federal government, rather than listening to the campesinos and Indigenous people of Mexico, would continue to implement policies devastating to their communities. While the neo-liberal reforms of Presidents Miguel de la Madrid and Carlos Salinas de Gortari had created massive displacement throughout the state of Chiapas and the nation, NAFTA would exacerbate the destructive motion-change of the previous decades. And so the people voted—the Indigenous Revolutionary Clandestine Committee voted and made it official; on January 1, the day on which NAFTA was scheduled to go into effect, they would go to war.[62]

Thus early on the morning of January 1, 1994, the military branch of EZLN entered the capital of Chiapas fully armed. They seized government offices, occupied thousands of acres of private land, and took control of several different municipalities.[63] They issued the First Declaration of the Lacandón Jungle:

> We are a product of 500 years of struggle: first against slavery, then . . . the War of Independence against Spain led by insurgents, then to avoid being absorbed by North American imperialism. . . . We have been denied the most elemental preparation so they can use us as cannon fodder and pillage the wealth of our country. They don't care that we have nothing, absolutely nothing. . . . Nor are we able to freely and democratically elect our political representatives, nor is there independence from foreigners, nor is there peace nor justice for ourselves and our children.
> But today, we say ENOUGH IS ENOUGH.
> We are the . . . true builders of our nation. The dispossessed, we are millions and we thereby call upon our brothers and sisters to join this struggle as the only path.[64]

The insurgents asked the people of Mexico to rise up and join them in fighting for "work, land, housing, food, health, education, independence, freedom, democracy, justice, and peace," and they declared war on the "supreme government" headed by Carlos Salinas de Gortari.[65]

The federal government responded by sending more troops to the state. They set up roadblocks and shot health-care workers; they even shot at Red Cross ambulances. They shelled communal populations, arrested people suspected of being Zapatistas, and detained and executed at least six people; others were tortured.[66] The armed resistance and violence between the troops lasted for twelve days, as did the federal army's harassment and attacks on the civilian population of the state. Then the government called for a cease-fire.

While the people of Mexico had not taken up arms, they had flooded the plazas and streets, demanding justice for the Zapatistas and an end to the violence. Students held solidarity demonstrations, nongovernmental organizations began to come to the area to observe and to report.[67] Initially the Salinas government offered a pardon to any Zapatistas who would lay down their arms. To this the EZLN published an open response titled "What Will We Be Pardoned For?" "What will they pardon us for? For not dying of hunger? For not remaining silent in our misery? . . . For having risen up in arms when we found all other roads closed off? . . . For having demonstrated to the rest of the country and the world that human dignity still lives and is present in its poorest inhabitants? . . . Who needs to ask for pardon and who can give it?"[68]

The EZLN entered into dialogue with the federal government, with Bishop Ruíz García acting as intermediary. The dialogues did not result in resolution but did help open further dialogue with the public, who asked the EZLN to engage in a nonviolent revolution. While the EZLN embraced the new strategy, the federal and state government continued its violent war against the EZLN and against the Indigenous people of Mexico. At the close of 1994 Ernesto Zedillo was elected to the presidency amid yet another fiscal crisis. He accepted a fifty-billion-dollar bailout package from the United States. It came with requirements for severe structural adjustments. In February 1995 Zedillo launched an offensive against EZLN communities, destroying houses and assaulting, arresting, and torturing those suspected of leadership or of knowing leaders. Approximately thirty thousand people were displaced.[69]

While the EZLN continued to grow both in numbers and in influence, the state and federal governments continued to engage in what can only be seen as yet another dirty war. On December 22, 1997, a paramilitary group armed and trained by state police went into the hamlet of Acteal, claiming to be looking for Zapatistas. They entered a church where forty-five men, women, and children had taken refuge from recent government-sponsored attacks on their village. The paramilitary group massacred them all, even the children. One child, an eleven-year-old girl, survived; she pretended to be dead after her mother fell on top of her.[70] The victims were not Zapatistas but Abejas, the pacifists of southern Mexico who also work for the empowerment of their communities. The violence against the EZLN and the Indigenous and peasant communities of the south continued, yet the numbers of Zapatistas and their allies continued to grow in Mexico and internationally. In Mexico the Zapatistas established caracoles (regional self-government structures) with good government councils to meet the growing administrative needs of their communities.[71] Internationally, organizations such as Schools for Chiapas and the Struggle continued and continue to keep the hope of resistance alive, as does the EZLN's own website and publications.[72] While organized violence against the EZLN and suspected allies continues to ebb and flow with each new federal and state election and each new economic crisis, the 1994 uprising both caused a further shift in gender roles in EZLN communities and brought about a national and international wave of hope that resistance is possible, that new ways of imagining what it means to be a citizen and, in fact, a human being are possible.

Generative Resistance II: The Factories

While the resistance of the EZLN and the rural communities of Mexico have inspired people throughout the hemisphere, their struggles remain just one critical strand in the weave of resistance that continues to move in and out of neoliberal policies and actions. Another critical weave of resistance is found in the factories of Mexico and the tens of thousands of workers affected by global capital. The violence to workers and to those living in Mexico's EPZs reached a point of saturation years ago. Local and some international organizations continue to struggle for basic human rights in EPZs where, as predicted, the companies building their factories and taking advantage of a burgeoning labor pool have not invested in the infrastructure from which they profit.

Confronting increased violence against women to the point of femicide is part of a larger struggle for justice in the unbalanced and violent spaces that result when profit is placed over people's lives. Such violence, as well as women's resistance to this violence, has been documented by Chicana feminist scholars such as Alicia Gaspar de Alba and Georgina Guzmán, and Kathleen Staudt and Zulma Y. Méndez.[73] Here I focus on the struggle of the workers in the factories of the EPZs for livable wages and safe working conditions within the world that NAFTA made. This refocusing shifts our gaze to the multiple strands of resistance that weave our times and, in relation, demonstrates the beautiful and complex weave of which trans activism is part; labor activism, at its best, is trans-ing, moving, shifting, and creating spaces where people can flourish as their authentic selves.

The Duro Bag incident of 2001 is among the most widely documented examples of worker struggles in the factories of the NAFTA era.[74] It reveals in structural terms both the lack of worker protections under NAFTA and the hope for worker rights and protections in international labor organizing. Located in Rio Bravo, Tamaulipas, Duro had a reputation for paying some of the lowest wages in the city, as Silvia Martínez, a former Duro worker noted: "Because of the salaries and bad working conditions it [was] the last resort."[75] But Duro was also one of the largest companies in the area, and so for many workers it was where they labored. Even as a last resort for many workers, the conditions of the post-NAFTA factory proved unbearable, and in June 2000 workers at its Tamaulipas plant held a demonstration demanding their right to form an independent union. Their goals were better wages and fewer hazardous work conditions.[76]

Two years prior, as a result of activism on the part of workers at Tijuana's Han Young plant, the Mexican government promised labor secret ballot elections; Lewis Karesh, the deputy secretary for the U.S. Department of Labor, whose job it was to hear NAFTA complaints, pointed to the promise as evidence of NAFTA's success.[77] The promise was the result of determination, sacrifice, and cross-border organizing on the part of labor. In June 1997, workers at Han Young, a subsidiary of Hyundai, began organizing and demanding better wages and the elimination of egregious safety hazards. They engaged in work stoppages and hunger strikes and chained themselves to the doors of the city hall. They gained support from the San Diego–based Support Committee for Maquiladora Workers (CJM), a trans-border organization founded at the time of NAFTA's birth and dedicated to improving "working conditions and living standards for workers in the maquiladora industry."[78] When their union, the Revolutionary Confederation of Workers and Farmers (CROC), with strong ties to the government, failed to help them, workers joined the independent Union for Workers in the Metal, Steel, Iron, and Allied Industries. Labor organizers held elections, and the independent union won. Not surprisingly, the state labor board refused to certify the results, and so workers filed a complaint under NAFTA's labor side agreement. It was because of this activism that Mexico's government promised to allow workers the right to organize and to hold secret ballot elections. NAFTA advocates, such as Karesh, pointed to the decision and the promise as an example of worker rights under NAFTA.[79] Two years later, at the Duro plant in Rio Bravo, this promise was put to the test.

Duro Bag was among the companies that manufactured the gift bags that became so popular throughout the United States in the late twentieth century. With its home office in Ludlow, Kentucky, Duro Bag had clients such as the U.S. companies Hallmark and Neiman Marcus. Prior to the strike, workers earned the equivalent of forty U.S. dollars a week for a forty-eight-hour workweek.[80] Workers were concerned about exposure to toxic solvents and unsafe machinery; several lost fingers in machinery where safety guards had been removed to increase production. When workers turned to their union, the Paper, Cardboard, and Wood Industry Union of the Confederation of Mexican Workers, it failed to represent them and instead signed a new contract that addressed none of their concerns. The union was known throughout the country for working "closely with the federal and state governments to guarantee labor peace."[81] Duro fired the workers who organized for better conditions; workers, in turn, stepped up demonstrations and began working with the Coalition for Justice in the Maquiladoras. The ten months of labor activism that followed was met with company and police brutality until finally, on August 14, 2000, as a result of international pressure, the local government allowed the Independent Worker's Union to register with the state. Yet the intimidation and violence continued. The house of one of the lead organizers was burned down. Finally a date was set for a union election: March 2, 2001.[82]

With a date set for the election, worker harassment increased. Police arrested organizers, managers told workers they would be fired if they voted for the independent union, and others were promised raises if they did not. On the day of the election, CROC employees escorted workers to vote and company managers sat to hear them speak their votes. Through fraud and intimidation, CROC won the day.[83] Duro workers then filed a complaint with the U.S. National Administrative Offices (NAO) under the North American Agreement of Labor Cooperation (NAALC—NAFTA's labor side agreement), which refused to hear their case, stating, "After consideration of the submission, the U.S. NAO determined that a review would not further the objectives of the NAALC and, on February 22, 2002, declined to accept it for review."[84] The decision demonstrated the ineffectiveness of the NAALC to protect workers. While Mexico's labor laws guarantee the right to unionize and to join the union of one's choice, the U.S. NAO chose to interpret the protection as narrowly as possible. Because the law did not explicitly state that secret balloting was necessary to ensure freedom of choice, under NAFTA workers are not guaranteed the right.[85] For Duro workers, NAFTA had devastating effects, yet the organizing that followed was and is inspiring and would bring hope to workers far beyond Duro's company walls.

When the U.S. Labor Department failed to recognize the rights of the Duro workers, the workers and CJM continued to organize—despite threats and violence. CJM worked with the Asociación de Abogados Democráticos to provide legal counsel for those arrested at protests or unjustly fired. CJM worked with faith-based groups such as the Interfaith Committee for Corporate Responsibility to make sure Duro representatives were aware of labor conditions in their Tamaulipas plant, and to pressure them to recognize the independent union; they also insisted on back pay for organizers who had been fired. Finally, on March 2003, two years after the U.S. Labor Department refused to hear their case, the workers were victorious. In the words of Paul Almeida and Hank Johnson, the organizing of the Duro workers with their allies at CJM "shows the effectiveness of mobilizing from below, and the inability of treaties like NAFTA to provide sufficient mechanisms to protect worker's rights."[86] That it was CJM, a trans-border organization that worked across the U.S.-Mexico border to help win the battle also points to the importance of trans-ing throughout times of global shift. It is motion across borders that allows workers to successfully strive for jobs with dignity in our time of nepantlan change.

NAFTA served as a destructive force of movement and change within Mexico and created waves of movement from Mexico to the U.S., providing a clear example of the many ways in which the weave of neoliberalism is indeed a global weave where no nation stands alone. While the EZLN and the Indigenous peoples of Mexico continue to fight for democracy and autonomy, and workers throughout EPZs fight to end exploitation, all of them fighting for dignity in a time of neoliberalism, many farmers and workers throughout Mexico have been exiled from their homelands, pulled and pushed into the fields and cities of a neighboring country, the big brother of NAFTA, the United States.

NAFTA generated destructive movement off small farms and into agro-maquilas, into the United States, and into EPZs with overextended infrastructures. In terms of movement from Mexico to the United States, initially numbers increased exponentially. The population of undocumented immigrants in the United States went from approximately 5.7 million in 1995 to 12.2 million in 2008.[87] Immigration from Mexico accounted for a significant portion of this increase. In 1995 there were approximately 2.9 million undocumented immigrants in the United States from Mexico; by 2007 that number grew to 6.9 million.[88] Then from 2008 to 2014, immigration from Mexico slowed.[89] The Pew Institute, as well as magazines such as the *Econo-*

mist, note that this change was due to anti-immigrant sentiment and a weak U.S. economy.[90]

In a sense, this slowdown of immigration was the consequence of predictions made in the 1990s when NAFTA was put forward: initially, as the movement of goods across borders increased, the trade agreement would fuel more movement of people across the border. But then immigration would slow as wages increased along the Mexican border and decreased in the United States.[91] While real wages for Mexican workers have not increased, wages for U.S. workers have in fact decreased since the passage of NAFTA. As the United States moved into the twenty-first century, real wages for working-class Americans continued to drop, with the wages of full-time workers in the lowest quarter of the wage scale losing a full 3 percent in earnings between 2000 and 2014.[92] As chapter 5 shows, the movement begun by the neoliberal policies of the late twentieth century did not stop as we moved into the twenty-first century but instead continued and continues to shape our world.

Faith, Hope, and Love

History demonstrates that resistance to a totalizing capitalist shift is found not only in Mexico but throughout the world, including the U.S. An obvious example of this resistance is the liberation movements of the 1960s and 1970s, out of which emerged much of our own Chicana feminist theory and activism. As will be discussed in chapter 5, the struggles over our immigration rights today have much in common with the activism that continues to shape and move resistance in Mexico and throughout the Americas. Yet with the continued economic shift into the next age of capital, increased destructive movement also continued into the twenty-first century.

NAFTA did, in fact, widen the gap between the top 1 percent in the U.S. and the large body of semiskilled and "unskilled" workers who fuel the economy.[93] U.S. manufacturing moved, in bold numbers, from the United States into the EPZs of Mexico. And, as is addressed in chapter 5, hundreds of thousands of small farmers were pushed off their land in Mexico. We live in nepantlan times—where the displacement of thousands of people from the Americas into the North is met with violence, at the same time that immigrant rights activism and support groups for immigrants, including queer immigrants, also grows. Yet this shift in capitalism is much like the last one. As in the shift to monopoly capitalism, as gender and culture shifted, the lives of people such as Jack Garland, who trans-ed gender, did so within the context of a constantly shifting landscape, so would those who trans gender now do so in a constantly shifting landscape. Their struggles for survival weave among the multiple strands of late twentieth- and early twenty-first-century resistance.

Not coincidentally, the theories we now develop to understand this, our nepantlan time, like the theory and activism of the Zapatistas, grow out of our specific social locations—whether we label this connection Theory in the Flesh, postpositivist realism, or Mestiza consciousness. As noted by Chela Sandoval almost four decades ago, growing up, living, and struggling "within similar realms of marginality" can give rise to coalitional and differential modes of consciousness and organizing.[94] Thus Anzaldúa's return to the global economy, to the home of Sor Juana, to Zapatismo gestures toward those knowledges we continue to need today. When we do not turn away from the simultaneously creative and destructive call of our time, we are able to see a unity in the movement and change that shapes our world. In chapter 4, as we shift our gaze, once again, to a specific life, we do so in the context of socioeconomic shift—destructive and creative, of autonomous movements, of the potential of humanity realized. As we will see in chapter 4, this shift, in the United States as in Mexico, has also brought great violence—woven through with resistance, and revolutionary love.

CHAPTER FOUR

Motion-Change in the Life and Times of Gwen Amber Rose Araujo

Look at me, I'm a person
Look at me, I'm my own person
So many different people
So many different kinds
—Gwen Stefani et al., "Different People"

Third world writers such as Guevara, Fanon, Anzaldúa, Emma Pérez,
Trinh Minh-ha, or Cherríe Moraga, to name only a few . . . understand
love as a "breaking" through whatever controls in order to find
"understanding and community." . . . These writers who theorize social
change understand "love" as a hermeneutic, as a set of practices and
procedures that can transit all citizen-subjects, regardless of social
class, toward a differential mode of consciousness and its accompanying
technologies of method and social movement.
—Chela Sandoval, *Methodology of the Oppressed*

Incorporated in 1955, Newark, California, shared much of the complex
history of Nueva Nepantla.[1] The first peoples of the region were the
Ohlone, today naming themselves Muwekma, or *the people*, as they
continue to rebuild their communities. Like other Costanoan peoples,
the Muwekma were a hunting and gathering society; they moved up
and down the region, trading and sharing culture with other nations
and tribes, but the areas that are now called Newark and Fremont were
their home.[2] Like other peoples who lived in the regions surrounding
San Francisco Bay, their community lost countless numbers to the
disease and colonial practices brought by Spanish and then Mexican

colonizers.³ With the secularization of the missions in the late 1840s some Muwekma became vaqueros on the land of Californios, while others moved north and inland, away from the settlers, only to be confronted by a new wave of settler-colonizers following the U.S. Invasion of 1846–48.⁴

The Euro-Americans who swept through Nueva Nepantla did not overlook the land of the Muwekma. By 1853 landings and warehouses had been built along the bay, and by 1856 Euro-Americans were fencing and farming the area. Railroads and railroad culture made inroads in the 1870s, bringing industry, hotels, and stores.⁵ Yet through that accelerated time of motion-change the Muwekma persisted, with many living and laboring on the Alisal Rancheria, farther inland from Newark; they were active in the Indigenous revivals of the 1870s. When, due to Euro-American incursions, outmigration, and a lack of seasonal work, the Alisal community dispersed, some families returned to Newark.⁶

As with other regions throughout Nueva Nepantla, Newark experienced two dramatic epochal shifts in capital: that of the U.S. Invasion, with its drive toward monopoly capitalism and railroad culture, and that to global capital. With the shift to global capital and the dot-com boom of the late twentieth century, Newark attracted Sun Microsystems, which brought with it a fourteen-million-square-foot campus along with two thousand employees and property taxes of $700,000. The company would close the campus a decade later, but while Gwen Amber Rose Araujo was a young teen living in Newark, Sun remained.⁷

In 1985, the child who would grow up to be Gwen Amber Rose Araujo was born into this world of motion-change. Her mother would remember her as "una joven creativa, llena de vida, divertida, platicadora y con una eterna sonrisa."⁸ She was given a male birth name, but as she grew up it became apparent to family and friends that it was a misnomer. She played with dolls, she wanted to be pretty—she was pretty. When she was in the eighth grade, she told a girlfriend that she was different, that she really was a girl. She gave her friend a ring—silver with bubbles on it—and asked if they could be best friends. Her girlfriend never took the ring off, even after the murder.⁹

4. Gwen Amber Rose Araujo. Courtesy of Sylvia Guerrero.

When she was fourteen she asked her family to call her Gwen, after Gwen Stefani, and so they did. Her mother promised that once she had sex-affirmation surgery, they would legally change her name.[10] Her family was accepting and supportive of her, even when they did not quite understand. Sometimes they used the wrong pronoun, but they kept trying. Her school was less supportive. In fact it was outside her family that she was most unsafe. Her mother asked that bath-room accommodations be made for her at school. The school refused. Students began to harass her; eventually she gave up and dropped out.[11] While the Catholic schools of Jack Garland's time policed gender through a curriculum designed to shape girls into Christian wives and mothers, the public schools in Gwen's time also policed gender—using sex and gender as weapons to drive trans and gender-creative young people from their campuses. Gender conformity, in the early twenty-first century, remained a requirement for survival in the hall-ways of Newark's public schools.

Gwen persisted. She continued to dream of growing up, having surgery, and becoming a makeup artist.[12] But before she was able to have the surgery she was killed by four men, "friends," all four of them five years her senior. At the time of her death, Gwen would have been a senior at Newark Memorial High School; her former campus had been getting ready to stage a production of *The Laramie Project*. Her girlhood friend, still wearing her ring, was in the play.[13]

Gwen was murdered by young men from her own town. Her life, cut short, demonstrated and reminds us that in times of nepantla, nep-antler@s are not safe. Hate crimes statistics from the late twentieth century affirm this finding.[14] Gwen's death also demonstrates a second truth of the nation-state: there are shades of queer. Gay and "just like you" and transgender and "could not pass for you if my life depended on it" remain at two very distinct ends of the queer spectrum.[15]

And so the death of this young woman raises many questions, critical questions, for all of us living in nepantlan times: How is it that in the twenty-first century, a young Latina could be murdered by "friends," young adult white and Latino men with whom she had socialized and dated? Why is it that, even with the growth of Latinx populations throughout the nation, when Matthew Shepard was murdered, vigils were held throughout the United States, yet for most violent crimes against queer people of color, especially transgender people of color, little attention is paid by the media or the larger U.S. public? How did gender roles and masculinity continue to shape lives amid the shift to global capitalism? In chapter 3 we witnessed how globalization and activism shifted gender roles among Indigenous women in southern

Chiapas. In this chapter I address these questions by placing the life and death of Gwen Araujo in a larger context of social and legal discourse about race and gender and by mapping the structural subordination of queers of color through the specific institutions of the media and the law. Thus I examine newspaper accounts of hate crimes as well as court decisions where violent crimes against LGBTQ people of color were prosecuted; I engage in what Deena González has termed "reading against the grain" to open up glimpses into the historical and lived realities of transgender mestiz@s in times of accelerated motion-change.[16] I close with the question, "How can and does revolutionary love survive amid the violence of this, our time of motion-change?"

In this chapter, in addition to the Chicana feminist and queer texts addressed in the opening chapters, I engage tools and scholarship from critical race theory more actively than I do elsewhere in the text. While Kimberlé Crenshaw, Derrick Bell, and Richard Delgado are foundational to this work, for queer analysis, it is the work of Francisco Valdes and Darren Lenard Hutchinson—especially Hutchinson, who addresses the ways the dominant U.S. culture has sexed and gendered communities of color—that are most useful when mapping queer realities in relation to law and power. Hutchinson specifically addresses the difference between discourses about racialized Black bodies in relation to U.S. slave and capitalist societies and those surrounding racialized Mexican and Chicanx bodies in relation to the U.S. Invasion of 1846–48.[17] It is Francisco Valdes who documented the multiple ways that queers of color, especially queer Latinx bodies, are rendered invisible both through legal discourse and through multiple heteropatriarchal institutions in U.S. society, calling for pragmatic scholarship to challenge those same institutions.[18]

Finally, this chapter argues that much of the violence that transgender Latin@s experience is due to heteropatriarchal violence asserted by white and Chicano men seeking to protect their masculine privilege, and that the nation-state allows such violence in its own attempt to stabilize capital and gender. As argued by Ramón A. Gutiérrez, it was Chicana feminists who first mapped and challenged constructions of Chicano masculinities.[19] Today scholars as diverse as Cherríe Moraga, Aida Hurtado, and Francisco Valdes continue to map and explore Chicano masculinities, praising what is useful, critiquing what is destructive, and imagining new ways of being Chicano, while queer crit scholars such as Dean Spade challenge us to mark gender as "an organizing principle of both the economy and the seemingly banal administrative systems that govern everyone's daily life."[20]

Constructing Race, Constructing Gender

On the morning she was murdered, Gwen Araujo was at a party. Michael Magidson, José Merel, Jason Cazares, and Jaron Nabors were also there. She had met the men a year before and had dated two of them.[21] Early in the morning of October 4, when the party had died down, some of the men began talking about Gwen and questioning her sex. José Merel shouted at Gwen, "Are you a fucking woman or a man?" Eventually Nicole Brown, who was female-identified, and who had been visiting with the group, suggested they bring Gwen into the bathroom to "check." Brown checked her, and then proclaimed Gwen a "fucking man."[22] The four men brutally murdered Gwen. They then drove to the Sierra foothills and buried her body in a shallow grave. Afterward they went to McDonald's for breakfast.[23]

Years after the event the violence of this crime is still unsettling. A young seventeen-year-old was murdered by "friends." Yet the actions of the perpetrators *and* the language of their attorney served to normalize the violence. The perpetrators of the violence exhibited little remorse; instead, after they buried Gwen's body, they went to breakfast together. At trial, attorney Michael Thorman, in asserting the innocence of Mike Magidson, constructed a similar normalizing and violent discourse. He argued that his client was not a bad person even though he behaved violently: "It's not because Mike's a bad guy with something to prove."[24] In the eyes of Thorman violence against a young woman such as Gwen was somehow understandable.

Such violence can be rationalized only in a social system where participating in normalized gender roles is central to what makes a person human. In the United States racialized and gendered ideologies construct what it means to be a man and what it means to be a woman. If a body fits into neither category, or crosses gender lines, it loses gender privilege and is assigned the label "it," often in conjunction with violence or threats of violence. On the night she was attacked, Gwen Araujo was called "it."[25] In another case, tried the same year that Araujo was murdered, the victim, nineteen-year-old Alina Barrigan, also Latina, was also referred to as "it" by her aggressors.[26]

Historically, as will be discussed below, U.S. ideologies of race and gender have been maintained through violence. Persons who cannot be identified as either male or female are subjected to violence. Men who do not perform masculinity and women who do not perform femininity face similar violence. Additionally, the dominant culture has stereotyped specific racialized communities as feminine or masculine, passive or aggressive, or sometimes as both. Many of these stereotypes were forged and reinforced with the U.S. Invasion of Mexico and following the U.S. Civil War, during the transition to monopoly capitalism; they continue to shape our world today, even while we plunge into yet another epochal shift in capital. To unravel the normalizing of violence against transgender persons, especially transgender Latinas, here I briefly map the relationships of race, gender, and personhood in U.S. history and society.

From its founding in systems of slavery and colonization, to wars of expansion, to Jim and Jane Crow, ideologies of manhood and womanhood in the United States constructed a culture of violence directed against men and women of color, especially men and women of color who did not meet the sex and gender expectations of these same ideologies. This is not a new theory but one found readily in Chicanx history and critical race feminism, but perhaps most clearly articulated in the work of James Baldwin writing for readers of *Playboy* magazine. His article, published 1985, the same year that Gwen was born, was written at a time when real wages for the working class were already in decline. The article reached out to an audience deeply in need of gendered critiques. Disrupting the gender binaries that structured the world of his readers, he explained,

> The American ideal . . . of sexuality appears to be rooted in the American ideal of masculinity. This ideal has created cowboys and Indians, good guys and bad guys . . . butch and faggot, black and white. . . .

The exigencies created by the triumph of the rise of Europe to global prominence . . . had, among many mighty effects, that of commercializing the roles of men and women. Men became the propagators, and perpetrators, of property, and women became the means by which that property was protected and handed down. . . . This pragmatic principle dictated the slaughter of the native American, the enslavement of the black and the monumental rape of Africa . . . as well as Latin America, and it controlled the pens of the men who signed the Declaration of Independence—a document more clearly commercial than moral.[27]

U.S. social structures, according to Baldwin, were constructed through binaries in which the dominant defined and exploited the weak. Thus dominant gender roles were and are inextricably tied to capital—to property and power in such a way that if one finds oneself on the wrong side, or outside, of a gender binary, one is subjected to unbounded violence. "Cowboys and Indians, butch and faggot, black and white," which side are you on? Historically, when subordinated groups challenged such binaries, they were subjected to brutal violence. Throughout the American South when, following the Civil War, African Americans registered to vote and founded schools and small businesses, whites responded with public and gruesome lynchings, mostly of Black men but also of Black women and a small number of white allies. Amid the rapid change from slavocracy to emergent capitalism, white southerners drew on a racialized discourse developed during the slave era, sexualized the bodies of Black men, projected their fears and desires onto them, and accused them of rape.[28] In the United States, manhood was constructed as white, as protecting property including white women, and as violent.

Yet it is not white men alone who are invested in ideologies of American masculinity. In Chicanx communities the other against which males often construct themselves are women and men who do not fit into traditional gender roles.[29] When, in the early twenty-first century, before brutally murdering Gwen Araujo, José Merel exclaimed, "I'm not gay, I don't like men," he graphically demonstrated the resilience of masculinist cultures in Chicanx lives.[30] In Chicanx communities as in white communities, "masculinity . . . continues to be a normative rubric that [polices] the sex/gender system." It normalizes male privilege at the same time that it requires adherence to gender roles in order to maintain that same privilege.[31] Merel, like most men, knew the price of finding himself outside accepted gender roles—he was willing to kill to avoid it.

The investment, especially of white women, in this culture has been noted by historians since the 1970s. The "Cult of True Womanhood" was in reality a cult of "True White Womanhood," and the bodies of women of color provided the "nonwoman" that countered the "true woman" of this ideology.[32] On the night of October 3, 2002, Nicole Brown, a white woman and mother of two young children, reconstructed her own gender status at the expense of Gwen Araujo. Three years later, in her testimony against Magidson, Merel, and Cazares, she recalled that when Araujo's sex was questioned, it was she who suggested that one of the men take Gwen into the bathroom and "find out . . . by checking her." When the men were slow to act, Brown testified, "I got frustrated and went over and checked myself. I put my hand between her legs and checked." Her verbal response was "I can't believe this is a fucking man. . . . I'm wigging out."[33]

Brown's "I can't believe this is a fucking man" and José Merel's "I don't like men" served to quickly place them within accepted gender binaries at the same time that they signaled to each other that Gwen had crossed a line. Merel's exclamation recalls Anzaldúa's argument that "we need a new masculinity."[34] Concurrently, it calls to mind Lisa Cacho's more recent argument that "we are all recruited often unwittingly and/or unwillingly to devalue lives, life choices, and lifestyles because valuing them would destabilize our own precarious claims to and uneasy desire for social value."[35] Over two decades have passed since Anzaldúa's call for a new masculinity. Despite work by Chicanx scholar-activists and gay and queer organizations such as the National Latina/o Lesbian, Gay, Bisexual, and Transgender Organization and GenderPac, we have yet to successfully disrupt the old masculinities, and we have yet to disrupt a system that values some lives at the expense of others.[36]

Brown and Merel's exclamations and the ensuing violence graphically support sociologists Witten and Eyer's study of anti-transgender violence where they argued:

> Violence against transgenders bears many similarities to violence against women and to anti-homosexual victimization. . . . Violence against women (committed by men) is often justified by the perpetrators as . . . a reasonable action to take against a woman who is transgressing social restraints. . . . Sexual violence against transgenders often receives similar justification. . . . Perpetrators often believe that a person who transgresses the norms of gendered sexuality, either by engaging in sexual relationships with members of the "non-opposite" gender, or by behaving as the other gender, is deviant or morally defective, and thus a deserving victim of violence and aggression.[37]

According to the language and actions of the men who murdered Gwen Araujo, she had "transgress[ed] the norms of gendered sexuality." Similar language was used against Alina Marie Barrigan when she was murdered in 1999 and against Brandon Teena in 1994, demonstrating an ongoing pattern of violence against people, including very young people, who disrupt the gender systems that structure and maintain the status quo. In a world of shifting economic systems and social mores, those who "move across a socially imposed boundary from an unchosen starting place" are constructed as "deserving of violence and aggression."[38]

Headlines from the turn of the century demonstrate that such violence was common and that when young people did not adhere to gender binaries, adults too often failed to protect them. This was the case in the murder of fifteen-year old Lawrence King—a murder committed *after* the introduction of California's Gwen Araujo Justice for Victims Act. The young King had come out as gay at the age of ten; the year he was murdered he had begun to dress in feminine clothing, at times wearing makeup or heels.[39] In fact, after King's murder, the majority of teachers at his school blamed King for his own death. One of the teachers went so far as to state, "I believe in heaven and hell," implying that King (not his killer) might go to hell.[40] Eventually the trial ended in a hung jury, even though the young killer had planned the murder, returned to his house to retrieve the weapon after leaving for school without it, and had shot King twice—point blank—in the head.[41]

At the turn of the century in Nueva Nepantla, as it was throughout the last epochal shift in capital, when white supremacists lynched Blacks in the South and ethnic Mexicans in the U.S. national West, the dominant social order was reinscribed through symbolic and very real acts of violence. Within these times of motion-change, there remained shades of queer.[42]

Shades of Queer

According to scholars as diverse as Harry Benjamin, Patrick Califia, and Bear Bergman, transsexualism is about gender, and homosexuality is about sexual orientation.[43] Yet they are related. In the law and in the media, transgender people are often referred to as "gay." The press sometimes wrote not of Araujo's gender identity but of her "sexual orientation."[44] Similarly, the courts also conflate sexual orientation and gender identity. In *People v. Michael Doktoreztk*, where Doktoreztk was tried for raping and brutally attacking a seventeen-year-old transgender youth named Dominique, the courts spoke of Dominique's "sexual orientation," not gender identity.[45] As is addressed in chapter 5, it was not until September 2015, with *Avendano-Hernandez v. Lynch*, that any federal court recognized transgender asylum seekers as a distinct class from gay and lesbian asylum seekers.[46] So while the lives of transgender and gay people demonstrate that gender and sexual orientation are two different aspects of personhood—there are lesbian transsexuals and gay transsexuals and heterosexual transsexuals—the media and the law often conflate the two.

Both transgender people and gay and lesbian people do violate gender roles, because, as Francisco Valdes explains, in most Western cultures sexuality is subsumed under gender.[47] Yet the rights of people who identify as gay, and their access to basic resources, are very different from the rights and access of those who identify as transgender. When the Human Rights Campaign, a national gay, lesbian, bisexual and, now, transgender rights organization initially refused to include transgender people as a protected class under the Employment Nondiscrimination Act, they acknowledged this difference. They were afraid that including transgender people would injure the chances of the bill's passage.[48] Likewise, in 2016–17 as many gay and lesbian communities celebrated the success of legal struggles for marriage equality, sixteen states throughout the nation considered antitransgender legislation.[49]

Clearly there are shades of queer. In the lives of transgender Latin@s and Chican@s the shades are magnified by the functions of structural racism, which marks some queer bodies as less valued than others, and constructs cisgender gay white males as "the boy next door." The political implications of the media blitz and public attention showered on the memory of Matthew Shepard is one example of this structural racism and can demonstrate how, just as there are different shades of blue, so are there different shades of queer. The reality of the queer spectrum, however, has ramifications beyond shade preference. The farther away a body moves from a mythic white cisgender everyman, the less valued that body is within U.S. society—in the words of Dean Spade, one's "life chances" are dramatically reduced. The media and popular treatment of the Matthew Shepard murder illustrates the importance of seeing shades of queer and demonstrates the function of racism in conjunction with heteropatriarchy to erase the realities of queer mestiz@ lives, thus contributing to the vulnerability of transgender mestiz@s in U.S. society.

When, in October 1998, Matthew Shepard was brutally murdered, the press labeled him "the perfect queer: young, pretty, and dead."[50] Even before his death, while he lay comatose in a Wyoming hospital, the website that had been set up to inform the public of his status received 815,000 hits and candlelight vigils were held throughout the nation.[51] After Shepard's death tens of thousands of newspaper articles reported on his life and death, his family, hate crimes activism, and court proceedings. In New York City alone over four thousand people attended his memorial service.[52] No fewer than forty-six different recording artists eulogized him in song.[53] Matthew Shepard's name became a household word in homes across America.

Why did the death of this young blond man garner so much visibility and sympathy from the media? The deaths of several queers of color around this same time gave rise to little or no public outcry. When Fred Martinez, a sixteen-year-old transgender Navajo youth, was murdered in Colorado, Arthur Warren, a gay Black man, was murdered in West Virginia, and five gay Black men were murdered in Washington, vigils were not mobilized throughout the United States. No one made a special recording for them.[54] A partial answer to this disturbing quandary can be found in the role of capital in U.S. society, in a nation where, as noted by James Baldwin, the founding documents are primarily economic, and the stability of the nation is rooted in race and gender binaries upholding the status quo.

There is an economics to queer visibility and queer invisibility. Who has access to the press? Who has the resources to memorialize their dead? Who has the socioeconomic status to demand and expect rights and protections in public and private spaces? Studies published from the late twentieth century through the early twenty-first demonstrate that white LGBTQ persons, on average, hold far more economic status than do queers of color. As the National Gay and Lesbian Task Force Policy Institute and the National Black Justice Coalition reported, at the turn of the century, Black same-sex couples earned, on average, $22,000 a year less than white same-sex couples.[55] This earning pattern was reflective of larger national race-based inequalities; according the U.S. Census of 2000, the average weekly earnings were $521 for white women, $451 for African American women, and $385 for Latinas. White women's earnings, at the close of the decade, were 15.5 percent higher than those for Black women, and 35.3 percent higher than Latinas'.[56] According to the U.S. Census Bureau, a white male with a high school diploma earned more, on the average, than a Latina with a bachelor's degree.[57] In a society with a racialized class system, families and communities of color have less access to media to solicit support or demand social action when tragedy strikes. Similarly, because the right to police protection has been and is increasingly tied to the ability to own and possess private space, it is those bodies that can afford such space who are afforded basic civil protections.[58]

Can socioeconomic class protect a queer body? What shade of queer would that body need to be in order to be protected? Matthew Shepard's middle-class status did not protect him from a brutal death. His father was a safety engineer for Aramco Oil, his family was Episcopalian, and Matthew had attended boarding school abroad, in Switzerland.[59] The public response surrounding his murder, however, referred to him as the "the all-American nice kid next door" and provided a new level of acceptability and personhood for his shade of queer.[60] The *Washington Post* wrote of the "nation's outrage." Students with armbands marched in homecoming parades to protest the violence he suffered.[61] Araujo's lower-middle-class family was also able to garner some public acknowledgment of the value of their daughter's life. Yet the contrast between the national vigils, music recordings, and television coverage of the one death in contrast to the other remains. The outrage and publicity following Shepard's murder created a strong counterdiscourse to the national narrative of masculinity, suggesting that if a queer body was the right shade of queer, it should, according to the national press, be spared. One month after the brutal murder of Matthew Shepard, Rita Hester, an economically poor transgender woman of color was brutally murdered in her own apartment. Unlike the Shepard murder, her death attracted little attention. She was loved by her family and by the trans community and African American LGBTQ community of Boston, yet her name merited less than half a dozen news articles. While LGBTQ communities in San Francisco mobilized a vigil, one that would grow into the Transgender Day of Remembrance, within a month, only transgender websites maintained information on her life and death. Her murder was never solved.[62]

While economic access to the media influences a community's larger visibility in the nation, the manner in which the media portrays communities, events, and lived realities also affects community visibility and, thus, access to rights and protections within the dominant society.[63] It is the news media that has the most direct influence on the dominant majority's "awareness and understanding of public problems and concerns." By selecting specific events as newsworthy and, equally important, deciding which aspects of a story to emphasize, the news media shapes policies and reality.[64] Initially the Matthew

Shepard story was not covered by the national media; it was only after two days, when his story proved itself marketable, that the national press created a media blitz. The story became newsworthy, in part, because Matthew Shepard was white and middle class, and in the words of Brian Ott and Eric Aoki, "because of his slight stature and . . . 'cherubic face,' even those uncomfortable with homosexuality saw him as an innocent (that is, sexually nonthreatening) victim. The public identified with Shepard, viewing him as a friend and a son."[65]

Because U.S. popular culture has traditionally portrayed bodies of color as sexually predatory or out of control, we might ask, Can a queer of color ever be identified and marketed as sexually non-threatening—"a friend and son"? Could the life and death of Gwen Araujo or of Rita Hester be as marketable as that of Matthew Shepard? Critical race scholars as diverse as Kimberlé Crenshaw, Darren Lenard Hutchinson, and Sumi K. Cho have demonstrated the deeply ingrained and sexualized stereotypes that white society holds of men and women of color.[66] While, as Hutchinson carefully articulates, these stereotypes arise out of specific historical circumstances and are thus unique to each racialized group, they all hold important and critical commonalities. They are constructed and reproduced, in part, through the media, and in all of them, bodies of color are constructed as oversexed, while white bodies are constructed as "innocent victims" or sexually restrained.[67] Thus the queer brown body remains typed as "threatening," newsworthy as perpetrator but seldom as victim.

Throughout the late twentieth century, whenever the news media did report on crimes against people of color, it reported almost exclusively on crimes against heterosexuals of color, thus creating a dichotomy where victims of hate crimes were either people of color or LGBTQ, but where both differences could not exist in the same body. Take for example the 1994 *Los Angeles Times* report on hate crimes. The article was among the most detailed and well-researched reports of its time and was one of the few news articles written in the 1990s that documented violence against queers of color. Yet even its headline, "Violence against Minorities on Rise: Gay Men Have Supplanted African Americans as the Primary Target of Hate Crimes in Los Angeles County," reinforced the fictive "Brown/Black is heterosexual, white is gay" model.[68] Throughout the 1990s, the news media consistently constructed and reproduced this split.[69] Only recently has there begun to be a shift in this rhetoric—this, in part, because of activism on the part of transgender communities who have noticed and noted the frightening number of hate crimes victims who are transgender women of color.[70]

At the time of Gwen's death, a dangerous myth remained deeply entrenched: queers are white, people of color are heterosexual. In the United States this myth was reinscribed through a legal system where Brown and queer could not exist in the same space.[71] When a queer person of color was assaulted or murdered, often victims, or their survivors, and their attorneys had to choose whether to prosecute on the basis of a race-based hate crime or a homophobic or transphobic hate crime. Darren Hutchinson demonstrated this split in his analysis of the 1993 Truong case. On a late winter evening, Loc Minh Truong, a working-class, gay Vietnamese American went for a walk through Mountain Street Beach, the gay section of Laguna Beach, California. Before the night was over, he lay alone and unconscious on a nearby beach, his face so disfigured police authorities could not identify his race, a rock "impaled in the back of his head."[72] All of the men who assaulted him were white, one of them an Eagle Scout. Yet both the police and prosecuting attorneys pursued the case exclusively as an antigay hate crime. Legal discourse, throughout the late twentieth century, functioned to reinscribe race, gender, and sexuality binaries that erased the lived realities of LGBTQ people of color.[73]

The death of Matthew Shepard was tragic. Yet in examining the media coverage surrounding his death in relation to the larger socioeconomic realities that shape the lives of LGBTQ people in the United States, it becomes clear that throughout the nation-state, there are shades of queer. The family of Gwen Araujo and friends of Rita Hester rallied to demand a public acknowledgment that Gwen and Rita were people to be valued. They used stories and histories of their lives and deaths to fight for protection and basic rights for all people; yet a national public outcry like the one that surrounded the murder of Shepard never surfaced.

Love in Times of Motion-Change

While the brutal assault of Loc Minh Truong and the murders of Rita Hester, Lawrence King, and Gwen Araujo demonstrate the resiliency of white supremacy and American masculinist culture through times of nepantlan motion-change, the mobilization of Gwen Araujo's family following her murder stands as an example of how resistance to violence through times of motion-change is also possible. Gwen's death also demonstrates the critical need for such resistance, rooted in revolutionary love, in confronting the violence that is directed against queer and minoritized communities.

It was a lawyer representing the interests of Gwen's family who, during the coverage of the trial, pointed out, "Los actos de violencia contra ciertos géneros, raza, color, religión, nacionalidad, discapacidad u orientación están relacionados entre sí y tienen que verse como un crimen de odio y como un crimen contra toda la comunidad entera."[74] Hate crimes are not individual acts of violence; all hate crimes are somehow structurally connected; they are attacks on our larger communities. In the words of Darren Lenard Hutchinson, a hate crime is part of a "system of subordination. . . . The multidimensional nature of oppressive violence also means that a number of social hierarchies will be informed and be reinforced through its occurrence."[75] When such crimes take place during times of motion-change, they play a powerful role in shaping the present and the future. They police bodies and intersect with administrative systems such as the police force, churches, and schools to reduce the life chances of trans people and other LGBTQ people of color.

The antihate activism following Gwen Araujo's murder was critical to confronting the structural effects of such violence. It demonstrated how activism that creates long-term change is almost always the result of multiple factors: the convergence of community resources, family commitment, and a drive for a better world and a more just society. And so here I focus on just three critical factors that resulted in a trial and a campaign to educate young people about gender differences: transgender activism, community coalition, and revolutionary love.

During the second half of the twentieth century, Sylvia Rivera was among the most noted of public transgender activists, for her involvement in the riots at the Stonewall Inn but also for her work to support LGBTQ street youth.[76] By the 1990s there were a handful of transgender rights organizations, including GenderPAC, Remembering Our Dead, and the Transgender Law and Policy Institute. While Rivera was Latina, most visible advocates and activists for these newer organizations were Euro-American, with Anne Ogborn and Riki Wilchins heading up some of the earliest actions in the 1990s. Wilchins founded GenderPac, a lobbying and education organization that worked to change public policies but also sought to empower transgender youth, sponsoring Youth Gender Leadership Summits.[77] Transgender activists were largely responsible for the publicity surrounding the murder of transgender youth Brandon Teena, as well as the less-publicized death of Tyra Hunter, a transgender woman who died from car accident injuries after an emergency medical technician refused to provide aid.[78]

It was transgender activists who, in the early twenty-first century, pushed to make Gwen's murder public. Initially activists stumbled through miscommunications with her family, then slowly and eventually established a connection. Disagreements between transgender activists and family members demonstrate the significant and hazardous gap that often exists between predominantly white LGBTQ organizers (and their resources) and racialized communities.[79]

As Gwen's mother, Sylvia Guerrero, became more public in her activism, local LGBTQ organizations mobilized. During the first of two trials Ms. Guerrero began working with the Transgender Law Center to have Gwen's name legally changed to Gwen posthumously. Because the press continued to use her old pronoun and her old name, it was difficult, as attorney Chris Daley explained, for the public to understand what had happened. For Gwen's mother, insisting on Gwen's chosen pronoun was part of keeping a promise to her daughter, but it was also about educating the public—for the long term.[80]

Community United against Violence (CUAV) was also among the first regional organizations to reach out to the family. CUAV traces its roots to the aftermath of the George Moscone and Harvey Milk assassinations. What began as an organization predominantly for gay men grew to include the needs of lesbian and transgender residents. Staff such as Tina D'Elia of CUAV's Hate Violence Programs worked with Guerrero and her family as an advocate when the case reached California's courts. After the first trial resulted in a hung jury, Andy Wong, also of CUAV, started a blog, *Court Watch*, to monitor the trial. Too many community and family members could not repeatedly take time away from work; others could not relive the violence in the space of a court room. And so Wong, Vanissar Tarakali, and Pablo Espinosa of CUAV, as well as Chris Daly of the Transgender Law Center, attended, kept watch, and entered transcripts. The trial took an emotional and physical toll on all those attending, but it was a community commitment and sitting with the family and listening with the family was a critical part of that commitment.[81]

Gwen's family and their insistence that their child be valued proved critical both to finding the perpetrators of the crime and to promoting larger educational projects. Here the work of Lisa Cacho comes to mind. For as the media and the larger economic system of the United States constructed Gwen as somebody unworthy of life within the nation, her family refused the negation.[82] In fact, Sylvia Guerrero's activism began long before Gwen's death. It was an activism rooted in love and commitment, the day-to-day activism of which Chicana feminists such as Gloria Anzaldúa, Cherríe Moraga, Aida Hurtado, and others have written. It is an activism noted by Chicanas writing at the beginning of the Chicano Movement where women respond to the everyday sexism, heterosexism, racism, and classism of U.S. society with a visible courage—a courage often overlooked by the mainstream media but which pushes back against these same institutions.[83] Such activism was and is rooted in the love of which Chela Sandoval writes, "It is love that can access and guide our theoretical and political 'movidas'—revolutionary maneuvers toward decolonized being."[84] It was an activism that meant, for example, walking away from her church community.

When Gwen was just fourteen and beginning to transition, the family went to church together: Sylvia and Gwen, Gwen's older sister Pearl, and Pearl's baby girl, Ariana. Gwen had begun to dye her hair pink and let it grow out—like Gwen Stefani. Years later Sylvia Guerrero recalled the day she confronted transphobia in her faith community: "We walked in as a family. It was Easter. And I will never forget the looks that we had—not us—I should say the looks that Gwen had from the church that I gave my tithe to—that we all attended. They all knew all of us, and I left. And I never went back. . . . That is not the kind of church I want my children or myself to attend."[85]

Sandoval writes of a love that is oppositional, and I would argue that it is such love that drove Guerrero to activism and gave her the strength to stand up and walk out and to love her children unconditionally. As she explained, "The God that I believe in and that I love, and that I grew up believing in and knowing would never close the door to anyone. God created all of us and we are all God's Children."[86]

After Gwen's death, her family spoke back to a violent culture and society at multiple levels. Initially, it was the family that pushed and aided police to locate her body, calling the station on a regular basis, pursuing leads they found and passing that information on to investigators. Local authorities acknowledged that the family and community played a key role in finding her body and locating the men who killed her.[87] At the level of public discourse Gwen's mother spoke to both the English- and Spanish-language press and insisted on doing so in such a way that the dominant language, so often used to maintain gender boundaries, was disrupted. Initially, she herself struggled with pronouns, but insisted Gwen be buried as Gwen. When she and the rest of the family, including Gwen's uncle and sisters, recognized the importance of naming Gwen by her self-identified gender, they met with reporters and discussed the importance of word choice before stories went to print.[88]

The above accounting is not intended to romanticize the struggles that followed the death of Gwen Amber Rose Araujo. The family persevered despite a marked lack of support from public institutions. Gwen was pushed out of high school by an administration that supported a harassing climate and that refused to acknowledge the necessity of using a bathroom. In nepantlan times, public institutions, such as schools, police borders of class and borders of sex and gender. At one point, following the murder, Sylvia Guerrero was so depressed it affected her job performance. She was fired, could no longer make house payments, and lost her home. Like Gwen, Gwen's little brother was not protected by the transphobic and racist school system of the U.S. nation-state. Following the murder of his sister he was taunted

10TH YEAR Anniversary

Remembrance of Gwen Araujo

"EMPOWERING AND TEACHING OTHERS ABOUT TRANSGENDER ISSUES"

In Loving Memory of

Eddie "Gwen" Araujo
Feb. 24, 1985
Oct. 03, 2002

**OCTOBER 6TH, 2012
AT 2:00PM
SAN FRANCISCO PUBLIC LIBRARY
VISITACION VALLEY BRANCH
COMMUNITY ROOM
201 LELAND AVENUE, SAN FRANCISCO, CA 94134**

JOIN US AS WE REMEMBER GWEN ARAUJO AND OTHERS. LET US SUPPORT LGBT'S AND
ALLIES ON "EQUALITY" AND BUILD LGBT SERVICES IN DISTRICT 10

Guest Speaker:

Sylvia Guerrero
"Gwen's Mother"

5. *A Mother's Activism.* Flyer for a library talk by Sylvia Guerrero in San Francisco. Courtesy of Sylvia Guerrero.

by his classmates at school. His grades dropped from As and Bs to Ds and Fs. His mother eventually sent him to live with his father, in another state.[89]

Yet the fact remains that Gwen's family fought back, and they did so in a manner that is highly reminiscent of the call of Chicana activists for oppositional politics; it was multivalent, aggressive and strategic; it disrupted gender discourse. For a few short months, in Northern California, self-representation was a field of struggle in the press and in the neighborhood where Gwen Amber Rose Araujo grew up. People learned to use the right pronouns. And Sylvia Guerrero helped found an educational fund that browned the transgender body. Local high school students organized a march to mourn Gwen's death.[90]

And then the unthinkable happened—Sylvia Guerrero forgave two of the perpetrators of the crime. Perhaps, given that her activism was so rooted in love, we should not be surprised that Ms. Guerrero would be able to see the humanity in the two young men—that somehow they were more than their fear and violence. Despite criticism from those who sought revenge, after hearing of their remorse, Sylvia Guerrero went to the jail and met with the young men; she spoke forgiveness. At the close of the second trial, Jaron Nabors apologized to Gwen's family, stating that he betrayed Gwen "in the worst way a human being could betray another." His mother and father came forward, Sylvia Guerrero joined them, and she and Mrs. Nabors embraced.[91]

The death of Gwen Araujo in this larger activist context reminds us that amid the incredible violence that so often plagues spaces of nepantla, resistance can confront violent spaces in queer communities and Latinx communities as they overlap and intersect in this, our world of motion-change. As a result of community action, change did happen: the California legislature passed AB 1160, the Gwen Araujo Justice for Victims Act, "the nation's first bill to address use of panic strategies." As the King case later demonstrated, the courts still struggle to enforce the law amid legal and educational institutions that degrade and devalue young transgender youth. Yet this act, fought for and supported by many organizations, including the Transgender Law Center, is a critical "granito de arena" in the struggle for a more just and safe society. At its passage, Sylvia Guerrero noted, "My family and friends received a life sentence when Gwen was murdered. This victory means that our loss is making a difference."[92] Clearly, "relations of domination can be effectively transformed through the agency of those whom the society subordinates."[93] As we continue to struggle against raced and gendered violence, the activism of Gwen's family reminds us that trans activism, like labor activism, is part of the fabric of our time, weaving through and pushing back against the totalizing violence of global capital. In the next chapter we will shift our gaze, once again, to a more hemispheric lens and the survival and resistance of trans immigrants in an age of global capital—for the local and the hemispheric remain part of the same cloth.

CHAPTER FIVE

Nepantler@s of the Sixth Sun

Most significant, however, is the construction of the immigration
system in the United States as a way to keep in desirables and to keep
out undesirables. The concept of "desirables" in the immigration context
is parallel to that of U.S. society in general. People of color, low-income
people, lesbian, gay, bisexual people, and transgender people . . . are
marginalized in our society whether or not they are immigrants. Thus it
logically follows that those immigrants who are already marginalized . . .
in our society are further marginalized. This dynamic has proven to be
especially powerful during times of "heightened national security."
 —Pooja Gehi, "Struggles from the Margins"

Borders are set up to define the places that are safe and unsafe, to
distinguish *us* from *them*.
 —Gloria Anzaldúa, *Borderlands / La Frontera: The New Mestiza*

As discussed in chapter 3, the late twentieth century brought with
it the dawn of a new age in capital, that of global capitalism. In the
western hemisphere neoliberal trade policies such as NAFTA set loose
a time of movement, oppression, and resistance. It was a powerful
disrupting and structural force within the larger neoliberal shift to a
totalizing global capital.[1] The FLN and then the EZLN were among the
many people's organizations rising up to challenge the neoliberal directives of multinationals and the governments that served them; and
workers such as the Duro Bag employees of Tamaulipas and those of
the Han Young plant fought for an end to worker exploitation despite
harassment, firings, intimidation, and violence.[2] The lies of stability
made by NAFTA's proponents had become apparent to many communities by the close of the century. And so movement continued into

the twenty-first century as destructive and creative forces continued to battle and weave into our own time.

The effects of neoliberalism, including NAFTA in Mexico and the Dominican Republic–Central America Free Trade Agreement (DR-CAFTA) throughout the Americas, created increased movement of people not only within their nation-states but from their homelands to the nations of the North. As noted by Saskia Sassen, the opening of borders to capital, in conjunction with foreign investment, necessarily increases immigration flow.[3] Clearly this was a function of NAFTA on the US-Mexico border. In addition, unequal power relationships embedded in free trade agreements resulted in pressure on developing countries to cut government subsidies to agriculture, while their more powerful counterparts were not required to do so. The result, throughout the late twentieth century, was an increase in poverty in the rural areas of Mexico and Central America, with a resulting increase in immigration to urban areas, often in the United States.[4]

In Mexico, the disruptive dynamics of NAFTA were clearly recognizable among small-scale corn farmers. While U.S. corn had begun to infiltrate the market the decade before the signing of the agreement, with NAFTA in effect, U.S. corn and other grains flooded the Mexican market, bankrupting hundreds of thousands of small farmers and cooperatives. With NAFTA, the Mexican government was required to phase out subsidies to its corn growers; the U.S. government made no promise to do the same.[5] According to Mexico's Ministry of Labor, from 1994 to 2012, 1,780,000 people left the countryside. It would be the men and women of families such as these who traveled north to EPZs and to the United States in search of a livelihood.[6] Clearly, this epochal shift in capital—that of monopoly capital to global capital—like the previous shift, was and is one of dramatic motion and motion-change.

In Mexico, by the second decade of the twenty-first century, the initial displacement of small farmers slowed. Yet with approximately two million small farmers stripped of their livelihoods, the sociopolitical vacuums left from widespread bankruptcies gutted social programs and disrupted cash flows, opening the doors to drug cartels.[7] With the collapse of the rural economy, drug cartels bought up property from those who went bankrupt, they expanded their ranches, added technology to their businesses, and built and expanded an infrastructure for production. They took over financing and lending and "diversified . . . beyond drugs, stealing machinery and equipment, robbing the wages of day laborers on pay day, requiring extortion payments from farmers and sales people, requiring a portion of the sale of the harvests."[8] They brought in a reign of terror, from which refugees today continue to flee. In this movement, as in the movement of the last epochal shift in capital, transgender lives were increasingly visible and vulnerable. A 2016 report by the Transgender Law Center and the Cornell University Law School noted, "Transgender women [fell] victim to cartel kidnappings, extortions, and human trafficking. One transgender woman described how cartel members forced her into sex work in Merida. Another transgender woman was targeted for rape and robbery while traveling by bus. In another case a transgender woman named Joahana in Cancun was tortured to death by drug traffickers who carved a letter "Z" for the Zeta cartel into her body."[9]

Violence against transgender women was exacerbated under Felipe Calderón's so-called war on drugs. With the rise of cartels in Mexico, Calderón gave targeted funding to the military to act as law enforcement in civilian matters. Soon violence against civilians increased generally but especially against transgender women, making them targets for "arbitrary arrests, beatings, extortions, and robberies." In Ciudad Juárez in 2007, military police assaulted a community of approximately forty transgender women, leaving many hospitalized.[10] In Chihuahua, Mercedes Fernández, president of the Chihuahua Lesbian Gay Movement, noted that transgender women "can't even go and buy their groceries because they are immediately transferred to the authorities where they are accused of engaging in prostitution. They take them away even if they are holding their grocery bags."[11]

By the second decade of the twenty-first century some of the displacement from NAFTA had slowed, yet immigration did not return to pre-NAFTA rates. The cycles set in motion by NAFTA could not be stopped by anti-immigrant bigotry, aggressive border policing, or a slow U.S. economy. As noted in a 2012 report by the Pew Institute, even if Mexican immigration to the United States never returned to prerecession numbers, "it has already secured a place in the record books.

The U.S., in 2012, had more immigrants from Mexico alone—twelve million—than any other county in the world has from all countries of the world."[12] In relation, as immigration from Mexico slowed, neoliberal trade agreements and policies, including DR-CAFTA, were signed by the United States and the governments of Central America and so movement continued. The disruption created by the intensification of neoliberal social policies and trade agreements further marginalized communities already fragile from years of civil strife. Immigration from Mexico's neighbors to the south, El Salvador, Guatemala, and Honduras, increased.[13] Those fleeing poverty and violence fled their home countries, traveling to Mexico in hopes of asylum there, or through Mexico in hopes of finding asylum in the United States.[14]

Like Mexico, these countries faced similar challenges in the shifting, weaving epoch of the late twentieth century to the early twenty-first. Such challenges were rooted in the history of violence named by Anzaldúa in her last published essay, where she wrote of the United States "using the military to advance economic and political interests around the world," and "a history of colonialism, imperialism, and support of right-wing dictatorships at the expense of freedom and democracy."[15] Throughout the hemisphere, the history of the United States is one of interference in national sovereignty, with neoliberal policies pushing people off lands and reducing social safety nets, and drug cartels filling vacuums left by displaced citizens. Lest we forget, the United States backed the 1973 overthrow of the democratically elected president of Chile, Salvador Allende; provided funds and arms to the Contras in Nicaragua; and through military and monetary aid, prolonged the dirty wars of El Salvador (1980–92). Much of the movement in this epoch of global capital was fueled by, with, and for U.S. economic interests.[16] Neoliberal economic policies throughout the hemisphere pushed people out of rural communities and into urban spaces where, often, they encountered stagnant labor markets.[17] And like so much movement in this epoch, the shortsighted actions of the United States gave rise to long-standing consequences with continued waves of violence; as a result, "devising ways to ensure personal safety, and ways to protect children and family members, [became] another element in people's survival strategies, which include migration to the United States."[18] Objects in motion do not always come to a peaceful stop.

Honduras would be one of several points of exit for refugees fleeing to the U.S. As in Mexico, the movement and violence pushing people from their homelands did not generate spontaneously. In Honduras, from the 1990s and into the early twenty-first century, neoliberal restructuring of the economy set lose violent motion-change throughout the country. "Gang violence, narco-trafficking, mass imprisonment, and state repression" accompanied the transformation of the urban labor market and the collapse of small farms through rural Honduras.[19] Initially the government of Honduras met violence with violence, including a war against young gang members and homeless children, but in 2006 this situation began to change. The people of Honduras chose Manuel Zelaya, the candidate who promised not a "strong arm" but social programs to improve employment and support the country's youth.[20]

Zelaya was not opposed to neoliberal trade policies; he signed onto DR-CAFTA but also insisted on limiting the exploitation of the people and land of Honduras. He banned open-pit mining, introduced legislation to protect national lands, raised the minimum wage by 60 percent, ended "voluntary" parent contributions for public education, and raised teacher salaries. He even refused to privatize the state-owned electric company. Socially progressive, he vetoed a bill that would have outlawed the morning-after pill—thus angering Evangelicals and conservative Roman Catholic groups such as Opus Dei.[21]

When, in the global economic crisis of 2008, Honduras suffered, Zelaya turned to his neighbors in the Alianza Boliviarana Para los Pueblos de Nuestra América, joining in the coalition and accepting support from Venezuela and Cuba to aid his struggling country. The result was a coup—military conservatives, the economic elite, and religious conservatives supported his overthrow. The United States was tepid in its response and then supported the "election" of Porfirio Lobo (Zelaya still being detained in the Brazilian embassy at the time of the election), and a new age of violence ensued.[22]

Lobo's inauguration brought with it a reign of oppression targeting progressive activists and those disenfranchised in the new neoliberal order. By March 2010, Honduras's Comité de Familiares Detenidos Desaparecidos en Honduras had documented 250 human rights violations.[23] "Security forces were responsible for thousands of illegal detentions, hundreds of injuries to peaceful protesters, dozens of murdered and disappeared individuals, and repeated uses of excessive force and intimidation against protesters, journalists, human rights defenders, and political activists."[24] Amid the backlash following the overthrow of Zelaya, LGBTQ people also became targets and "the killing of transgender women and gay men skyrocketed to unprecedented levels." Honduras was never a safe haven for transgender women; between 2004 and 2009 the murders of seventeen transgender individuals were reported. But with Lobo's election, violence escalated and in 2009 alone there were twenty-two such murders.[25] According to a 2009 article in the *Nation*, one of the first activists murdered on the night of the coup was Vicky Hernández Castillo, a transgender woman and LGBTQ rights activist.[26] The murders were not investigated.

Even while the violence continued, President Barack Obama welcomed Lobo to the White House, praising his government and asserting, "Two years ago, we saw a coup in Honduras that threatened to move the country away from democracy, and in part because of pressure from the international community, but also because of strong commitment to democracy and leadership by President Lobo, what we've been seeing is a restoration of democratic practices and a commitment to reconciliation that gives us great hope."[27]

And so the movement continued. Refugees fled Honduras to Mexico and to the United States. Their displacement was driven indirectly and directly by the needs of global capital and its relationship to neoliberalism in the late twentieth century—that is to say, the strategic deregulation of trade and production across borders, with few to no protections for the citizens who might be displaced by such economic shifts. Those fleeing to Mexico encountered struggles similar to those at home. Those who went on to the United States encountered yet new struggles, many as detainees in the U.S. prison industrial complex—a system that, since the anti-immigrant backlash and growth of Immigration and Customs Enforcement, has come to include immigration detention centers and a web of private and public jails and prisons contracted to house undocumented immigrants.

Here, the confrontation of immigrants with the prison industrial complex should not be a surprise, for as noted by both Sassen and Cohen, the rise of neoliberalism constituted not a reduction in state power but instead a shift from the regulation of businesses to the regulation of bodies. New legislation on the part of the state continued to play a critical role in shaping world power, but now it served to open borders to trade and foreign investment.[28] While the state legislates to facilitate the movement of capital, it also passes laws restricting the movement of people, through immigration restrictions and through the growth of the carceral state.

Fabric Torn Asunder: Movement, Immigration, and the Rise of the Carceral State

While the destructive weave wrought by trade agreements, neoliberal elimination of social programs, and the concomitant rise of cartels drove tens of thousands of people north, upon arrival in the United States they encountered a system that not only refused to protect them but also viewed the incarceration of immigrants as a deterrent. As noted by Alisa Solomon, the expansion of the U.S. immigrant detention system helped fuel the rapid growth of the prison industrial complex, with detention centers "at the crossroads of anti-immigrant anxiety and the roaring economy of incarceration, raking in profits and, at the same time barring the supposed threat of teeming masses coming to snatch those profits."[29] For those fleeing the violence wrought by neoliberal policies and economic shift, the struggle for asylum and safety within the United States would be a perilous one.

Clearly most immigrants and refugees coming north shared a vulnerable status, yet because of the manner in which vectors of inequality and privilege intersect in public, private, and legal discourses, LGBTQ populations have been marked by international forums as needing extra protections. Guideline 9 of the United Nations' detention guidelines, for example addresses LGBTQ refugees, insisting "that detention personnel and all other officials in the public and private sector who are engaged in detention facilities [must be] trained and qualified regarding international human rights standards and principles of equality and non-discrimination, including in relation to sexual orientation or gender identity. Where their security cannot be assured in detention, release or referral to alternatives to detention would need to be considered."[30]

While international organizations such as the United Nations recommended alternatives to detention centers, and studies such as those by Taback and Levitan have demonstrated that detention and threats of detention do not deter people from fleeing their countries, the use of detention centers on the part of the United States and European countries has increased since 1994 and into the twenty-first century. In the U.S. in 1994, according to the Department of Homeland Security, 6,785 people were held in immigrant detention centers per day. By 2012 that number had swelled to 32,953.[31] Likewise, the duration of detention increased from an average of less than four days in 1981 to over sixty days in 2003.[32] While global capital continued to move people north through capital shifts and international trade agreements, clearly the modern nation-state, as demonstrated by the carceral state, remained critical to organizing and controlling bodies.[33] Transgender mestiz@s were among the thousands fleeing their countries, and despite directives from the United Nations to protect the safety of vulnerable immigrants, including LGBTQ immigrants, or to seek alternatives to detention, they were also among the increasing numbers of immigrants being detained.

As with the push factors for so many people leaving their home countries, at the root of much of the move to incarceration was global capital as it intersected with U.S. economic interests. With new federal policies favoring immigrant detention, the numbers of detainees quickly surpassed the federal capacity for detaining people. The federal government then turned to state and private facilities, as well as some county facilities, to house detainees. By 2011, according to the Harvard Law Review Association, such facilities were housing 84 percent of all immigrant detainees—a system had developed that "benefited both the federal government and the nonfederal facilities: the facilities had beds to spare and a desire for additional revenue, while the INS met its demand for beds at a relatively low cost."[34] And

Immigration and Customs Enforcement (ICE) was given economic incentives to increase and sustain its number of immigrant detainees. In 2007 the Department of Homeland Security placed a quota of detainees that ICE would have to meet to receive full funding. While the stated purpose of detention was to ensure that immigrants made their trial dates or to protect the public from violent offenders, the numbers belie such a narrative. Between 2009 and 2011 over half of those detained by ICE had no criminal records. With economic incentives built into the system where detention benefits both ICE and private facilities, less expensive, more humane compliance measures were discouraged.[35] Despite its own role in creating crisis situations throughout the hemisphere, the United States maintained a restrictive annual quota of four thousand refugees from all of Latin America and the Caribbean.[36]

Even while an increasing number of LGBTQ people fled their homelands, the scrutiny under which all residents of the United States lived increased, making undocumented immigrants perhaps more vulnerable to deportation than at any time since the anti-immigrant sweeps of the 1930s. The 1996 Illegal Immigration Reform and Immigration Responsibility Act and its companion bill, the Anti-terrorism and Effective Death Penalty Act, created a climate of crisis for undocumented transgender immigrants. The laws reduced opportunities to seek relief from deportation and made detention mandatory for most awaiting deportation proceedings, at the same time they expanded the crimes for which a person could be deported.[37] Today, use of a stolen social security number can be prosecuted as an aggravated felony.[38] People can be deported for crimes of "moral turpitude" as well as felonies—and in some states felonies include nonviolent crimes such as forging a check. The wide net of deportable crimes includes a number of survival crimes, or crimes in which an unemployed or marginalized person might engage to feed themselves.[39]

Six years after the 1996 acts, on October 26, 2001, George W. Bush signed the Uniting and Strengthening America by Providing Appropriate Tools Required to Intercept and Obstruct Terrorism Act, also called the Patriot Act. The Patriot Act "reduce[d] constraints on the government's ability to conduct searches, deport suspects, eavesdrop on Internet communications, monitor financial transactions, and crack down on immigrant violations."[40] The destructive weaving of the late twentieth century accelerated when, as part of the formation of the Department of Homeland Security, the Immigration and Naturalization Service was abolished and a new department was created, that of Immigration and Customs Enforcement. Soon ICE agents would be collaborating with local law enforcement "to help facilitate deportations by assisting ICE in identifying individuals who have committed crimes, regardless of gravity, as well as by providing records of individuals who have been stopped, fingerprinted, and found not to have committed any crime."[41] The absorption of the Immigration and Naturalization Service by Homeland Security and the bolstering of border security resulted in increased surveillance of all immigrants and an exponential growth in immigrant detention. For transgender immigrants the acts and related measures exacerbated identity policing already enacted in 1996, placing all in greater risk of detention and deportation.

The weave and battle of destructive forces continues in our time; in fact it is this weave that is, at present, weaving our world. A draconian amount of tax dollars are utilized in an attempt to stop the movement fueled by nation-states and corporate politics. In 2014, with a budget of $3.6 billion, the U.S. Border Patrol had 18,156 agents along the U.S.-Mexico border, equipping them with ground radar, motion detectors, thermal imaging sensors, helicopters, drones, and more.[42] Equally disturbing, the U.S. federal government began pouring money into Mexico to turn back immigrants and refugees from its borders. As of October 2014, according to the American Immigration Council, the United States had sent approximately $1.3 billion to Mexico to secure its southern border. Police and the military raid trains, restaurants, and hotels, and the government is working with companies that run cargo trains to increase their speed so that immigrants and refugees cannot use them to travel north.[43] The number of refugees deported by Mexican authorities dramatically increased so that in 2015 the federal government deported over 118,000 people fleeing the violent motion-change of their home countries.[44]

Yet these are nepantlan times, and such times are woven not by destructive forces alone but also by creative and life-affirming forces that push through the violence. Thus, amid the destructive forces of ICE and the flourishing of private for-profit carceral institutions, positive forces reacted and pushed back and pushed through—creating countermovements and counterdiscourses, and weaving a more livable world. Among these counterforces was the Transgender Law Center and the many vectors of resistance it helped to fuel.

Making Revolution: The Transgender Law Center

I crush the patriarchy by leaving a seed of consciousness behind at every space that I navigate. I crush the patriarchy all the times that I'm the first trans Latina to speak at an event or a school, which is often. I crush the patriarchy by ensuring that I'm not the last trans Latina to have these talks. I make sure the people in my community also hold the keys to crush the systems that keep us down, in place and silent. We all have some truth to speak.

—Isa Noyola in *Latina Magazine*, 2016

The Transgender Law Center (TLC) was founded in 2001, five years after the passage of the Illegal Immigration of the Illegal Immigration Reform and Immigration Responsibility Act and the Anti-terrorism and Effective Death Penalty Act of 1996, and one year after the Patriot Act. According to cofounder Christopher Daley, the groundwork for TLC had begun decades before. As with most efforts toward structural change, years of struggle at multiple levels were necessary before any kind of infrastructure could be developed. So it was that decades after the founding of Vanguard, a community organization for LGBTQ youth, in 1965 and the Compton's Cafeteria Riot in 1966, TLC began as the Transgender Law Project under the umbrella of the Center for Lesbian Rights (CLR).[45]

It is not surprising that San Francisco would be a point of generative energy for nepantlan rights. As noted by Ilona M. Turner, legal director for TLC, San Francisco had been at the forefront of transgender rights for decades.[46] One could argue that at the same time the destructive forces of totalizing capital were gathering, human rights struggles were also creating sites of disruption and change in this often generative site by the sea. As early as 1961, gender rights were visible in a renewed call for human rights. In that year the burgeoning homophile rights movement in San Francisco received a dramatic boost when the politically astute drag performer José Sarria ran for public office.[47] Roughly five years later the Compton's Cafeteria Riot rocked the city.

The Compton's Riot was, perhaps more radical than Sarria's run for office, for it was transgender youth and street youth who were at the forefront. Many of the youths were members of Vanguard, supported by Glide Memorial, a progressive church in San Francisco's Tenderloin district.[48] In 1965 Glide had begun outreach to LGBTQ communities, including young people. Joel Roberts, one of Vanguard's founders, would later recall "storming into Glide Methodist Church. . . . [They] had hired a Texas black Pastor named Cecil Williams, . . . and I stormed in and said there's kids on the fucking street selling their ass. There's kids sleeping eight in a hotel room at night and you people talk about social change. . . . And Cecil Williams came out and said[,] 'Young man, anybody that can swear like you I want to talk to.'"[49] Glide hired a seminarian, Edward Hansen, as an intern to develop street outreach, and Hansen immediately went out into the neighborhood to "listen." From those early exchanges Vanguard would emerge, eventually holding dances, drag balls, coffeehouses, and direct action protests, and publishing a newsletter.[50] At the cutting edge of gay and trans organizing, Vanguard called for "Street Power." The newsletter they published was of, by, and for the young queer street youth of the neighborhood. They wrote it, they circulated it, and they published it with the support of organizations such as Glide, the Mattachine Society, and the Society for Individual Rights.[51] The support of the older, more established homophile organizations would remain clear over the course of Vanguard's magazine; similar support would also play a role in the Compton's Cafeteria riot that soon rocked the neighborhood and city.

Compton's Cafeteria had been one of the few places where drag queens, sex workers, and queer youth, including young people involved in Vanguard, could informally gather and be safe. In the early 1960s the manager, like other older gay men in urban areas, had informally provided a safe space for queer youth to gather. But he died, and the new manager hired private security guards to drive the youth from the establishment.[52] When the guards began harassing the youth and pushing them out of the space, Vanguard members worked with Glide Memorial and older homophile organizations to organize a picket.[53] When the picket failed to change management's discriminatory practices, the infamous Compton's Riot ensued. Predominantly young street youth and trans youth rose up, creating a cultural shift by forcing the population of San Francisco to note the very real needs and demands of its transgender residents.[54]

San Francisco would continue to be at the forefront of transgender organizing. After the riot, Conversion Our Goal (COG), one of the first transgender peer-support groups, was founded in San Francisco with the support of Glide Memorial; and a police liaison, officer Elliot Blackstone, was assigned to address the needs of the homophile communities in the Tenderloin. Louise Ergestrasse, a trans activist in the neighborhood, insisted that the assigned officer educate himself about transsexual lives and needs and provided him with some resources to do so.[55] Such forces of change, pushing and weaving through the cultural backlash that resulted in the election of Richard Nixon in 1968 and into the backlash of the 1980s would keep San Francisco at the forefront of transgender organizing and transgender rights for decades.[56]

Indeed, the city continued to weave forward into the era of global trade agreements and hemispheric displacement of LGBTQ people. As Ilona M. Turner noted, "In the 1980s, San Francisco was also the home base of the first national organization that focused solely on trans men, FTM International, and in 1992, of Transgender Nation. The city also subsequently pioneered municipal protections for trans people including issuing a groundbreaking report on discrimination faced by the trans community in 1994, enacting an ordinance prohibiting discrimination based on gender identity in 1994, and in 2001, becoming the first municipality in the nation to provide health insurance coverage for transition-related care for city employees."[57] Had Jack Mugarrieta Garland lived in this second wave of nepantlan movement, his ability to support himself would have been significantly stronger than during his own nepantlan time, yet he would have also seen that for transgender women of color, movement toward a realization of rights remained very slow.

Grounded in this larger history of transgender rights and liberation, TLC emerged as a force within multiple vectors of movement. Shannon Minter had been working on transgender rights cases with the CLR, so when Christopher Daley was awarded a Tom Steel fellowship, he was able to build on that work.[58] For the first three years of its existence, the Transgender Law Project operated under the umbrella of the CLR.[59] Daley and Minter worked collaboratively, producing *Trans Realities: A Legal Needs Assessment of San Francisco's Transgender Communities*, a study addressing immigration rights as well as the many other critical needs of transgender people.[60] Constructive forces of resistance continued to meet and challenge the destructive forces of a reactionary nation-state and the disruptive winds of totalizing capital.

While still under CLR's umbrella, the Transgender Law Project released a pamphlet, *Know Your Rights*, in both English and Spanish, that included information about asylum rights, among other issues.[61] In 2004, with Noemi Calonje, the immigration clinic coordinator at CLR, TLC represented Adriana Turcios as she applied for asylum.[62] TLC later developed "cultural competency" training for immigration service providers and immigration attorneys.[63]

Yet as the country moved forward regarding many aspects of gender rights, the rights of transgender immigrants, especially women immigrants, remained remarkably vulnerable. As noted in *Authentic Lives*, the government "increasingly recognized and upheld certain rights of transgender people, while continuing to sanction the horrific abuse of transgender immigrants held in detention centers across the country."[64] And so, in 2014, TLC stepped up its efforts, hiring Isa Noyola, an activist and organizer with extensive experience working locally for transgender immigrant rights to manage the center's outreach and programming.[65] The hiring of Noyola exemplified the complex strategy that had come to dominate the center: advocating and providing "legal assistance and information to transgender individuals and their families [and engaging] in impact litigation and policy advocacy to advance transgender rights." Such advocacy would grow to be as broad as facilitating networking among transgender activists in the U.S., supporting protests at detention centers, and finding pro bono legal support for transgender refugees even while continuing to engage in impact litigation.[66]

Fresh out of college, Noyola had not intended to do national work; instead she had focused her efforts on local communities and local needs. She worked with Marcia Ochoa at Proyecto ContraSIDA Por Vida creating Habla la Jotería, a queer- and trans-friendly program in English as a second language.[67] Proyecto ContraSIDA was a vibrant, holistic center with programming that included community forums, creative educational courses, career guidance workshops, and a soccer team for young women.[68] It is not surprising that Ochoa and Noyola would find it the perfect place to house the ESL program. Yet Proyecto ContraSIDA, like so many critical spaces in the San Francisco Bay area, would face the debilitating effects of gentrification as it intersected with shrinking government aid. It closed its doors in August 2005.[69]

When Proyecto ContraSIDA closed, Noyola continued to work with El/La Para TransLatinas, where she did everything from database work to fundraising to program planning.[70] Noyola worked tirelessly, organizing protests at detention centers, heading education programs, and supervising projects. Her labor, like that of queer Chicanas of the twentieth century, was clearly rooted in a "politics of necessity."[71] That necessity became even more urgent with the murder of Ruby Ordeñana. Ruby was just twenty-seven years old when she was killed. As noted in her CUAV memorial, "she left her native Nicaragua in search of a place she could call home. She wanted to be able to live a life free of violence and stigma where she could express herself without fear for her safety. At twenty-seven-years old, she had created her own family from various communities in the Bay Area."[72] With Ruby's passing Noyola ardently embraced El/La, later noting, "I just really made my home at El/La where . . . it is in many ways a home for many of us. . . . This beautiful respite and holistic space that we have created, in which we honor our community members that have passed and also honor our folks that are living by providing services and space and providing—un cafecito con pan, you know, in the everyday ways we build community."[73] Noyola's work with El/La would continue long after she joined the TLC.

Yet, working in advocacy, Noyola noted the absence of trans women of color in leadership, even in advocacy organizations themselves. As she continued her work, the absence became increasingly and glaringly apparent, even in places and organizations dedicated to making policies and implementing change on behalf of transgender women. Thus, when the opportunity to work at the TLC presented itself, she knew she had to make the shift. And so her outreach became more national in scope, even while maintaining her ties with local organizations.[74] At the time she was hired as program manager for TLC she had also been working as the program manager of LYRIC's LGBTQQ youth leadership and workforce department. As she shifted to TLC, she continued to serve as a national advocate for El/La Para Trans-Latinas and on the steering committee of Familia Trans Queer Liberation Movement.[75] Only one year later she would be promoted to director of programs at TLC. As the organization grew into its role as a leading "multi-disciplinary organization committed to creating concrete change in the lives of those members of our communities who are most marginalized," it was nepantleras such as Noyola who held the experience, insight, and vision to facilitate that growth.[76]

Throughout the 1990s and into the twenty-first century, the motion-change within which Noyola moved, like the motion-change of the last epochal shift in capital, was and is not one to be romanticized. Her appointment, in fact, came within a context of multiple violences: physical and emotional violence targeting trans women and, in relation, spatial violence—destructive motion-change. As Noyola herself noted in the press release announcing her promotion, "My decision to do this work was not a career choice but a matter of survival, and I am committed to picking up the torch that has been violently taken away from my sisters."[77]

Motion-change in the form of spatial violence—gentrification—rocked the Bay Area, San Francisco, and beyond. Notably, some of the workers and families displaced from the fields of Mexico due to the structural adjustment programs of the 1980s and 1990s had settled in the Bay Area—into cities of movement.[78] For cities, like the fields of southern Mexico, are not static spaces. Instead, they are "shaken up repeatedly by the dynamic forces of capitalism and modernity."[79]

Thus, like the displacement of Mexico's farmers due to neoliberal policies and trade agreements, the gentrification of the Bay Area was also driven by shifts in global capital. Neighborhoods that had survived the urban gentrification movements of the 1990s were once again vulnerable. In this next wave of gentrification, even the landmark queer Latinx gathering place of Esta Noche closed, as did Proyecto ContraSIDA Por Vida.[80] Nancy Raquel Mirabal, a professor at San Francisco State University, noted, "San Francisco was changing once again. A familiar and yet disturbing process, the gentrification of working-class neighborhoods, had resurfaced with a speed and precision that had not been seen for years. Housing prices soared, new businesses opened, rents were at their peak, and thousands moved into the city to participate in what newspapers, politicians, academics, and business leaders were calling the dot-com boom."[81]

Noyola came to TLC at about the same time that the organization moved to Oakland. Throughout the San Francisco Bay Area, globalizing forces of capital moved industrial jobs offshore while dot-com businesses moved into traditionally working-class and immigrant communities. One study estimated that two hundred dot-com businesses had set up in San Francisco's Mission District and the area surrounding it. In that same neighborhood, by the year 2000, more than one thousand Latinx families had been pushed out.[82] Likewise, between 1990 and 2011, in the city of Oakland, the African American population decreased by 40 percent.[83] Gentrification created a widening gap between the haves and the have-nots. Many LGBTQ people, especially the most vulnerable, could not afford to live in San Francisco; and service and support organizations could expand their ability to serve their communities only by relocating elsewhere.[84] As Noyola herself would note in an interview on *Democracy Now*, that was a time when gentrification in urban areas north and south was closing down queer havens; safe spaces for queers of color, clubs and LGBTQ centers that were once "spaces to mobilize and to organize," were no longer available.[85]

Within this context of capital-driven motion-change, the TLC moved from one space of gentrification to another. As noted by Causa Justa, a grassroots organization that works for housing and racial justice in

Oakland and San Francisco, "much of what develops in San Francisco ends up crossing the Bay." While, in 2000, in San Francisco, two thousand evictions were reported, in Oakland between 1998 and 2002 "no fault" evictions, where landlords provided no reason for the eviction, tripled and rents increased 100 percent. As in San Francisco, the first wave was fueled largely by venture capital, tech companies, and the dot-com boom but also by local politicians such as Jerry Brown with his "10K initiative for Downtown Oakland."[86] It would also be exacerbated by displaced persons crossing the bay. It was in this larger context of motion-change that the TLC leased offices on Telegraph Avenue in downtown Oakland, near a rapid-transit stop and in an area that itself was undergoing transition. It was here that they would continue to labor until they outgrew the space in 2017.

Today TLC engages in advocacy as well as direct actions targeting ICE and detention centers.[87] As in their early years, when they worked in collaboration with organizations such as Community United against Violence, the San Francisco Human Rights Commission, and the Asylum Project, today they work collaboratively with the same organizations but also with Familia QTLM and GetEQUAL. It was working with Not1More Deportation, in collaboration with Familia QTLM and GetEQUAL that they successfully fought alongside Christina López for her release from the Santa Ana Detention Center.[88] The next year they appealed a deportation ruling on behalf of Marianna, a transgender woman from Mexico who had fled the country fearing for her life. Their appeal was successful, and Marianna's case was remanded.[89]

And so the weave continues. Marianna's case was remanded, but only after she was detained for eleven months. With the success of her appeal she still faced the long and difficult process of applying for asylum. Struggles for justice and struggles for profit clash and weave and create the world around us. In the twenty-first century the forces of a totalizing capital continue to grow strong as the nation-state functions to facilitate the globalizing of capital: moving, controlling, and incarcerating bodies in its service. In this movement it is the lives of queer mestiz@s that become visible but also vulnerable. And yet there is hope. For the forces of mobilizing capital are met with resistance by labor movements and by the activism of organizations such as TLC, Causa Justa, and the workers of Duro Bag. The weave does continue, and we do continue to strive to shape the weave, to build upon the work of nepantler@s past and present in order to shape a better present and a livable future, one where those of us who live in between genders, races, cultures, and spaces might flourish.

Conclusion

Into the Sixth Sun

> Gloria was an unassuming philosopher-poet whose words will inspire generations. She articulated our past to make sense of our present; however, she didn't just look to Nahuatl culture because she was merely seeking origins. She looked to that past to excavate hope for our future.
> —Emma Pérez, "Gloria Anzaldúa"

> Today, we are facing a devastating reality. A demagogue who has pledged to destroy our communities and campaigned on open and enthusiastic contempt for our lives—as transgender people, as people of color, as people of different faiths and abilities and citizenship status—has been elected to the highest office in our country.
> —Kris Hayashi, executive director, Transgender Law Center, November 6, 2016

The struggle for transgender survival and flourishing has a long history that is woven through with the strains and threads of global movement and local and global energy. Transgender mestiz@s are part of a great weave, shaping it while concurrently being shaped by it. In nineteenth-century California, or Nueva Nepantla, people moved and shifted and were moved and shifted. Displaced Chinese and Irish laborers came to the space of movement and further fueled cultural and economic *remolinos*; their motion added to the already-in-motion lives of Indigenous peoples and Californios/ianas struggling to survive amid a Euro-American invasion that brought with it a new culture: the culture of the railroad and monopoly capitalism. Within this time-space of motion-change, trans men such as Jack Garland strove to survive, living as men and working in a man's world. Jack's life was one of transition as he moved from living as a masculine woman in a semiurban space to living as a man in the teeming city of San Francisco. While the Stockton where he lived as a masculine woman did not yet have a law against cross-dressing, that time was quickly passing. By the time he returned to live in San Francisco as Jack Garland, cross-dressing carried with it penalties of not only fines but jail time. And yet capital and gender identities did not become etched in stone. Capital and gender remained part of the same great weave, yet the weave again underwent a dramatic change at the turn of the century.

With the dawn of global capital, transgender lives again were very visible and very vulnerable. Yet while monopoly capital insisted on stable gender roles to people its economic system, the role of gender in this, our new emerging economic epoch, remains somewhat unclear. Thus, mapping global capitalism and resistance to its totalizing forces since its emergence in the late twentieth century remains a useful tool for attempting to understand the present and to shape the future. The neoliberal policies of governments throughout the western hemisphere, as exemplified by the North American Free Trade Agreement, created accelerated motion-change not seen since the epochal shift to monopoly capitalism. Even before NAFTA, structural adjustment programs globally pushed people from traditional lifeways and into factories. In Mexico the Salinas government pushed Indigenous peoples and peasants from their communal landholdings, going so far as to change the constitution to free up land for "development."

By the time NAFTA was signed, Indigenous and working communities were well organized and pushed back. The resistance of EZLN and of the workers of Duro Bag are just two bold examples of people fighting back and rejecting a world of totalizing capitalism. In Chiapas the Zapatistas called on people everywhere to find their own style of organizing "from the bottom and to the left."[1] To some, including many Chicanx communities, their organizing embodied and embodies hope for a better world. As noted by Yaotl, a vocalist with Aztlán Underground, "Zapatismo is the Sixth Sun, the rebirth of our culture. . . . [They] have taught us that the struggle is global."[2] The activism of the Zapatistas and the Duro Bag workers demonstrated and demonstrates how the trans-ing of gender is part of a great weave where gender, labor, oppression, and resistance push up against each other and push and pull through each other to create the past, present, and future. Where we find gender, we find political economy; where we find political economy, we find gender.

Within the shift to global capitalism, a young trans woman by the name of Gwen Amber Rose Araujo struggled for survival. Her life, like that of Jack Garland, was one amid motion-change. Yet there were dramatic differences between her life and that of Jack because of their very different times and their very different movements. As Jack moved into manhood he was able to disappear into the working class and the displaced masses of San Francisco. Like Gwen he came from a loving family who did not quite understand him, but their ongoing attempts at support, from his mother bringing him home from the state asylum after his brief incarceration to his sister slipping him cash to aid in his survival near the close of his life, meant that he was able to live to be an elder—Uncle Jack—dying from a treatable illness at the age of sixty-seven.

Gwen lived in a very different world—one transitioning from the world of monopoly capitalism in which Jack lived. It was the world of hemispheric and global trade agreements, of neoliberalism and Zapatismo. As in Jack's time, capital displaced people and people resisted. Yet while Gwen, like Jack, had a supportive family, as in Jack's time her world treated people who trans-ed gender as surplus. She was pushed from those public institutions created to shape, condition, and support youth: schools and places of worship. Moving into womanhood she faced the violent misogyny directed at trans women in Western society where, as Valencia notes, "trans and gender-variant women are not only killed as women, with overflowing sexual brutality, but also killed socially for disobeying the biologist mandate of conforming to live in a body whose gender has been assigned medically and with which they do not identify."[3]

Gwen's life and death and her mother's activism became critical strands in the weave of resistance that pushed through the violent motion-change of global capitalism. Organizations such as Community

United against Violence and the Transgender Law Center worked with her mother and family in seeking justice for her death but also sought to educate the public and create structural change, improving the life chances of transgender and gender nonconforming people in the years to come. The TLC grew to be the largest trans-led rights organization in the United States. Yet even as organizations such as TLC and EZLN continued to grow and flourish, the disruptive and destructive shifts of global capital also continued to grow and flourish.

The Hope of Edin Avendaño-Hernández and the Weave of the Sixth Sun

As we passed the year 2012, some of us continued to hope for the realization of the Sixth Sun. The words of Gloria E. Anzaldúa echoed in our hearts: "In terms of evolutionary stages, the world is presently between el quinto sol y el sexto. According to Maya knowledge, the sixth world starts December 2012. It is this nuevo mundo, this new order, we need to create with the choices we make, the acts we perform, and the futures we dream."[4] Anzaldúa was writing in the context of the 2001 attacks on the Pentagon and the World Trade Center. Thousands of people had lost their lives. Anzaldúa placed the loss and violence within the context of global and local violences that shaped the last age and that continue to shape this new age, calling us to shift, to make this sun different from the last. For many of us the Sixth Sun was not and is not an empty myth but contemporary prophecy. We are here in the weaving of a new world, and we must weave it.

We continued to struggle. In 2012 the gap between the wealthiest 1 percent of U.S. families and the rest of society was greater than it had been since 1928, with "the top 1% receiving 22.5% of all pretax income, while the bottom 90% share [was] below 50% for the first time ever."[5] President Obama issued an executive order, Deferred Action for Childhood Arrivals, offering temporary protections to young undocumented immigrants while at the same continuing to deport more immigrants each year than did George W. Bush.[6] And the earth continued to warm. Yet resistance continued to build and weave, and as we moved into the next age, people continued to resist the totalizing forces of neoliberalism, anti-immigrant rhetoric, and scapegoating.

Then, in March 2015, the U.S. Ninth Circuit Court decided a case that brought hope to many.

Amid the motion-change that continued to shape our world, transgender immigrants still were among the most vulnerable people in our hemisphere. Those who sought refuge in the United States often faced further abuse on their arrival; in some jurisdictions, such as Orange County, immigration judges had denial rates as high as 93.8 percent.[7] But on March 6, 2015, in *Avendano-Hernandez v. Lynch*, the Ninth Circuit rendered a decision giving hope to those who continue to work for a safer world for all, ruling that transgender refugees hold a status distinct from that of gay immigrants, and that the passage of marriage equality rights in a country was not evidence of safety for transgender or gay people. Edin C. Avendaño-Hernández, a transgender refugee from Mexico, was allowed to remain in the United States.

The journey for Avendaño-Hernández was long and arduous. She grew up in a rural town in the state of Oaxaca. As a child she knew she was different, preferring her sister's clothes to those her parents bought for her.[8] As with so many gender-creative children, as she grew, violence on the part of schoolmates and even family members grew. Her brothers and cousins assaulted and harassed her. School was not a refuge; it was a place where classmates attacked her for being "gay." The adults in her life, instead of protecting her, also participated in the violence. Her father beat her, throwing homophobic and transphobic language at her; a schoolteacher harassed her and tried to force her to have sex with him. She lived with the abuse until secondary school and then fled, at age sixteen, to Mexico City.[9]

Yet Mexico City was not and is not the paradise that so many think of when they imagine queer communities in central Mexico. Yes, it is the home of Jesusa Rodríguez and her edgy-fabulous performances—the home of the Resistencia Creativa movement.[10] It is also the place where in 2009 the city legalized same-sex marriage and adoption. Yet, as in the United States, such legislation did nothing to protect transgender women; in fact, it appears to have made things worse. As noted by the Ninth Circuit, violence against transgender people increased following the legalization of marriage and adoption: "Indeed, the country's highest number of hate crimes in 2010 took place in Mexico City—where arguably the most efforts have been made to protect the rights of sexual minorities."[11]

In Mexico City Avendaño-Hernández found work at a nightclub but also found that even cities such as the Federal District did not provide a safe haven for transgender women. When her mother was diagnosed with cancer Avendaño-Hernández went home to live with her for a year but, due to her brother's continued threats of violence, left immediately after her mother's passing. This time she headed for the United States and was able to successfully cross into California, settling in Fresno. Yet there she struggled with alcohol addiction and was arrested twice for drunk driving. After her second conviction she was sentenced to 364 days in jail. Upon her release she was deported to Mexico. Due to the violence she faced in Mexico she again struggled to find a way to come to the United States. This time she faced violence at the hands of not only family and civilians but also police and the military. En route to visit family in the city of Oaxaca she was stopped, beaten, and raped by uniformed police officers. Again she fled north.

When, in 2011, she was arrested and detained, and removal proceedings began, it was because, on being deported to Mexico, she failed to report to her probation officer in the United States.[12] Yet this time she was not alone. In applying for withholding of removal due to fear of torture under the Convention against Torture, a United Nations agreement the United States signed in April 1988, she found legal support through the Equal Justice Works Public Law Center and pro bono representation from the firm of Manatt, Phelps, and Phillips. A team of four lawyers—Andrea Ruth Bird, Matthew Williamson, Janine Weiss, and Munmeeth Soni—from the two firms went to work for her, and six different rights organizations signed on as amici curiae.[13] While the Board of Immigration Appeals ruled against her, claiming that progress toward gay rights in Mexico negated her claims of fear for her safety, her appeal to the Ninth Circuit succeeded.

In deciding *Avendano-Hernandez v. Lynch* the court found that the violence inflicted on Avendaño-Hernández by uniformed police and military officers constituted a threat of government-sanctioned torture. Equally important, it found that "the BIA [Board of Immigration Appeals] primarily relied on Mexico's passage of laws purporting to protect the gay and lesbian community. The agency's analysis, however, is fundamentally flawed because it mistakenly assumed that these laws would also benefit Avendaño-Hernández, who faces unique challenges as a transgender woman. . . . While the relationship between gender identity and sexual orientation is complex and sometimes overlapping, the two identities are distinct."[14] The court also noted that following the passage of rights legislation, violence against minorities often increases. Her case was remanded to the Board of Immigration Appeals to grant deferral relief under the Convention against Torture. For transgender immigrants, *Avendano-Hernandez v. Lynch* established a precedent on which advocates continue to build.

No Turning Back

We are not gathered here today in order to change the world. . . . We are here with a more modest proposal . . . which proposes to create a new world.

—Comandanta Ramóna, International Meeting for Humanity, 1996

November 6, 2016, was a devastating morning for many of us. Even while we were well aware that the country remained in a time of backlash, we remained hopeful that the dream of a better world for all was still on the horizon. We saw the signs of destruction around us but hoped and worked for a weave in which we could all live and flourish. The facts, of course, remained. Both the decision of *Avendano Hernandez v. Lynch* and the appointment of a working-class Latina to the U.S. Supreme Court occurred in the context of mass deportations of immigrants from the Americas and the continued flourishing of political communities such as the Tea Party. Hate crimes against transgender women of color remained rampant in the United States and in countries to the south from which refugees continued to flee. In 2015 alone twenty-one transgender women were killed in the United States; the majority of the victims were women of color. In 2016 the violence increased, and by November 9, when the Gay and Lesbian Alliance against Defamation had updated its website, twenty-seven people had been murdered.[15] It appeared that the Sixth Sun would be equally violent, if not more so, than the Fifth Sun.

The base for the reactionary turn of the 2016 election, like the work behind successful battles such as *Avendano-Hernandez*, ran deep. Many saw the roots of this latest wave of backlash in the Tea Party movement of the early twenty-first century. The Tea Party had emerged amid a sea of cultural conservatism and anti-immigrant sentiment. Conservative white Americans, in 2009, in response to the election of Barak Obama and some of his economic policies, organized at local and national levels. The movement was fueled by national forces such as Fox News and Americans for Prosperity but also by local communities of voters who already knew each other through Republican organizations, faith communities, and neighborhood organizations. While many mark the bailouts of the early years of the administration as the impetus for the Tea Party, a common sentiment among Tea Party organizations across the nation was a belief that the nation was in economic and cultural decline. Christian prayer, the Pledge of Allegiance, and fear were central themes and practices among many of the grassroots organizations.[16]

The result of the 2016 election, then, should not have been a surprise. The shift to global capitalism, addressed in chapters 3 and 5, resulted in large-scale displacement of workers throughout the hemisphere, including the United States. In the United States both working- and middle-class Euro-Americans felt vulnerable. As noted by clinical psychologist Jay Einhorn,

> Money . . . is a form of stored social energy that affords its possessors agency in their lives, status in their communities[,] and coherence, or at least a sense of coherence[,] in their identities. Individuals, families, and communities, who were solidly in the middle class and then lost their ability to remain middle class, with impairment in their member's sense of agency, status, and self-coherence, are psychoeconomically disenfranchised. Others, while not yet having lost their middle class status, are threatened with losing it, and insecure. . . . Psychoeconomic disfranchisement fosters a host of negative experiences . . . feelings of intense inadequacy and victimization, and vulnerability to malignant authoritarian leaders, who promise to restore lost status and blame scapegoat groups for the problem, while in reality seeking power as an end it itself.[17]

A study by the Center for Social Inclusion showed that the Tea Party of the early twenty-first century flourished at the intersection of white supremacy and economic insecurity: "in districts with economic insecurity, Tea Party candidates won 9 of 10 races where the White population is above 60 percent, while losing 7 of 10 races where the population of color is above 40%." In districts not suffering economic stagnation or downturns, the Tea Party did poorly.[18]

Thus it should not be surprising that in the 2016 election 53 percent of white women voted for Donald Trump while 84 percent of Black women voted for Clinton.[19] The anti-immigrant sentiment that ebbs and flows through U.S. history manifested itself with increasing fierceness for a solid decade; candidate Trump simply fed into Euro-Americans' fear of loss of economic and cultural status. With the 2016 election such sentiment resulted in increased violence against immigrants, with policies from the Trump administration violating basic human rights conventions, tearing children from their parents and holding them in cages, and ICE officials neglecting to observe the basic human rights of people seeking refuge in the United States.[20] While Indigenous and peasant communities, such as the Zapatistas of Chiapas, rose up to challenge the systems that would oppress them, and community groups such as the Franciscans in southern Mexico continued to reach out to LGBTQ refugees and migrants, far too many Euro-American working- and middle-class Americans, men and women alike, fell to scapegoating and other self-destructive behaviors.[21]

Yet Zapatista communities did continue to organize, as did organizations such as TLC. In July 2018 the five caracoles, or regional self-government structures, of the Zapatistas celebrated their fifteenth anniversary. Days of workshops, poetry, history, organizing, and dance brought together community members from the areas of self-government as well as guests from the United States, Europe, and Mexico.[22] Also in southern Mexico, in Tenosique, Tabasco, Fr. Tomás González Castillo continued to welcome LGBTQ refugees and migrants to La 72, a shelter named for the seventy-two Central and South American refugees massacred by members of a cartel in 2010.[23] Today La 72 welcomes all refugees, with attention paid to the unique needs of LGBTQ people.[24]

In the United States in 2017, the Transgender Law Center expanded its work to increase support of transgender immigrants and refugees. In announcing the founding of their Trans Immigrant Defense Effort (TIDE), executive director Kris Hayashi noted, "The Trump administration has pledged to devastate immigrant communities on an unprecedented scale, at a time when our government already deports people in record numbers and holds transgender immigrants in inhumane, abusive conditions. . . . We have a duty to launch a vigorous defense against this attack on some of the most vulnerable members of our community."[25] TIDE went on to recruit, train, and connect culturally competent pro bono attorneys with transgender and gender-nonconforming immigrants and refugees and to work with grassroots organizations to help support their autonomous and networked organizations. Staff from TLC's TIDE went to Nogales to ensure that the Rainbow 17, the caravan of Central American and Mexican refugees who traveled to the Mexico-United States border in September 2017, had legal representation.[26] The struggle continues, and organizations such as TLC have become more critical than ever in the fight for transgender survival and flourishing and for a more just world. In the words of Francisco Galarte, . . . "the whole range of travesti-trans interventions being made across las Américas that teem with creativity, refusal, and vitality in the face of precarity are anything but utopian or idealistic; they set the stage for myriad forms of transformation."[27]

As this work went to print the man elected on a wave of anti-immigrant scapegoating, misogyny, and fear succeeded in replacing the North American Free Trade Agreement with yet another neoliberal agreement destined to eliminate "economic borders while reinforcing . . . internal borders and beefing up . . . surveillance systems."[28] The United States, Mexico, Canada agreement (USMCA) also called NAFTA 2.0, was ratified by the U.S. Congress as the copyedits arrived in my inbox. The negotiation of NAFTA 2.0 was itself an example of the nepantlan time in which we continue to live. The U.S. House of Representatives was successful in forcing the removal of a provision that would have given pharmaceutical companies a ten-year monopoly on any biologics they developed. Other provisions, or lack of provisions, however, will continue to push people from their homes and into motion.[29] As noted by Ronald Labonté the USMCA

> opens up markets in both Canada and Mexico for US food exports without reducing the subsidies the US provides to its own producers, and introduces a number of new regulatory reforms that weaken public health oversight of food safety. . . . Its labour and environmental chapters contain a few improvements but overall do little to ensure either worker's rights or environmental protections.[30]

And so the struggle continues. We live in a time of motion-change. This is not to argue that previous ages were devoid of motion and weaving but that this, our age, is a time of accelerated motion. In looking to the past we can see other times of rapid motion-change such as California's late nineteenth-century shift to monopoly capital. That change too brought about rapid shifts in culture and power, displacing thousands of people prior to its settling. Today, the shift to global capital remains incomplete. Culture again is shifting, and communities are being torn from their homelands. There is no guarantee the world that emerges from this shift will be any better than the last. The words of Gloria Anzaldúa are hopeful, yet also call us to action: "It is this nuevo mundo, this new order, we need to create with the choices we make, the acts we perform, and the futures we dream."[31] If we are not to repeat the violence of the late nineteenth century, we need to learn from the past. If we seek to participate in the weaving of a more just society—to realize the prophecy of the Sixth Sun—then all of us must leave fear behind, learn from communities such as the EZLN and TLC, and with our dreams and our labor create a new world.

NOTES

Introduction

1. Maffie, *Aztec Philosophy*, 479–512.
2. Snorton, *Black on Both Sides*, 2–14. Fajardo, "Transportation," 406.
3. Snorton, *Black on Both Sides*, 7.
4. Anzaldúa, "Aliens: The Dynamic Construction of US Chicana/Latina Experience," talk at the University of Milwaukee, Wisconsin, October 6, 1995, MS 112.1, Gloria Evangelina Anzaldúa Papers, Benson Latin American Collection, University of Texas at Austin (hereafter cited as Benson); Gloria E. Anzaldúa, interview, in Karin Rosa Ikas, *Chicana Ways: Conversations with Ten Chicana Writers* (Reno: University of Nevada Press, 2002), 13.
5. Anzaldúa, "Exploring Cultural Legacies," MS 112.2, Benson.
6. Indigenous and mestiz@ scholars today note that Spanish as well as English is a colonizing language. Ortiz, "Indigenous Continuance." Ortiz provides examples of using colonial language with an indigenous consciousness, as well as the dangers of taking colonial language for granted.
7. Wiegers, "Managing Disaster," 145; Martínez, "Black Blood of New Spain," 483. Wiegers notes that in 1611 a royal decree was issued to expel not only recent converts but also *Antiguos*—Moriscos whose history in Spain preceded those who claimed a Christian identity. After 1611 only Moriscos who could pass as Old Christians remained. This action of course gives rise to questions of passing and queering early Christian Spain. Martínez notes that the concept of *limpieza de sangre* originally designated one free of "Jewish, Muslim, and heretical antecedents" and was used primarily against Jewish and Muslim converts.
8. Gaspar de Alba, *[Un]Framing the 'Bad Woman,'* 2.
9. Stryker, *Transgender History*, 1.
10. Snorton, *Black on Both Sides*, 2.
11. Fajardo, "Transportation," 407.

12. Twenty-two trans women were murdered between January 1 and November 19 of 2015, the year I began drafting this introduction. In the United States and globally, violence against trans women remains an epidemic. See National Center for Transgender Equality, "With Heavy Hearts, Remembering Those Lost and Pressing for Change"; see also Terry, "In the Crosshairs," 27–35.
13. Long live motion-change.
14. Acuña, *Sometimes There Is No Other Side*, 109–14.
15. Ferguson, *Aberrations in Black*, 149n1. See also page 3.
16. Sandoval, "U.S. Third World Feminism," 1–24.
17. Anzaldúa, "To(o) Queer the Writer."
18. Sánchez, *Forgotten People*; González, *Woman Who Lost Her Soul*; Galarza, *Merchants of Labor*; Paredes, *With His Pistol in His Hand*. For historiographies addressing this foundational generation, see García, "Turning Points"; González, "Gender on the Borderlands"; Gutiérrez, "Significant to Whom?"
19. Cotera, *Diosa y Hembra*; García, *Chicana Feminist Thought*, 4–8.
20. Soldatenko, *Chicano Studies*, 145; Blackwell, *¡Chicana Power!* 4–9, 195–205.
21. Cotera, *Diosa y Hembra*, 164–65. García, *Chicana Feminist Thought*, 4–8. See also Committee for the Development of Subject Access to Chicano Literatures, *Chicano Periodical Index*, for 1969–73. Both *Regeneración* and *Encuentro Feminíl* were Chicana feminist journals. *El Grito del Norte* was edited by Enriqueta Longeaux Vasquez and Elizabeth Martínez.
22. Cotera, *Diosa y Hembra*, 31–35. Blackwell *¡Chicana Power!*, 100–25. It is Blackwell who applied the term "retrofitting" to the work of many of these women.
23. Esquibel, *With Her Machete in Her Hand*, 23–34. Blackwell, *¡Chicana Power!*, 145–56. See also Ruiz, *From Out of the Shadows*; Del Castillo, "Matlintzín Tenepal."
24. Esquibel, *With Her Machete in Her Hand*, 25–26.
25. Apodaca, "Chicana Woman," 72. For an example of this scholarship in relation to Chicana literary and interdisciplinary studies see Sánchez, "Chicana Labor Force," in Sánchez and Martinez Cruz, *Essays on La Mujer*. See also the introduction to that same volume.
26. Ruiz, *Cannery Women, Cannery Lives*; Castañeda, "Comparative Frontiers"; González, "Widowed Women of Santa Fe"; Sánchez and Martinez Cruz, *Essays on La Mujer*.
27. Anzaldúa, "La Prieta," 232; Anzaldúa, *Borderlands*; Moraga, *Loving in the War Years*.
28. Morgensen, "Unsettling Queer Politics."
29. Luna, "Indigenous Knowledge for Resistance."

30. See, for example, Muños, *Disidentifications*; Foster, *El Ambiente Nuestro*; Esquibel, *With Her Machete in Her Hand*; Ramírez, "Claiming Queer Cultural Citizenship," and "'That's My Place.'"
31. Feinberg, *Transgender Warriors*; Feinberg, *Trans Liberation*.
32. *Hetero-patriarchy* was coined by LatCrit scholar Francisco Valdes to describe the manner in which androsexism and heterosexism function to maintain systems of privilege for masculine heterosexual men in U.S. society. See Valdes, "Queers, Sissies, Dykes, and Tomboys."
33. Califia, *Sex Changes*, Stryker, *Transgender History*; Stryker and Whittle, *Transgender Studies Reader*; Halberstam, *Female Masculinity*.
34. Califia, *Sex Changes*, 120–62.
35. Boag, *Re-Dressing America's Frontier Past*; Sears, *Arresting Dress*; Skidmore, *True Sex*.
36. Gaspar de Alba, *[Un]Framing the "Bad Woman,"* 2.
37. Fajardo, "Transportation," 406.
38. Fajardo, "Transportation," 407.
39. Snorton, *Black on Both Sides*, 2.
40. Snorton, *Black on Both Sides*, ix.
41. Valdes, "'We Are Now of the View,'" 1407–63; Valdes, "Queers, Sissies, Dykes, and Tomboys."
42. Spade, *Normal Life*, 89.
43. Spade, *Normal Life*, 87–89. See also Spade and Willse, "Confronting the Limits of Gay Hate Crimes Activism."
44. Rebolledo, "Politics of Poetics," 354.
45. Partida, "Abordar la Impunidad de la *Guerra Sucia* Ayuda a Analizar la Actualidad." I did not make this connection; Anzaldúa did. It is found in her notes at the Benson Latin American Collection. "Exploring Cultural Legacies, notes," 1999, box 112, folder 2.
46. Transgender Law Center, "Adriana Turcios," *Legal Translations/Traducciones Legales*; National Coalition of Anti-Violence Programs, "Lesbian, Gay, Bisexual, Transgender, Queer, HIV-Affected Hate Violence in 2012."
47. Gehi, "Gendered (In)Security," 357.

1. A World Created through Motion

1. Maffie, *Aztec Philosophy*, 14.
2. Dodds Penncock, *Bonds of Blood*, 2.
3. Vásquez, "Aztec Epistemology," 79.
4. Curl, *Ancient American Poets*, 6–11; Maffie, *Aztec Philosophy*, 2–3. Maffie notes that Aztec philosophy was not a matter for the elites alone but instead was shared throughout Mexica society.
5. Vásquez, "Aztec Epistemology," 74–79; León-Portilla, *Aztec Thought and Culture*, 102.

6. Carrasco, *Religions of Mesoamerica*, 30–45. Carrasco and others note that the belief in the Feathered Serpent and Rain God as well as the use of jaguar motifs and the ball court can all be traced to the Olmecas.

7. León-Portilla, *Aztec Thought and Culture*, xvi, 23.

8. Curl, *Ancient American Poets*, 3, 49–50.

9. Curl, *Ancient American Poets*, 3.

10. Carrasco, *Religions*, 12. Carrasco notes that Zumaraga burned hundreds of books. Today only eleven remain.

11. Vásquez, "Aztec Epistemology," 76; Maffie, *Aztec Philosophy*, 14–24.

12. Maffie, *Aztec Philosophy*, 480.

13. Burkhart, "Mexica Women on the Home Front," 25; Townsend, "What Have You Done to Me?," 373.

14. Kellogg, "Woman's Room," 564. For marriage and divorce see also Dodds Pennock, *Bonds of Blood*, 133–37.

15. Burkhart, "Mexica Women on the Home Front," 28; Dodds Pennock, *Bonds of Blood*, 42.

16. Maffie, *Aztec Philosophy*, 21.

17. Burkhart, "Mexica Women on the Home Front," 34.

18. Dodds Pennock, *Bonds of Blood*, 10–18, 36; León-Portilla, *Aztec Thought and Culture*, 102.

19. Kellogg, "Woman's Room," 566.

20. Maffie, *Aztec Philosophy*, 495.

21. Maffie, *Aztec Philosophy*, 479.

22. Maffie, *Aztec Philosophy*, 493.

23. Townsend, "What Have You Done to Me?," 355. For Cihuacoatl, see Maffie, *Aztec Philosophy*, 493.

24. Lara, "Goddess of the Americas," 99–127. Lara also notes that *ichpochtli*, the word Franciscans would come to use for "virgin," simply meant "postpubescent girl."

25. Messinger Cypess, *La Malinche in Mexican Literature*. Sandra Messinger Cypess was one of the first scholars to map the mobilization of historical figures as symbol in the political movements of Mexico. For the later mobilizations and retrofittings during the Chicano movement and by Chicana feminists, see Baca, "Chicano Codex"; Sauer, *Accidental Archives of the Royal Chicano Air Force*; and Blackwell, *¡Chicana Power!*.

26. Anzaldúa in Ikas, *Chicana Ways*, 13, 14.

27. Pérez, "Gloria Anzaldúa," 1.

28. Soldatenko, *Chicano Studies*, 24, 73, 89–92. Soldatenko notes the heterogeneity and contested intellectual territories among Chicanx scholars even in its early years.

29. The most famous iteration is Gonzalez's "Yo Soy Joaquin," but his work, while exemplary of the time, was part of a much larger genre.
30. Apodaca, "Chicana Woman"; Del Castillo, "Malintzín Tenepal"; Alarcón, "Chicana Feminist Literature"; Soto, "Tres Modelos Culturales"; Candelaria, "La Malinche."
31. Saldívar-Hull, "Before Borderlands," 8.
32. Anzaldúa, "La Prieta," 221; Ikas, *Chicana Ways*, 2.
33. Anzaldúa, *Interviews/Entrevistas*, 22–23.
34. Anzaldúa, "La Prieta," 222.
35. Anzaldúa, "La Prieta," 222; Ikas, *Chicana Ways*, 3. Anzaldúa would go on to serve as a bilingual and migrant director for the state of Indiana.
36. Anzaldúa, "La Prieta," 222; See also Anzaldúa, "Turning Points," in *Interviews/Entrevistas*, 29.
37. Anzaldúa, "Turning Points," 30–32.
38. In her last published interview Anzaldúa spoke to the dynamics of identity, with the need for creating new categories as we shift, and of changes in Chicana identities. See Lara, "Daughter of Coatlicue," for an analysis of Anzaldúa's work on Coyolxauhqui as symbolic of ongoing reconstruction of our selves; see also Alarcón, "Anzaldúan Textualities."
39. Hernández, "With Heart in Hand." Anzaldúa earned a bachelor's degree in English, art, and secondary education from Pan American University and went on to earn a master's in English and education from the University of Texas; she then supported herself through teaching, while writing and producing a number of critical works (see Ikas, *Chicana Ways*, 3–4).
40. Moya, *Learning from Experience*, 62–88; Sandoval, *Methodology of the Oppressed*, 41–46, 153–54; Lara, "Sensing the Serpent in the Mother"; Pérez, "Gloria Anzaldúa."
41. Anzaldúa, *Borderlands*, 104.
42. Sandoval, *Methodology*, 153–54.
43. Sandoval, *Methodology*, 180–84.
44. The difficulty Moraga and Anzaldúa had in finding a publisher for the volume was symptomatic of the sexism and racism embedded in the publishing world of the time. Persephone Press, a white feminist publishing house, published the first edition, only to fold the next year. Barbara Smith, at this time, was pulling and pooling women of color into a collective to found their own press, forged into reality the next year; both Anzaldúa and Moraga would be among its founding members. Kitchen Table would go on to publish the second edition of *This Bridge*, ultimately selling over a million copies. While few women of color found publishers prior to this, a flurry of publications followed.

45. Anzaldúa, "La Prieta," 232–33.
46. Anzaldúa, "El Mundo Zurdo," 218.
47. Pérez, "Performance of Spirituality," 14.
48. Anzaldúa, *Borderlands*, 103.
49. Lara, "Daughter of Coatlicue," 41.
50. Lara, "Daughter of Coatlicue," 44.
51. Arrizón, *Queering Mestizaje*, 75.
52. Joysmith and Lomas, prologue, *One Wound for Another*, 21–23.
53. Anzaldúa, "Let Us Be the Healing of the Wound," 99.
54. Gaspar de Alba, *[Un]Framing the "Bad Woman,"* 2.
55. Katz, *Gay American History*; Boag, *Re-Dressing America's Frontier Past*.
56. National Conference of State Legislatures, "Federal and State Recognized Tribes"; Fixico, *Indian Resilience and Rebuilding*. In the words of Donald Fixico, "After four hundred years of colonized suppression, the indigenous responded but not in the way that those in power thought. Certainly not overnight, but within a century's stretch, the Native nations arose from the ashes of near ethnic cleansing and third-world neglect" (218).
57. Hinton, "Advocates for Indigenous California," 53–55. Advocates for Indigenous California Language Survival has trained almost two hundred teams in forty different California languages.
58. Kewanhaptewa-Dixon, "Preservation and Sustainability."
59. Coonrod Martínez, "New Century for Indigenous Writing," 1.
60. Apodaca, "Chicana Woman," 80. See also Martin et al., *Concise History of America*, 427–30; Glenn, *Unequal Freedom*, 105. According to Martin et al., government subsidies to the railroads began before the Civil War. Then, during the 1860s, Congress gave the Union Pacific and the Central Pacific twenty square miles of public land for each mile of track they laid.
61. Gómez, *Manifest Destinies*, 4.
62. Acuña, *Occupied America*, 9–27; Paredes, "Origins of Anti-Mexican Sentiment," 139–57; Pitti, *Devil in the Silicon Valley*, 26–32; Gómez, *Manifest Destinies*, 15–41. See also Heidenreich, *"This Land Was Mexican Once,"* 82–88.
63. Carrigan and Webb, "Lynching of Persons of Mexican Origin."
64. Carrigan and Webb, *Forgotten Dead*, 17–61. Carrigan and Webb note that Euro-Americans did not distinguish Californios, or even Chileans, from "Mexicans" (57–58).
65. Hurtado, *Intimate Frontiers*, 132–36; Pitt, *Devil in the Silicon Valley*, 73–74. Carrigan and Webb, *Forgotten Dead*, 69–74. Carrigan and Webb cite Frederick Douglass as writing that if Juana Loaiza were white she would

have been lauded for defending her honor, noting that her "cast and Mexican blood" determined her fate (70).

66. Chávez-García, *Negotiating Conquest*, 175.
67. Menchaca, *Recovering History*, 217–23. See also Almaguer, *Racial Fault Lines*, 17–74.
68. Molina, *How Race Is Made in America*, 25–26.
69. Almaguer, *Racial Fault Lines*, 30.
70. Robinson, *Theory of Global Capitalism*, 41–58.
71. White, "Railroad Reaches California," 131; Polanyi, *Great Transformation*, 45–70, 226.
72. White, "Railroad Reaches California," 137; Almaguer, *Racial Fault Lines*, 167.
73. Glenn, *Unequal Freedom*, 150–54.
74. Chan, *Asian Californians*, 10–12.
75. Takaki, *Different Mirror*, 140–45. Takaki notes, "Between 1815 and 1910, five and a half million Irish immigrated to America" (140).
76. Takaki, *Different Mirror*, 150–54.
77. Almaguer, *Racial Fault Lines*, 166.
78. Menchaca, *Recovering History*, 256–76. See also Robert Heizer's classic *Destruction of the California Indians*.
79. Takaki, *Different Mirror*, 166–85.
80. Saxton, *Indispensable Enemy*, 117–32.
81. McLeod, "Transubstantiation of Andrew Johnson," 88–101. Cacho, *Social Death*, 23–25.
82. Takaki, *Different Mirror*, 31.
83. Glenn, *Unequal Freedom*, 151.
84. Almaguer, *Racial Fault Lines*, 192–99.
85. Street, *Beasts of the Field*, 464–65.
86. Camarillo, *Chicanos in a Changing Society*, 1–35, 146–54; Gutiérrez, "Migration, Emergent Ethnicity," 488–89.
87. Polanyi, *Great Transformation*, 38–40.

2. Life and Times of Jack Mugarrieta Garland

1. I use masculine pronouns for Garland throughout this chapter out of respect for his chosen gender at the close of his life, and because it appears that, as early as his life as a reporter in Stockton, he wished to live socially as a man.
2. In reading though the correspondence of Louis Sullivan, housed in the California Room of the San Francisco Public Library, it became clear that he learned he was HIV-positive about the same time that he won his contract with Alyson Publications, which published his book *From*

Female to Male: The Life of Jack Bee Garland. Given the reality of the times, he would not have had time to develop his analysis beyond the initial work that he submitted. The book remains a foundational text on this historical figure. Earlier works that contained passing reference to Jack's life include Robbins, *Tales of Love and Hate in Old San Francisco*, 52–52, and De Ford, *They Were San Franciscans*, 34–36.

3. For discussions of transsexual and transgender biography and autobiography, see Califia, *Sex Changes*, 163–94.

4. Boyd, "Bodies in Motion," 424

5. Skidmore, *True Sex*, 101–11. Skidmore's work addressing the life of Jack Garland appeared after the publication of an earlier version of this chapter and, while citing the work in her footnotes, does not address those times in Jack's life where he seems to have utilized, if not embraced, his biracial upbringing.

6. Molina, *How Race Is Made in America*, 22.

7. See the introduction to this work for more information about the foundational work of this generation of historians.

8. Anzaldúa, *Borderlands/La Frontera*, 25.

9. Castañeda, "Gender, Race, and Culture," 153–54; Kaplan, "Manifest Domesticity"; Glenn, *Unequal Freedom*, 170–71. Glenn notes the attitude of white women toward Mexican American domestic workers reinforced ideologies of white supremacy: "The only situation in which most Anglo women felt comfortable with Mexican women was one that clearly affirmed the Anglo's superior status. As in the South and Hawaii, the most common such situation was that of employer and domestic servant" (170).

10. Kessler-Harris, *Women Have Always Worked*, 62–69; Foner, *Women and the American Labor Movement*.

11. Juárez Rose, *Past Is Father of the Present*, 12, 32; Weber, *Mexican Frontier*, 216; Reyes, *Private Women, Public Lives*, 86–133.

12. Apodaca, "Chicana Woman," 78. Castañeda, "Engendering the History of Alta California," 232–33, 242–51; Reyes, *Private Women, Public Lives*, 86–133.

13. Glenn, *Unequal Freedom*, 172.

14. Hurtado, in *Intimate Frontiers*, maps the ways in which the processes through which the new system became established necessarily included violence against Californianas and other women of color. See also Kaplan, "Manifest Domesticity."

15. Kaplan, "Manifest Domesticity."

16. Castañeda, "Women of Color and the Rewriting," 114–17.

17. Castañeda, "Political Economy."

18. Menchaca, *Recovering History*, 272.

19. Pitti, *Devil in the Silicon Valley*, 51.

20. Chávez-García, *Negotiating Conquest*, 176.

21. Castañeda, "Gender, Race, and Culture," 164–65. For an article that maps this phenomenon in Australia and notes a pattern similar to that of white women claiming power in the United States, see Haskins, "Domestic Service and Frontier Feminism."

22. Sears, *Arresting Dress*, 54–57.

23. Siemers and Phillips, "City Hall Historian's Office Report," box 4, folder 139, Sullivan Collection, Daniel E. Koshland San Francisco History Center at the San Francisco Library, San Francisco, California (hereafter cited as SC). In the Catholic tradition *sisters* engage in active community work, teaching, social service, and so on; *nuns* are contemplative and tied to a monastery or cloister. Both are *women religious*.

24. Borunda, "Mexican Nationhood Context," 43–45.

25. Alba, "Reforms," 139–40.

26. Key to manuscript notes, Jose Marcos Mugarrieta Collection, MSS 69/93m, Bancroft Library, Berkeley, CA (hereafter cited as Bancroft).

27. *Biographical Directory of the United States Congress*, s.v. "Rice Garland," accessed July 13, 2017, http://bioguide.congress.gov.

28. Wilder, "Reins, Riggings, and Reatas," 369.

29. Wilder, "Reins, Riggings, and Reatas"; Alonzo, "Mexican-American Land Grant Adjudication."

30. Letter to Virginia Garland, June 22, 1859, and letter to "Amadisima Meca," January 20, 1860. In most of his letters Mugarrieta referred to Eliza as "Amadisima" and "querida rubia." Mugarrieta Collection, MSS 69/93m Outgoing Letters, folders Jan.–June 1859 and Jan.–June 1860, Bancroft.

31. "Babe Bean Has a Visitor," *Stockton Evening Mail*, December 9, 1897, 5.

32. Siemers and Phillips, "City Hall Historian's Office Report," SC.

33. "Babe Bean Has a Visitor"; Siemers and Phillips, "City Hall Historian's Office Report," SC.

34. Adelman, "Empowerment and Submission"; O'Brien, "French Nuns in Nineteenth-Century England." See also Deggs, *No Cross, No Crown*. Deggs's *No Cross, No Crown* is of particular use to historians interested in the limits of Catholic women's communities in the nineteenth century, as it notes their varied approaches in New Orleans, from challenging unjust laws to working within the system and offering only minimal education and services to racial minorities.

35. O'Brien, "French Nuns in Nineteenth-Century England," 142–43.

36. O'Brien, "French Nuns in Nineteenth-Century England," 154.

37. O'Brien, "French Nuns in Nineteenth-Century England," 144, 153.

38. Fajardo, "Transportation."

39. Here the exact school is not certain—once I narrowed the school to the most likely based on the school's location and the socioeconomic class of the girls who attended it, I contacted the order's archivist. She, Sr. Billie Olin, O.P., explained to me that they do not have rosters for either St. Rose or St. Catherine's for the 1800s. She was good enough to send me information on the curriculum of the time.

40. Dougherty, "Dominican Sisters of San Rafael."

41. Clarke, *Life of Reverend Mother Mary*, 145. Clarke also notes that for the Sisters of the Good Shepherd, the first missionaries sent to America were women from four different countries (255).

42. Adelman, "Empowerment and Submission," 139.

43. Dougherty, "Dominican Sisters of San Rafael,"5.

44. Pagliarini, "And the Word Was Made Flesh," 228.

45. Sr. Billie Olin to author, March 19, 2007, correspondence in possession of author.

46. "Was Dressed as a Boy," *Stockton Daily News*, August 23, 1897, 1.

47. Sears, *Arresting Dress*, 74–75.

48. Krafft-Ebing, *Psychopathia Sexualis*, 188–221.

49. Sears, *Arresting Dress*, 82–83.

50. Starr, "Stockton State Hospital," 116, 118.

51. "Director's Report," *Appendix to the Journals of the Senate and Assembly*, 6 (1889): 27.

52. Magennis and Lacy, "Demography and Social Epidemiology," 266–69.

53. "Director's Report," 27.

54. "Superintendent's Report, Year Ending June 30, 1888," *Appendix to the Journals of the Senate and Assembly*, 6 (1889): 18.

55. "Daily Medical Reports," Department of Mental Hygiene, Stockton State Medical Records, February 1895, California State Archives.

56. Commitment register, vols. 9 and 10, 1886–94, Stockton State Hospital, California State Archives. The entry noted that he was committed by Judge J. F. Sullivan of San Francisco. The register lists his age as eighteen, but also lists his birth date as "about 1870." Elvira Mugarrieta did not appear in the Stockton State Hospital Female Patient Index, 1857–1903; in fact, my initial lead for his internment was a copy of the commitment register at Ancestry.com.

57. Feldberg, "Comparable Worth," 315–16. For information on Eliza Garland's employment, see Siemers and Phillips, "City Hall Historian's Office Report," SC.

58. *Langley's San Francisco Directory for the Year 1888*, Daniel E. Koshland San Francisco History Center, San Francisco.

59. Siemers and Phillips, "City Hall Historian's Office Report," SC.

60. "Pardoned but Dying, William Mugarrieta Has Only Escaped San Quentin to End His Life at Home," *San Francisco Call*, March 14, 1896.

61. Siemers and Phillips, "City Hall Historian's Office Report," SC. See also Sullivan, *From Female to Male*, 168–69.

62. Katz, *Gay American History*, 317–422. For more recent work see Peter Boag's output as well as Sears, *Arresting Sex*, and Skidmore, *True Sex*.

63. See Boag, *Re-Dressing America's Frontier Past*, 50–53 for his discussion of Garland, and page 34 for his brief discussion of Cathay.

64. "Girl Lives as Man and Weds," *Milwaukee Journal*, May 3, 1914, 2. Kerwineo was exposed because his wife took him to court for abandonment. At trial she explained that as women of color they had not been able to support themselves, thus Kerwineo adopted the dress of a man to earn a man's wage. For more accounts of people who crossed genders to marry, see Katz, *Gay American History*, or http://www.npr.org/blogs/npr -history-dept/2015/01/29/382230187/-female-husbands-in-the-19th -century, for a popular accounting of such couples.

65. "Babe Bean Has a Visitor."

66. "Has Babe Bean Skipped Out? Said That the Girl-Boy Has Disappeared," *Stockton Daily Record*, August 27, 1897, 1.

67. "'Babe' Bean Bruised: She Somersaults from a Street Car in Motion, and Two Doctors Tell the Rest," *Stockton Daily Record*, August 30, 1897, 1.

68. Davis, *Stockton*, 10–14.

69. For an excellent discussion of gender and power among the first peoples of the Stockton area, see Dick-Bissonnette, "Gender and Authority among the Yokoch, Mono, and Miwok of Central California."

70. Kennedy, *It Happened in Stockton*, 1:28.

71. Streeby, *American Sensations*, 5, 90–118.

72. Kennedy, *It Happened in Stockton*, 2:223.

73. Kennedy, *It Happened in Stockton*, 1:25.

74. Sullivan, "Elvira Mugarrieta alias Jack Bee Garland," 5–6.

75. "'Babe' Bean in Her Pantaloons. It Is Probable That She Has the Right to Wear Them," *Sacramento Evening Bee*, September 16, 1897, 1, SC.

76. "Wears Trousers but Her Tongue Is Silent," *San Francisco Examiner*, August 24, 1897, SC.

77. In San Francisco, at this time, cross-dressing was a misdemeanor penalized with a fine; more severe laws would be passed in 1903. See Sullivan, *From Female to Male*, 146, and Sears, "Electric Brilliancy," 171.

78. "A Little Miss Adventure," *Stockton Evening Mail*, August 23, 1987, 1, SC; "Has Babe Bean Skipped Out?," *Stockton Daily Record*, August 27, 1897, 1, SC. "Male Clad Girl of the Lake," *Stockton Evening Mail*, August 17, 1897, 1, SC.

79. *The Mail* (Stockton), September 17, 1897, 6, SC; "'Babe' Bean and Her Pantaloons," *Evening Bee*, September 16, 1897, 1, SC.

80. "Oh Babe, Babe, Look Out!," *Stockton Evening Mail*, September 29, 1897, 1, SC.

81. "Male-Clad Girl at the Lake," *Stockton Evening Mail*, August 27, 1897, 1.

82. "Babe Bean on Deck Again," *Stockton Evening Call*, January 26, 1898, 1.

83. "Burying the Asylum Dead," *Stockton Evening Mail*, March 10, 1898; "Babe Bean in Tuolume: The Mail's Lady Correspondent Is Engaged on a Railroad Detail," *Stockton Evening Mail*, April 12, 1898.

84. Boyd, "Bodies in Motion," 424.

85. "Babe Beam Is Clara Garcia: So Says a Man Who Knows her Husband," *Stockton Daily Record*, September 15, 1897; "Not Clara Garcia: Babe Beam Indignantly Denies the Story to the Effect," *Stockton Daily Record*, September 19, 1897. While Skidmore sees the "indignant" rejection of this identity as a rejection of Bean's Mexican heritage, the article itself accounts for his indignation as due to the accusation of "doing anything wrong" or "criminal or immoral." Had Bean objected to the ethnic label it seems that the article, or perhaps a later article would have stated as much. It did not. See the *Stockton Evening Record*, September 19, as well as Skidmore, 103.

86. "Babe Bean in the Asylum," *Stockton Evening Mail*, December 30, 1897.

87. Siemers and Phillips, "City Hall Historian's Office Report"; "Exploits of an Extraordinary Woman: 'Babe Bean' Now Known as 'Jack,'" *Stockton Evening Mail*, April 28, 1900, 10, SC.

88. "Claimed to Be Born in the South," *San Francisco Call*, August 24, 1897, 3.

89. Kennedy, *It Happened in Stockton*, 1:25–28.

90. "Stockton's History," *Stockton Full of Flavor*. The page notes that the depot was built in 1898 and the bank in 1906.

91. The reporter Carl Schurz wrote of this as the "new Manifest Destiny." See Quince, *Resistance to the Spanish-American and Philippine Wars*, 9.

92. Siemers and Phillips, City Hall Historian's Office Report.

93. While, at the time of his passing, some newspapers wrote of his tattoo as having the number 29, as if to recognize the regiment, government records list the regiment on the ship *Para* as the 24th. It is possible that with time the tattoo blurred so that the 4 appeared to be a 9. "Summary of the Principle Events," *Annual Reports of the War Department* 1 (part 2): xv.

94. Boag, *Re-Dressing America's Frontier Past*, 34.

95. "Girl Lives as Man and Weds," *Milwaukee Journal*, May 3, 1914, 2, SC.

96. Skidmore, *True Sex*, 116–26.

97. Sullivan, *From Female to Male*, 119–30.

98. "'Babe Bean' Now Known as 'Jack,'" *Stockton Evening Mail*, April 28, 1900, 10, SC; Beebe Bean, "My Life as a Soldier," *Sunday Examiner Magazine*, October 21, 1900, SC.

99. Sullivan's notes from *Stockton Daily Record* and *San Francisco Examiner*, box 4, folder 134, SC.

100. Fr. Pio Pi to his superior general, Manila, September 30, 1896, quoted in Arcilla, "Jesuits during the Philippine Revolution," 300.

101. Beebe Bean, "My Life as a Soldier," *Sunday Examiner Magazine*, October 21, 1900, SC; Siemers and Phillips, "City Hall Historian's Report"; "Exploits of an Extraordinary Woman," *Stockton Evening Mail*, April 28, 1900, 10, SC. The Jesuits also held an in-between position in the Philippines. While Spanish, they were one of only two religious orders that did not own haciendas. Thus they received less vitriol from revolutionaries than the landholding orders such as the Augustinians and Dominicans. See Pilapil, "Nineteenth-Century Philippines and the Friar-Problem," 127–48, esp. 141.

102. Schoonover, *Uncle Sam's War of 1898*, 99.

103. Katz, *Invention of Heterosexuality*.

104. Sears, "Electric Brilliancy," 171; Sullivan, *From Male to Female*, 146.

105. Sullivan, *From Male to Female*, 146–49.

106. López, *White by Law*, 17.

107. Boyd, *Wide Open Town*, 13–14.

108. Death certificate, Elvira Virginia Mugarrieta, folder 135, SC. "Death Reveals San Francisco Writer's Spouse as a Man," *San Francisco Examiner*, September 21, 1936, 1, 8; "Confirms Masquerade: Says Sister was 'Jack Garland,'" *San Francisco Call Bulletin*, September 21, 1936, A2, SC.

3. NAFTA and Generative Movement in the Sixth Sun

1. Anzaldúa, "Nepantla, Creative Acts of Vision," n.d., box 112, folder 19, "Speeches," Benson; Medina, "Nepantla Spirituality," 205–14; Gaspar de Alba, *[Un]framing the "Bad Woman,"* 105.

2. Anzaldúa, "Nepantla, Creative Acts of Vision."

3. Anzaldúa, "La Prieta," 232–33.

4. Joysmith, "'Let Us Be the Healing of the Wound,'" 97.

5. See Robinson, *Theory of Global Capitalism*, for aspects of this shift rooted in the decades just prior to the agreement.

6. Quintana, "How NAFTA Unleashed the Violence in Mexico"; Ruiz-Marrero, "Contras and Drugs," 15.

7. Anzaldúa, "Exploring Cultural Legacies," box 112.2, Benson.

8. Herrera Calderon and Cedillo, "Introduction." Herrera Calderon and Cedillo note that Mexico's Dirty War remains the most understudied of the dirty wars of the late twentieth century. It was not until the Zapatista uprising of 1994 that scholars began to map the violence and resistance of late twentieth-century Mexico.

9. Artemusicayvideo, "Nepantla, la insurreccion de la memoria 1"; Cedillo, "Armed Struggle without Revolution," 149.

10. Treviso, *Rural Protest and the Making of Democracy*, 67–73. On October 2, 1968, approximately three hundred military snipers infiltrated a student rally at the Plaza de las Tres Culturales. Convinced by the government that the five thousand to ten thousand students wanted to overthrow the government, they opened fire and continued to shoot into the crowds for an hour. Students arrested at the rally were later tortured. Many consider the massacre the turning point in urban activism, radicalizing Mexico's reformist organizations.

11. Herrera Calderon and Cedillo, "Introduction," 6–8, quotation and numbers from page 8; Treviso, *Rural Protest and the Making of Democracy*, 12–13.

12. Harvey, *Chiapas Rebellion*, 60. Lal, "Rebellion in Chiapas," 1515. See also Harvey, "Rebellion in Chiapas," 50. Harvey notes that in the state of Chiapas ranch owners rebelled against agrarian reform and elected Tiburcio Fernández Ruiz as governor in 1920. Ruiz prevented land redistribution into the 1930s and decreed that ranchers could retain up to eight thousand hectares (almost twenty thousand acres) of land. When Cárdenas moved redistribution forward, ranchers continued to hold the choice pieces of land, leaving forest areas for redistribution.

13. Harvey, "Rebellion," 42.

14. Lal, "Rebellion in Chiapas," 1515.

15. Harvey, "Rebellion," 49–50.

16. Harvey, *Chiapas*, 58.

17. Fox, "Roots of Chiapas," 119.

18. Harvey, *Chiapas*, 62–65. See also Lal, "Rebellion in Chiapas," n. 26.

19. Hernández Castillo, "Between Feminist Ethnocentricity and Ethnic Essentialism," 60.

20. Alvarez, "Peasant Movements in Chiapas," 286–88. In 2016, when the state sought to build yet another dam by expropriating yet more ejido land, residents who were interviewed pointed out that the promises of land, piped water, and a health clinic made in 1976 were never kept. See Godoy, "Rural Community Fights a Second Dam and a New Expropriation of Land."

21. By 1972 they had also begun to establish an armed branch in the Cañadas region of the Lacandón jungle; they posed as chile dealers and so called the ranch El Chilar. The endeavor failed due to reasons mapped by Cedillo in "Armed Struggle without Revolution."
22. Cedillo, "Armed Struggle without Revolution," 153–56.
23. Cedillo, "Armed Struggle without Revolution," 152–54.
24. Harvey, *Chiapas*, 62–63, 76–79. At the congress the governor addressed the delegates, stating that "in no way should you feel your freedom threatened, so that you may express your reality as you live it," yet soon after the congress the army continued to suppress local communities with violent evictions from Lacandón communities (quotation from Harvey, *Chiapas*, 78). See also Hidalgo-Monroy Wohlgemuth, "Alternatives to Rural Development," 73, and Kampwirth, *Women and Guerilla Movements*, 96.
25. Hernández Castillo, "Between Feminist Ethnocentricity and Ethnic Essentialism," 59.
26. Cedillo, "Armed Struggle without Revolution," 155; Dillingham, "Indigenismo Occupied," 557. Harvey (*Chiapas*, 79) notes that among the lawyers and teachers that Bishop Ruiz invited to run workshops prior to the congress were members of the Unión del Pueblo.
27. Hidalgo-Monroy Wohlgemuth, "Alternatives to Rural Development," 73. Las Abejas, for example, also worked toward liberation and indigenous rights but embraced nonviolence.
28. Kovic, "Demanding Their Dignity as Daughters of God," 132–44.
29. Klein, *Compañeras*, 60.
30. Paré in Treviso, *Rural Protest and the Making of Democracy*, 34–35.
31. Klein, *Compañeras*, 33–34.
32. Here I intentionally use the terms *insurgent*, the English translation of the Zapatista term *insurgente/a*, to describe those Zapatistas who are actively engaged in building the armed resistance of the movement, in contrast to the comandantes/as, whose work was and is primarily political and community organizing and leadership.
33. Klein, *Compañeras*, 35.
34. Marcos quoted in Muños Ramírez, *Fire and the Word*, 20–22.
35. Comandante Abraham quoted in Muños Ramírez, *Fire and the Word*, 51.
36. And into the present. At the time this chapter was being drafted, the government of Mexico was building yet another military base in Chiapas. See Chiapas Support Committee, "Construction of New Military Base."
37. Gilly, "Chiapas and the Rebellion of the Enchanted World," 289–90.
38. Klein, *Compañeras*, 35.

39. Klein, *Compañeras*, 1–21.

40. Rayas, "Subjugating the Nation," 168–69.

41. Klein, *Compañeras*, 144–46.

42. Millan Moncayo, "Indigenous Women and Zapatismo," 85.

43. Klein. *Compañeras*, 68–70.

44. Quoted in Klein, *Compañeras*, 70, and Millan Moncayo, "Indigenous Women and Zapatismo," 85–86. Full text available at http://palabra.ezln .org.mx/comunicados/1994/1994_01_26.htm.

45. Harvey, *Chiapas*, 195–98.

46. Stephen, *Zapata Lives!*, 138–40; Khasnabish, "They Are Our Brothers and Sisters," 107.

47. Harvey, *Chiapas*, 198.

48. Subcomandante Marcos and the Zapatistas, *Other Campaign*, 109–11; Olivera and Pérez, "From Integrationist 'Indigenismo' to Neoliberal De-Ethnification," 105. Olivera and Pérez note that part of the late twentieth-century agrarian reforms, particularly in Chiapas, "created dependence on credit and chemical pesticides."

49. For specific examples of women's leadership in the EZLN military and in the civilian government, see Klein, *Compañeras*.

50. Acevedo and Espenshade, "Implications of the North American Free Trade Agreement," 229.

51. Bertrab, *Negotiating NAFTA*, 1–5. Bertrab, an alumnus of the economics department at the University of Texas, Austin, headed Mexico's negotiating team in the United States.

52. Peña, *Terror of the Machine*, 309. Bertrab, *Negotiating NAFTA*, 22–24. The opposition groups also included the AFL-CIO and the Child Labor Coalition. In Mexico, NAFTA is called the Tratado de Libre Comercio (TLC).

53. Bertrab, *Negotiating NAFTA*, 34. The vote was 231-192 in the House and 59-36 in the Senate. Mexico had made the formal request as part of the legal process necessary for fast-track negotiations.

54. Bertrab, *Negotiating NAFTA*, 91–95; Garvey, "Trade Law and Quality of Life," 439–44. While minimal mention of the environment is in the central trade agreement, labor was largely ignored until the side agreements.

55. Bertrab, *Negotiating NAFTA*, 95; see also Peña, *Terror of the Machine*, 311–12.

56. Peña, *Terror of the Machine*, 310–18.

57. Bertrab, *Negotiating NAFTA*, 116–26.

58. Bertrab, *Negotiating NAFTA*, 131–44; Kahane, "Congressional Voting Patterns on NAFTA", 395–96.

59. Ruiz-Marrero, "Contras and Drugs," 15; Quintana, "How NAFTA Unleashed the Violence in Mexico."

60. Insurgent First Infantry Captain Noé in Muños Ramírez, *Fire and the Word*, 65–66.
61. Comandante Abraham in Muños Ramírez, *Fire and the Word*, 71.
62. Harvey, *Chiapas*, 197; Gilly, "Chiapas and the Rebellion of the Enchanted World," 300–301.
63. Harvey, *Chiapas*, 105–6; Stephen, *Zapata Lives!*, 144–45.
64. "First Declaration of the Lacandón Jungle."
65. Muños Ramírez, *Fire and the Word*, 105–6.
66. Muños Ramírez, *Fire and the Word*, 107; Stephen, *Zapata Lives!*, 145. Drawing on the work of Human Rights Watch, Stephen suspects the number was higher.
67. Harvey, *Chiapas*, 204; Gilly, "Chiapas and the Rebellion," 304.
68. Muños Ramírez, *Fire and the Word*, 115.
69. Muños Ramírez, *Fire and the Word*, 117–26; Harvey, *Chiapas*, 206–7.
70. Olivera and Pérez, "From Integrationist 'Indigenismo,'" 109; Stephen, *Zapata Lives!*, 172–73.
71. Klein, *Compañeras*, 177–79.
72. See Schools for Chiapas, http://www.schoolsforchiapas.org/; EZLN website, http://www.ezln.org.mx. See also *Revista Rebeldía* at http://www .cgtchiapas.org/revista-rebeld%C3%ADa.
73. Gaspar de Alba and Guzmán, *Making a Killing*; Staudt and Méndez, *Courage and Resistance in Ciudad Juárez*.
74. See, for example, Bacon, "Union Ballot Exposes NAFTA's Broken Labour Promises"; Hennessy, "Duro Bag Workers"; Finbow, *Limits of Regionalism*, 127–28; Graubart, *Legalizing Transnational Activism*.
75. Quoted in Hennessy, "Duro Bag Workers."
76. Hennessy, "Duro Bag Workers."
77. Bacon, "Testing NAFTA's Labor Side Agreement," 6.
78. "Coalition for Justice in the Maquiladoras," Coalition for Justice in the Maquiladoras Annual Report 2010, 2. For CJM, also see Bacon, "Health, Safety," 339.
79. Bacon, "Union Ballot Exposes."
80. Hennessy, "Duro Bag Workers." In 2014, Duro Bag was acquired by Hilex Poly, creating the Duro Hilex Poly company. Hilex Poly, in November of 2014, changed its name to Novalex but continues to produce bags under the name of Duro Bag. See "Hilex Poly Announces Name Change and New Brand Structure," *Novalex News and Blog*, November 3, 2014, https://novolex.com/news/hilex-poly-announces-name-change-and -new-brand-structure/.
81. Hennessy, "Duro Bag Workers."
82. Hennessy, "Duro Bag Workers."

83. Hennessy, "Duro Bag Workers." Finbow, *Limits of Regionalism*, 127–28.
84. United States Department of Labor, "Submission under the North American Agreement on Labor Cooperation."
85. Weiss, "Two Steps Forward, One Step Back," 743.
86. Quoted in Carty, "Transnational Labor Mobilization," 301–2.
87. Passel and Cohn, "Unauthorized Immigrant Population."
88. Passel, "Written Testimony Submitted to the U.S. Senate Committee."
89. Passel and Cohn, "Unauthorized Immigrant Population."
90. "The Border Closes," *Economist*, December 18, 2008, 51.
91. Acevedo and Espenshade, "Implications of the North American Free Trade Agreement," 229–45.
92. Desilver, "For Most Workers, Real Wages Have Barely Budged."
93. Kitaoka, "Effect of U.S. Import Tariff Reductions," 6.
94. Sandoval, "U.S. Third World Feminism," 10–11, 27–35; Moya, *Learning from Experience*.

4. Life and Times of Gwen Amber Rose Araujo

1. "Newark Demographics and Community Outlook," 3–9.
2. Field et al., "Contemporary Ohlone Tribal Revitalization," 414.
3. Milliken, *Time of Little Choice*, 153, 194–95. Field et al., "Contemporary Ohlone Tribal Revitalization," 415. Mission San José was established in 1797 in what is today Fremont, California. During the mission's early years, the death rate there was higher than that of either Mission San Francisco or Mission Santa Clara. Then in 1806 measles overtook the mission, killing nearly three-quarters of all children under the age of five, half of the adult women, and 25 percent of adult men.
4. Field et al., "Contemporary Ohlone Tribal Revitalization," 424–25.
5. "History of Newark California."
6. Field et al., "Contemporary Ohlone Tribal Revitalization," 426.
7. Woodall, "Sun Microsystems Shuts Down Newark Campus," *East Bay Times*, May 12, 2006, http://www.eastbaytimes.com/2006/05/12/sun-microsystems-shuts-down-newark-campus/; Todd R. Brown, "Newark Mayor Remains Optimistic," *East Bay Times*, April 18, 2008, http://www.eastbaytimes.com/2008/04/18/newark-mayor-remains-optimistic/.
8. Araceli Martínez, "Recuerdan a Gwen Araujo," *La Opinión*, April 19, 2003, 6.
9. Moser, "Killing Gwen," *Rolling Stone*, accessed March 11, 2005, http://www.rollingstone.com/news/story.
10. Kelly St. John, "Posthumous Request for a Name Change, Slain Transgender Teen's Mom Wants 'Gwen' to be Official," *San Francisco Chronicle*, May 26, 2004, B1.

11. Moser, "Killing Gwen"; Califia, "Sex with the Imperfect Stranger"; de Sá, "Teen's Sad Tale," 21–22.

12. Califia, "Sex with the Imperfect Stranger."

13. Henry K. Lee, "One Year Since Transgender Teen's Death," *San Francisco Chronicle*, October 3, 2003, A17; Moser, "Killing Gwen."

14. At the turn of the century, an increase in violence against people of color and LGBTQ people was documented by watch groups such as the Southern Poverty Law Center. See Russell, "FBI Reports," 9; Potok, "Rage on the Right"; after 2004 the numbers stabilized despite the passage of hate crimes legislation. From 2004 to 2015, the U.S. Department of Justice noted that the rate of hate crimes "was not significantly different from the rate in 2004." See U.S. Department of Justice, Bureau of Justice Statistics, *Hate Crime Victimization*, 1.

15. The incidence of hate crimes against queers of color also increased in Britain. The support group Victim Support, London, found that queers of color experienced a higher incidence of hate crimes than did white queers. Given the similar colonial histories of these two countries, parallels in homophobic and transphobic racism are not surprising. See "Figures of Hate," *Community Care*, 35.

16. González, "Gender on the Borderlands," 15.

17. Hutchinson, "Ignoring the Sexualization of Race," 80–97.

18. Valdes, "Queer Margins, Queer Ethics"; Valdes, "'We Are Now of the View'"; Iglesias and Valdez, "Religion, Gender, Sexuality."

19. Gutiérrez, "Community, Patriarchy, and Individualism," 47–49. Gutiérrez's article is also one of the first queer Chicano articles to see print, locating lesbian Chicana and gay Chicano literatures within a larger body of Chicanx resistance.

20. Spade, *Normal Life*, 11.

21. Michelle Locke, "Defense Lawyer: Client 'Not a Bad Guy,'" *Associated Press and Local Wire*, April 15, 2004.

22. Ivan Delventhal, "Witness Recounts Night of Araujo Killing," *Argus*, April 21, 2004.

23. Marisa Lago, "Mistrial Declared in Teen's Killing: Prosecutor Says He Will Move to Retry Three Men Accused of Killing the Transgender Student," *Los Angeles Times*, June 23, 2004.

24. Locke, "Defense Lawyer."

25. Nicole Brown, in part of her diatribe against Gwen, stated, "It's a man." See Margie Mason, "1 of 3 Suspects Pleads Innocent: Transgender Teen's Death Lamented," *AZCentral.com*, October 25, 2002, reprinted in *The Channel* 21, no. 11 (November 2002), 17.

26. People v. Scott (Kozi Santino), 2003 Cal. LEXIS 4363 (Supreme Court of California, June 25, 2003, filed).

27. Baldwin, "Freaks and the American Ideal of Manhood," 815–16.

28. Barnard, "Application of Critical Race Feminism," 15–17. The study, of course, was Ida B. Wells's *Southern Horrors: Lynch Law in All Its Phases* (New York Age Print, 1892; available through Project Gutenberg).

29. Foster, *El Ambiente Nuestro*, 45–60. See also González, *Muy Macho*, for discussions of multiple and varied Chicano masculinities as well as Chicano challenges to gender binaries. See also Saldívar-Hull, *Feminism on the Border*, 29–57; García, *Chicana Feminist Thought*; Hurtado, *Color of Privilege*, 91–122.

30. Delventhal, "Witness Recounts."

31. Muños, *Disidentifications*, 57.

32. White women may have been contained by the ideology, but women of color did not have its protection. See Sanchez, "'Go after the Women'"; Anzaldúa, "La Conciencia de la Mestiza," 382–86.

33. Delventhal, "Witness Recounts."

34. Anzaldúa, "La Conciencia," 383.

35. Cacho, *Social Death*, 27.

36. For more information on LLEGÓ or GenderPac, see www.llego.com or www.gpac.org, respectively.

37. Eyler and Witten, "Hate Crimes and Violence against the Transgendered," 466.

38. Stryker, *Transgender History*, 1.

39. Perkiss, "New Strategy for Neutralizing the Gay Panic," 278, 285–86; Reis, "Making Sense of the Senseless."

40. Cunningham, *Valentine Road*.

41. Perkiss, "New Strategy," 782; Broverman, "System Failure," 13. See also Sloop, "Disciplining the Transgendered"; *People v. Kozi Santino Scott*.

42. The phrase "shades of queer" is a deliberate attempt to paint the conflation of class, race, sex, and gender in the multivalent discourses that continue to structure dominant U.S. society as well as many decolonial communities, while at the same time drawing attention to the different material realities that queers experience based on our specific location within those conflations.

43. Califia, *Sex Changes*, 14–15; Benjamin, *Transsexual Phenomenon*; Bergman, *Butch Is a Noun*.

44. Joe Rodriguez, "See Newark Teen for What He Was: Still Just a Kid," *Mercury News*, October 24, 2002, in *The Channel* 21, no. 11 (November 2002), 17.

45. Hunter, "Transcending Pathology," 25–26.

46. Isa Noyla, interview by author; Farrell, "Ninth Circuit Grants CAT Protection to Transgender Applicant from Mexico" 1, 7.

47. Valdes, "Queers, Sissies, Dykes," 20–24.

48. Califia, *Sex Changes*, 240.

49. Thankfully not all discussions resulted in new legislation. In the state of Washington, for example, where the proposed legislation was driven by voter initiative, the organizers failed to gather enough signatures to place the item on the ballot. In Texas and North Carolina, on the other hand, such "considerations" resulted in passing discriminatory laws. The sixteen states included Alabama, Arkansas, Illinois, Kansas, Kentucky, Minnesota, Missouri, Montana, New York, South Carolina, South Dakota, Tennessee, Texas, Virginia, Washington, and Wyoming. See Kralik, "'Bathroom Bill' Legislative Tracking."

50. Joann Wypijewski, quoted in Ott and Aoki, "Politics of Negotiating," 495.

51. Ott and Aoki, "Politics of Negotiating," 488.

52. Michael Cooper, "96 Arrested during Rally Protesting Gay Man's Killing in Wyoming," *New York Times*, October 20, 1998, B1; Yeoman, "Mother Finds Her Voice"; Patrick, "Call Haters to Account," 6.

53. "Songs for Matthew Shepard." The author of the list noted that it was most probably incomplete.

54. Ott and Aoki, "Politics of Negotiating," 495; Barrett, "Getting Along in Cortez," 27. In the town where Martinez was murdered, white youth had beat an Indigenous youth to death "several years" earlier ("several years" was the word choice of the Cortez state representative).

55. Dang and Frazer, *Black Same-Sex Households in the United States*, 3, 15–16.

56. U.S. Department of Labor, Bureau of Labor Statistics, *Highlights of Women's Earnings in 2001*, 1.

57. National Committee on Pay Equity, which used data from U.S. Census Bureau, "Current Population Survey, March 2002," for persons twenty-five years and older.

58. Williams, *Alchemy of Race and Rights*, 67–69.

59. Sheff-Cahan, "Matthew's Legacy," 95–97; Wil Haygood, "Channeling a Nation's Outrage; Son's Murder Propelled Judy Shepard into Activism," *Washington Post*, August 10, 2003, F01.

60. Brian Levin, director of the Center on Hate and Extremism at Richard Stockton College in Pomona, New Jersey, quoted in Ott and Aoki, "Politics of Negotiating," 499.

61. Ott and Aoki, "Politics of Negotiating," 488; Haygood, "Channeling a Nation's Outrage," F01.

62. Donlan, "Friends of Murdered Transvestite Recall Pal, Mourn Loss," *Boston Herald*, November 30, 1998, 5; Jesse Brooks, "Hate Crimes against

Transgenders, Especially of Color, Increasing," *Oakland Post*, April 27, 2011, 4, 7. A search for news articles about her death was performed on the Lexis-Nexis news database. See also Allen, "Trans Murder That Started a Movement."

63. In this context I define media as including television situation comedies, where the gay folk are not only white but wealthy, vacuous, and, at times, racist; and I also include our news media. *Will and Grace*, first aired in 1999, was among the most problematic. In this situation comedy two middle-class white males and their white and middle-class to wealthy heterosexual girlfriends spent money and made fun of people less fortunate than themselves. That the show was able to stay on the air during such a time of backlash is indicative that it was nonthreatening to the status quo. One decade later ABC aired *Modern Family*, yet another sit-com where the lead gay characters were overconsuming middle-class white males.

64. Husselbee and Elliot, "Looking beyond Hate," 835; Spade, *Normal Life*, 108–9; Cacho, *Social Death*, 8–21.

65. Ott and Aoki, "Politics of Negotiating," 489.

66. Crenshaw, "Demarginalizing the Intersection of Race and Sex"; Cho, "Converging Stereotypes in Racialized Sexual Harassment."

67. Hutchinson, "Ignoring the Sexualization of Race," 80–97.

68. Denise Hamilton, "Violence against Minorities on Rise: Gay Men have Supplanted African Americans as the Primary Target of Hate Crimes in Los Angeles County," *Los Angeles Times*, May 17, 1994, 1.

69. See, for example, Andrew Blankstein, "Attacks at Gay Center Probed as Hates Crimes," *Los Angeles Times*, September 15, 2004, B4; Michael Krikorian, "Hate Crimes against Gays, Lesbians Up 7%," *Los Angeles Times*, December 18, 2003, B4. An exception to this was the *Times* coverage of a campaign to address hate crimes against gay Latinos (see Bob Pool, "Campaign Launched Urging Gay Latinos to Report Hate Crimes," *Los Angeles Times*, August 4, 2000, 5).

70. Brooks, "Hate Crimes against Transgenders," 4, 7. See also Southern Poverty Law Center, "*Ebony* Publishes SPLC Report on Violence"; Southern Poverty Law Center, "Murders of Trans Women This Year Hits New High"; Transgender Law Center, "Hundreds of LGBT People of Color and Immigrants to Rally."

71. In 1994, in *Lam v. University of Hawaii*, the Ninth Circuit Court, utilizing the work of critical race feminists, recognized intersectionality in a raced gender case. See Valdes, "Queer Margins, Queer Ethics," 1321.

72. Hutchinson, "Ignoring the Sexualization of Race," 21–22.

73. Hutchinson, "Ignoring the Sexualization of Race," 27–29.

74. Araceli Martínez, "Recuerdan a Gwen Araujo," *La Opinión*, April 19, 2003, 6A.

75. Hutchinson, "Ignoring the Sexualization of Race," 22.

76. Duberman, *Stonewall*, 122–39.

77. Theophano, "Gender Public Advocacy Coalition"; Wilchins, *Queer Theory, Gender Theory*, 146–57; Theophano, "Gender Public Advocacy Coalition."

78. Califia, *Sex Changes*, 221–34; Gender Public Advocacy Coalition.

79. Rodriguez, "See Newark Teen for What He Was"; Mason, "Transgender Teen's Death Lamented," 17; Wronge, "Newark Teen's Family, Activists Differ on Memorials."

80. Christopher Daley, interview by author, November 8, 2006.

81. Connie Champagne, interview by author, November 7, 2006.

82. Cacho, *Social Death*, 6–8.

83. Aida Hurtado, "Underground Feminisms." See also García, *Chicana Feminist Thought*; Oropeza and Espinosa, *Enriqueta Vasquez and the Chicano Movement*; Pardo, *Mexican American Women Activists*.

84. Sandoval, *Methodology of the Oppressed*, 140.

85. Sylvia Guerrero, interview by author, June 6, 2007.

86. Guerrero, interview.

87. Robert Airoldi, "Family Provided Police with Leads," *The Argus*, September 29, 2003. See also Chakko, Wronge, Fernandez, and Reang, "Many Knew, None Told Killing Story," 18.

88. Patrick Letellier, "A Mother's Pain and Defiance," *Advocate*, March 30, 2004, 20; "Advocate Report," *Advocate*, April 13, 2004, 21; Kelly St. John, "Posthumous Request for a Name Change," *San Francisco Chronicle*, May 26, 2004, B1; Kelly St. John, "Slain Teen Officially Renamed," *San Francisco Chronicle*, July 2, 2004, B5.

89. Letellier, "Mother's Pain and Defiance," 20; de Sá, "Teen's Sad Tale," 21.

90. Moser, "Killing Gwen"; Wronge, "Newark Teen's Family," 20.

91. Guerrero, interview; Champagne, interview.

92. Daley, "Gwen Araujo Justice for Victims Act Becomes Law!"

93. Iglesias, "Structures of Subordination," 317.

5. Nepantler@s of the Sixth Sun

1. Robinson, *Modernization of Sex*, 9–21; Martínez-Salazar, "'Poisoning' of Indigenous Migrant Women Workers and Children," 100–111.

2. Bacon, "Union Ballot Exposes"; Hennessy, "Duro Bag Workers"; Finbow, *Limits of Regionalism*.

3. Sassen, *Globalization and Its Discontents*, 7–43.

4. Flynn and Kofman, "Women, Trade, and Migration," 67.

5. Bacon, *Illegal People*, 62–63.

6. Quintana, "How NAFTA Unleashed the Violence in Mexico"; Healey, "NAFTA Corn Fuels Immigration," 23.
7. Ruiz-Marrero, "Contras and Drugs."
8. Quintana, "How NAFTA Unleashed the Violence in Mexico." See also Valencia, "Necropolitics."
9. Transgender Law Center and Cornell University Law School, *Report on Human Rights*, 19–20.
10. Transgender Law Center and Cornell University Law School, *Report on Human Rights*, 18–19.
11. Transgender Law Center and Cornell University Law School, *Report on Human Rights*, 19.
12. Passel, Cohn, and Gonzalez-Barrera, "Net Migration from Mexico Falls to Zero."
13. Passel, "Written Testimony Submitted," 4.
14. Amnesty International, *Report: No Safe Place*; "Mexican Shelter Welcomes LGBTI Refugees."
15. Anzaldúa, "Let Us Be the Healing of the Wound," 95.
16. Hernández, "Alliances and Dis-alliances." See also Anzaldúa, "Let Us Be the Healing of the Wound."
17. Wood et al., "Crime Victimization in Latin America," 20.
18. Wood et al., "Crime Victimization in Latin America," 6–7. The authors note that the United States is the primary destination of most immigrants pushed from these countries.
19. Gordon and Webber, "Overthrow of a Moderate," 357.
20. Gordon and Webber, "Overthrow of a Moderate," 362–63.
21. Gordon and Webber, "Overthrow of a Moderate," 363. The influence of conservative groups such as Opus Dei on politics in Honduras is not unique to the country but can be found throughout Latin America. Nara Milanich noted the efforts of members of Opus Dei to block the passage of natal equality laws in Chile, arguing that such laws would undermine the family. As in Honduras, Opus Dei had "a significant following among Chilean elites." (Milanich, "In the Power Structure of Society," 793–94).
22. Gordon and Weber, "Overthrow of a Moderate," 364–65. Grandin, "Waiting for Zelaya." The work by Gordon and Weber and that by Grandin note the role of evangelicals and Opus Dei, a conservative Roman Catholic organization, in supporting the overthrow of Zelaya.
23. Gordon and Webber, "Overthrow of a Moderate," 372.
24. Brondo, *Land Grab*, 168.
25. Suyapa Villeda Portillo, "'Outing' Honduras," 6. See also "Mexico/Central America: Authorities Turning Their Backs on LGBTI Refugees." Amnesty International, in *No Safe Place*, notes that between 2009 and July 2017, 264 LGBTQI people were killed in Honduras (9).

26. Grandin, "Waiting for Zelaya."
27. United States Office of the Press Secretary, "Remarks by President Obama and President Lobo." See also Portillo, "New 'Success' in Post-Coup Honduras." Grandin notes that the business backers of the coup hired a former adviser to Hillary Clinton, Lanny Davis, "to lobby his old boss to recognize the new regime."
28. Sassen, *Globalization and Its Discontents*, xxvii, 34.
29. Solomon, "Trans/Migrant," 8.
30. United Nations High Commission for Refugees, *Detention Guidelines*. From the guidelines: "As a principle, UNHCR opposes detention of people seeking international protection. The new guidelines make clear that seeking asylum is not a criminal act, and that indefinite and mandatory forms of detention are prohibited under international law." See also Taback and Levitan, "LGBTI Migrants in Immigration Detention," 4.
31. Taback and Levitan, "LGBTI Migrants in Immigration Detention," 10.
32. Harvard Law Review Association, "Improving the Carceral Conditions," 1478.
33. Solomon notes the compulsion of the neoliberal state to police its national and gender borders; see especially page 4 of "Trans/Migrant." This dynamic is a concrete example of William I. Robinson's theory that the nation-state does not become obsolete under global capital but instead shifts to facilitate its functioning. See Robinson, *Theory of Global Capitalism*, especially chapter 3, "The Transnational State."
34. Harvard Law Review Association, "Improving the Carceral Conditions."
35. Brickenstein, "Making Bail and Melting ICE," 240–41. Brickenstein notes measures such as ankle bracelets and supervised release as effective and less costly.
36. American Immigration Council, *Guide to Children Arriving at the Border*, 6.
37. Anello, "Due Process and Temporal Limits," 365. Anello notes that "the number of people being detained on a given day has risen from about 6,600 in fiscal year 1996 to at least 34,000 in 2012." For detention in relation to deportation proceedings, see Solomon, "Trans/Migrant," 8.
38. Mejívar and Abrego, "Legal Violence."
39. Gehi, "Struggles from the Margins," 315–46. Gehi notes that in regions where people can be sentenced to more than one year for crimes of "moral turpitude," people have been deported for misdemeanor crimes.
40. Platt and O'Leary, "Patriot Acts."
41. González Fernández, "Immigration Detention in America," 4.
42. American Immigration Council, *Guide to Children*, 3.
43. American Immigration Council, *Guide to Children*, 5–6.

44. Portillo, "New 'Success' in Post-Coup Honduras."

45. Stryker, *Transgender History*, 63–75. Daley, "Trans Rights Come of Age." The National Center for Lesbian Rights continues to include the rights of transgender people as part of its agenda.

46. Turner, "Pioneering Strategies to Win Trans Rights," 5–6.

47. Imperial Court de San Diego, "Empress I Jose Sarria." In 1965 Sarria went on to become Empress I of San Francisco, founding the International Court System, a philanthropic organization of drag kings and queens. The author benefited from a scholarship from the Imperial Court de San Diego when they were a graduate student.

48. Glide was also the faith community at the core of the Council on Religion and the Homosexual, now famous for their sponsoring of the 1964 New Year's Eve dance at California Hall in San Francisco. See Hillman, "Most Profoundly Revolutionary Act," 160, and D'Emilio, "Gay Politics, Gay Community," 83–84.

49. Roberts and Williams quoted in Worley, "'Street Power' and the Claiming of Public Space," 48.

50. Marat and Forrester, "Touchstone," 2. Marat and Forrester listed the many projects founded or supported by Hansen, but then noted, "In all of this, Rev. Hansen played a very important part. But most of all, it was the way he cared about other human beings that counted. That was what he felt his real ministry to be. And it was." See also Worley, "'Street Power,'" 48–49.

51. Worley, "'Street Power,'" 55. Here Worley does not note that SIR aided with the publication of the journal, but extant copies of the journal indicate that SIR did provide aid. In the earlier issues the editors thank "Mr. Hal Call, Mr. Donald Lucas, and Mr. Kerry Bowman, from Mattachine, S.F.; Miss Phyllis Lyons, Administrative Assistant to Rev. Cecil Williams, Glide Church; Miss Janice Mirikitani, Secretary, Glide Church, and to many other people who gave us the moral support we needed." Later issues include advertisements by SIR and Mattachine.

52. Worley, "'Street Power,'" 49, 53–54.

53. Hillman, "'Most Profoundly Revolutionary Act,'" 162–63; Stryker, *Transgender History*, 68–75.

54. Stryker, *Transgender History*, 68–75.

55. Stryker, *Transgender History*, 75. In the documentary *Screaming Queens: The Riot at Compton's Cafeteria*, Victor Silverman and Susan Stryker note that Blackstone was eventually forced out of the department due to his advocacy.

56. The decade of the 1980s, much like the Nixon years, would see pushback to the gains made during the liberation movements of the 1960s. The

Reagan administration promoted abstinence-only curricula in public schools, reduced funding to social programs, and in relation, according to Anderson and Shapiro, during the Reagan years discrimination law was poorly enforced. See Perrin and DeJoy, "Abstinence Only," for the origins of the Adolescent Family Life Act; and Hoover, "Rise of Conservative Capitalism," especially pages 255–56, for cuts to social programs.

57. Turner, "Pioneering Strategies," 6.
58. Daley, interview. Each year the Pride Law Fund awards a Tom Steel Legal Fellowship "to build an innovative civil rights project on behalf of the LGBT and HIV/AIDS communities." See the Pride Law Fund (www.pridelawfund.org).
59. Connell, *Legal Translations*, 1.
60. Minter and Daley, *Trans Realities*.
61. Transgender Law Center, "Sylvia Guerrero, Client."
62. Transgender Law Center, "Adriana Turcios."
63. Transgender Law Center, "Immigration."
64. Transgender Law Center, "Fresh and Evolving Perspective."
65. Transgender Law Center, "TLC Welcomes New Program Manager."
66. Transgender Law Center and Cornell University Law School LGBT Clinic, *Report on Human Rights*, 3.
67. Isa Noyola, interview by author, May 17, 2016.
68. Rodríguez, *Queer Latinidad*, 54–83.
69. Gabriel, "Lessons to Learn."
70. Noyola, interview. Noyola noted that the list was actually more extensive: "going to the grocery store, running errands, and fundraising and logistics and database work and program planning."
71. Moraga, "Entering the Lives of Others."
72. "Demanding True Justice in the Face of Violence," 1, 3.
73. Noyola, interview.
74. Noyola, interview.
75. Transgender Law Center, "TLC Welcomes."
76. Transgender Law Center, "Isa Noyola Becomes."
77. Transgender Law Center, "Isa Noyola Becomes."
78. Causa Justa, *Development without Displacement*, 20.
79. Richard Walker, in Causa Justa, *Development without Displacement*, 3.
80. Causa Justa, *Development without Displacement*, 25.
81. Mirabal, "Geographies of Displacement," 12.
82. Mirabal, "Geographies of Displacement," 13. Between 1990 and 2011 Latinx households in the Mission "decreased by 1,400 while the number of White households increased by 2,900." See Causa Justa, *Development without Displacement*, 7.

83. Tulio Ospina, "Neighborhood Coalition Awaits City Council Action of East 12th Street Development," *Oakland Post*, December 2, 2015. See also Causa Justa, *Development without Displacement*, 7. A later article in the *Oakland Post* noted that some neighborhoods were successfully pushing back: the 16th and Wood Train Station Development would now include low-income housing and the preservation of the train station, a building of historical significance, marking the legacy of black porters in the region and the social economy of the nation. See "Gentrification Focus of West Oakland Tour," *Oakland Post*, December 20, 2006, and Carolyn Jones, "Gentrification Transforming Face of Oakland," sFGate, April 9, 2014, http://www.sfgate.com/bayarea/article/Gentrification-transforming-face-of-Oakland-5387273.php.

84. Sam Levin, "Too Straight, White, and Corporate: Why Some Queer People Are Skipping sF Pride," *The Guardian*, June 26, 2016, https://www.theguardian.com/us-news/2016/jun/25/san-francisco-gay-pride-corporate-orlando-shooting.

85. Noyola, interview by Amy Goodman.

86. Causa Justa, *Development without Displacement*, 22. Governor Brown's 10K plan sought to bring ten thousand new residents to downtown Oakland.

87. To learn more about TLC's current programs see Transgender Law Center, "Programs," at https://transgenderlawcenter.org/programs.

88. Minter and Daley, "Creating a Transgender Law Project," 46; Transgender Law Center, "Victory for #FreeChristina."

89. "TLC Challenges Order to Deport Transgender Immigrant"; "TLC Wins BIA Appeal."

Conclusion

1. "Abajo a la izquierda," that lasting change must come from the roots, not the elites. See Marcos, "Abajo a la Izquierda."

2. Quoted in Melendez, "Globalize This," 45.

3. Valencia, "Necropolitics," 182.

4. Anzaldúa, "Let Us Be the Healing," 99. She went on to write, "In addition to community-building we can transform our world by imagining it differently, dreaming it passionately via all our senses, and willing it into creation" (101). For Anzaldúa, the shift needs concrete, on-the-ground community building with imagination and spiritual labor.

5. Desilver, "U.S. Income Inequality, on Rise."

6. According to Pew, by 2013 Obama had already deported about as many immigrants as Bush had in his eight years in office. See Gonzalez-Barrera and Krogstad, "U.S. Deportations of Immigrants Reach Record High in 2013."

7. Soni, "Call to Service," 35.

8. Farrell, "Ninth Circuit Grants CAT Protection," 1.

9. Avendano-Hernandez v. Lynch, 800 F. 3d (2015).

10. Vega, "Nupcias de Liliana y Jesusa."

11. Avendano-Hernandez v. Lynch, 800 F. 3d (2015), 22.

12. Avendano-Hernandez v. Lynch, 800 F. 3d (2015); Rumph, "Avendano-Hernandez v. Lynch," 391–93.

13. Avendano-Hernandez v. Lynch, 800 F. 3d (2015); "Clay Awards."

14. Avendano-Hernandez v. Lynch, 800 F. 3d (2015).

15. Schmider, "Doubly Victimized."

16. Westermeyer, "Local Tea Party Groups," 125–27.

17. Einhorn, "Election 2016," 194.

18. Scher and Berlet, "Tea Party Moment," 108.

19. Ferguson, "Trump Is a Feminist, and Other Cautionary Tales," 54; Davis, "Polling Results Estimate 94 Percent of Black Women Voters."

20. For an overview of the growth of anti-immigrant sentiment in the twenty-first century, especially on the part of the Tea Party and the far right, see Williams, "Immigration and National Identity in Obama's America." For Trump's immigration policies see Williams, "Blood, Soil, and Trauma," 10; Rhodan, "Facts about Trump's Border Policy," 31.

21. This scapegoating too was tied to white cultural backlash. A 2016 study by the Public Religion Research Institute and the Brookings Institute found that 70 percent of white evangelical Protestants felt "the American way of life" had declined since the 1950s and "approximately six in ten (57%) white Americans and roughly two-thirds (66%) of white working-class Americans agree[d] that discrimination against whites is as big a problem today as discrimination against blacks and other minorities." See Jones et al., *How Immigration and Concerns about Cultural Changes are Shaping the 2016 Election*, 16.

22. Martín Pérez, "EZLN Inicia Actividades para Celebrar el 15 Aniversario." In 2003, following dialogue and community meetings, the Zapatistas reorganized their self-government into a structure of five caracoles to which representatives from each autonomous region would travel to consult and decide issues of import to their larger regions.

23. "Mexican Shelter Welcomes LGBTI Refugees." See also "Fray Tomás, Haz que se Vean."

24. Amnesty International, *Report: No Safe Place*.

25. Transgender Law Center, "Transgender Law Center Launches Trans Immigrant Defense Effort (TIDE)."

26. Taracena, "Displaced LGBT People from Central America."

27. Galarte, "General Editor's Introduction," 143.

28. Valencia, *Gore Capitalism*, 41. This, according to Valencia, is the function of the state within systems of globalization.
29. Levitz, "Trump's NAFTA"; Wallach, "Battle over NAFTA"; Wiseman, Johnson, and Freking, "North America Trade Pact Deals."
30. Labonté et al., "USMCA (NAFTA 2.0)."
31. Anzaldúa, "Let Us Be the Healing," 99.

BIBLIOGRAPHY

Archives

Bancroft Library, Berkeley, California
  José Mugarrieta Letters
California State Archives, Sacramento
  Daily Medical Reports, Department of Mental Hygiene, Stockton Medical
    Records, 1895
  Journals of the Senate and Assembly
  Stockton State Hospital, Commitment Register, 1886–94
  Stockton State Hospital, Female Patient Index, 1857–1903
Daniel E. Koshland San Francisco History Center, San Francisco
  Louis Sullivan Collection (GLBT Historical Society)
  Langley's San Francisco Directory for the Year 1888
Nettie Lee Benson Latin American Collection, University of Texas at Austin
  Gloria Evangelina Anzaldúa Papers

Published Works

Acevedo, Dolores, and Thomas J. Espenshade. "Implications of the North
    American Free Trade Agreement for Migration into the United States."
    In *Between Two Worlds: Mexican Immigrants in the United States*, edited
    by David Gutiérrez, 229–45. Lanham MD: Rowman and Littlefield, 1996.
Acuña, Rodolfo. *Occupied America: A History of Chicanos*. 3rd ed. New York:
    Harper Collins, 1988.
———. *Occupied America: The Chicano's Struggle toward Liberation*. San Fran-
    cisco: Canfield, 1972.
———. *Sometimes There Is No Other Side: Chicanos and the Myth of Equality*.
    Notre Dame IN: University of Notre Dame Press, 1998.
Adelman, Sarah Mulhall. "Empowerment and Submission: The Political
    Culture of Catholic Women's Religious Communities in Nineteenth-
    Century America." *Journal of Women's History* 23, no. 3 (2011): 138–61.

Alarcón, Norma. "Anzaldúan Textualities: A Hermeneutic of the Self and the Coyolxauhqui Imperative." In *El Mundo Zurdo 3: Selected Works from the Meetings of the Society for the Study of Gloria Anzaldúa 2012*, edited by Larissa M. Mercado-López, Sonia Saldívar-Hull, and Antonia Castañeda, 189–208. San Francisco: Aunt Lute, 2013.

———. "Chicana Feminism: In the Tracks of 'the' Native Woman." *Cultural Studies* 4, no. 3 (October 1990): 248–56.

———. "Chicana Feminist Literature: A Re-vision through Malintzin/or Malintzin; Putting Flesh Back on the Object." In Moraga and Anzaldúa, *This Bridge Called My Back*, 202–11.

———. "Traductora, Traditora: A Paradigmatic Figure of Chicana Feminism." *Cultural Critique* 13 (Autumn 1989): 57–87.

Alarcón, Norma, Ana Castillo, and Cherríe Moraga, eds. *The Sexuality of Latinas*. Berkeley CA: Third Woman Press, 1983.

Alba, Víctor. "Reforms." In *Mexico: From Independence to Revolution*, edited by W. Dirk Raat, 139–52. Lincoln: University of Nebraska Press, 1982.

Allen, Samantha. "The Trans Murder That Started a Movement." *Daily Beast*, July 12, 2017. https://www.thedailybeast.com/the-trans-murder-that-started-a-movement.

Almaguer, Tomás. *Racial Fault Lines: The Historical Origins of White Supremacy in California*. Berkeley: University of California Press, 1994.

Alonzo, Armando C. "Mexican-American Land Grant Adjudication." *Handbook of Texas Online*. Texas State Historical Association. Accessed August 11, 2017. https://tshaonline.org/handbook/online/articles/pqmck.

Alvarez, Fernando. "Peasant Movements in Chiapas." *Bulletin of Latina American Research* 7, no. 2 (1988): 277–98.

American Immigration Council. *A Guide to Children Arriving at the Border: Laws, Policies and Responses*. 2015. http://immigrationpolicy.org/sites/default/files/docs/a_guide_to_children_arriving_at_the_border_and_the_laws_and_policies_governing_our_response.pdf.

Amnesty International. *Report: No Safe Place; Salvadorans, Guatemalans, and Hondurans Seeking Asylum in Mexico Based on their Sexual Orientation and/or Gender Identity*. 2017. https://www.amnestyusa.org/wp-content/uploads/2017/11/No-Safe-Place-Briefing-eng-1.pdf.

Anderson, Debora, and David Shapiro. "Racial Difference in Access to High-Paying Jobs and the Wage Gap between Black and White Women." *Industrial and Labor Relations Review* 49, no. 2 (January 1996): 273–86.

Anderson, Henry P. *The Bracero Program in California*. New York: Arno Press, 1976.

Anello, Farrin R. "Due Process and Temporal Limits on Mandatory Immigration Detention." *Hastings Law Journal* 65 (February 2014): 365.

Anzaldúa, Gloria. *Borderlands: The New Mestiza*. San Francisco: Aunt Lute, 1999.

———. *Interviews/Entrevistas*, edited by Ana Louise Keating. New York: Routledge, 2000.

———. "La Conciencia de la Mestiza: Towards a Critical Consciousness." In Anzaldúa, *Making Face, Making Soul*, 377–89.

———. "La Prieta." In Moraga and Anzaldúa, *This Bridge Called My Back*, 220–33.

———. "Let Us Be the Healing of the Wound: The Coyolxauhqui Imperative—La Sombra y el Sueño." In Joysmith and Lomas, *One Wound for Another/Una Herida Por Otra*, 92–103.

———, ed. *Making Face, Making Soul: Haciendo Caras*. San Francisco: Aunt Lute, 1990.

———. "To(o) Queer the Writer—Loca, escritora y chicana." In *Living Chicana Theory*, edited by Carla Trujillo, 263–76. Berkeley CA: Third Woman Press, 1998.

Apodaca, María Linda. "The Chicana Woman: An Historical Materialist Perspective." *Latin American Perspectives* 4, nos. 1, 2 (Winter–Spring 1977): 70–89.

Arcilla, José S. "The Jesuits during the Philippine Revolution." *Philippine Studies* 35 (1987): 296–315.

Arriola, Elvia. "Difference, Solidarity, and Law: Building Latina/o Communities through LatCrit Theory." *Chicano-Latino Law Review* 19 (Spring 1998): 1–12.

Arrizón, Alicia. *Queering Mestizaje: Transculturation and Performance*. Ann Arbor: University of Michigan Press, 2006.

Arroyo, Laura E. "Industrial and Occupational Distribution of Chicana Workers." *Aztlán* 4, no. 2 (Fall 1973): 343–82.

———. "Queering the Painted Ladies: Gender, Race, Class, and Sexual Identity at the Mexican Border in the Case of Two Paulas." *Seattle Journal for Social Justice* 1, no. 3 (December 2002): 679–724.

Artemusicayvideo. "Nepantla, la insurreccion de la memoria 1." *YouTube*. January 18, 2012. https://www.youtube.com/watch?v=gdu8ijkUyiU.

Baca, Damián. "The Chicano Codex: Writing against Historical and Pedagogical Colonization." *College English* 71, no. 6 (July 2009): 564–83.

Bacon, David. "Health, Safety, and Worker's Rights in the Maquiladoras." *Journal of Public Health and Policy* 22, no. 3 (2001): 338–48.

———. *Illegal People: How Globalization Creates Migration and Criminalizes Immigrants*. Boston: Beacon Press, 2008.

———. "Testing NAFTA's Labor Side Agreement." *NACLA Report on the Americas* 31, no. 6 (May–June 1998): 6–9.

———. "Union Ballot Exposes NAFTA's Broken Labour Promises." *Green Left*, March 28, 2001. https://www.greenleft.org.au/node/25419.

Baldwin, James. "Freaks and the American Ideal of Manhood." In *James Baldwin: Collected Essays*, edited by Toni Morrison. New York: Penguin, 1998.

Barnard, Amii Larkin. "The Application of Critical Race Feminism to the Anti-Lynching Movement: Black Women's Fight against Race and Gender Ideology, 1892–1920." *UCLA Women's Law Journal* 3, no. 1 (Spring 1993): 1–38.

Barrett, Jon. "Getting Along in Cortez: In the Aftermath of the Murder of Transgendered Navajo Fred Martinez Jr., a Colorado Town Faces Its Dark Side, and Martinez's Mother Faces Life without Her Best Friend." *Advocate* 27 (September 9, 2001): 27–30.

Bedi, Sheila A. "The Constructed Identities of Asian and African Americans: A Story of Two Races and the Criminal Justice System." *Harvard Blackletter Journal* 19 (Spring 2003): 181–99.

Bell, Derrick A. "Brown v. Board of Education and the Interest-Convergence Dilemma." *Harvard Law Review* 93 (1979–80): 518–33.

Benjamin, Harry. *The Transsexual Phenomenon*. New York: Paul D. Erikson, 1967.

Bergman, Bear. *Butch Is a Noun*. San Francisco: Suspect Thoughts Press, 2006.

Bertrab, Hermann von. *Negotiating NAFTA: A Mexican Envoy's Account*. Westport CT: Praeger, 1997.

Blackwell, Maylei. *¡Chicana Power! Contested Histories of Feminism in the Chicano Movement*. Austin: University of Texas Press, 2011.

Boag, Peter. *Re-Dressing America's Frontier Past*. Berkeley: University of California Press, 2011.

Borunda, Rose. "A Mexican Nationhood Context." In *Speaking from the Heart: Herstories of Chicana, Latina, and Amerindian Women*, edited by Rose M. Borunda and Melissa Moreno, 25–46. Dubuque IA: Kendall Hunt, 2014.

Boyd, Nan Alamilla. "Bodies in Motion: Lesbian and Transsexual Histories." In *The Transgender Studies Reader*, edited by Susan Stryker and Stephen Whittle, 420–33. New York: Routledge, 2006.

———. *Wide Open Town: A History of Queer San Francisco to 1965*. Berkeley: University of California Press, 2003.

Brickenstein, Eric. "Making Bail and Melting ICE." *Lewis and Clark Law Review* 19 (2015): 240–41.

Brondo, Keri Vacanti. *Land Grab: Green Neoliberalism, Gender, and Garifunda Resistance in Honduras*. Tucson: University of Arizona Press, 2013.

Buchanan, Kim Shayo. "Our Prisons, Ourselves: Race, Gender, and the Rule of Law." *Yale Law and Policy Review* 29, no. 1 (Fall 2010): 1–82.

Bullough, Bonnie, Vern L. Bullough, and James Elias, eds. *Gender Blending*. Amherst NY: Prometheus Books, 1997.

Burkhart, Louise M. "Mexica Women on the Home Front: Housework and Religion in Aztec Mexico." In *Indian Women of Early Mexico*, edited by Susan Schroeder, Stephanie Wood, and Robert Haskett, 25–54. Norman: University of Oklahoma Press, 1997.

Butler, Octavia E. *Parable of the Sower*. New York: Grand Central Publishing, 1993.

Cacho, Lisa Marie. *Social Death: Racialized Rightlessness and the Criminalization of the Unprotected*. New York: New York University Press, 2012.

Califia, Patrick. *Sex Changes: The Politics of Transgenderism*. San Francisco: Cleis, 1997.

———. "Sex with the Imperfect Stranger." *Good Vibes Magazine*, December 9, 2002. www.passionpress.com.

Camarillo, Albert. *Chicanos in a Changing Society: From Mexican Pueblos to American Barrios in Santa Barbara and Southern California, 1848–1930*. Cambridge: Harvard University Press, 1979.

Candelaria, Cordelia. "La Malinche, Feminist Prototype." *Frontiers* 5, no. 2 (1980): 1–6.

Carrasco, Davíd. *Religions of Mesoamerica: Cosmovision and Ceremonial Centers*. Long Grove IL: Waveland Press, 1990.

Carrigan, William D., and Clive Webb. *Forgotten Dead: Mob Violence against Mexicans in the United States, 1848–1928*. New York: Oxford University Press, 2017.

———. "The Lynching of Persons of Mexican Origin or Descent in the United States, 1848–1928." *Journal of Social History* 37, no. 2 (2003): 411–38.

Carty, Victoria. "Transnational Labor Mobilization in Two Mexican Maquiladoras: The Struggle for Democratic Globalization." *Mobilization* 9, no. 3 (October 2004): 295–310.

Castañeda, Antonia. "Comparative Frontiers: The Migration of Women to Alta California and New Zealand." In *Western Women and Their Land, Their Lives*, edited by Lillian Schlissel, Vicki L. Ruiz, and Janice Monk, 283–301. Albuquerque: University of New Mexico Press, 1988.

———. "Engendering the History of Alta California, 1769–1848: Gender, Sexuality, and the Family." In Heidenreich, *Three Decades*, 229–72. First published in *California History* 76, nos. 2, 3 (Summer-Fall 1997): 230–59.

———. "Gender, Race, and Culture: Spanish Mexican Women in the Historiography of Frontier California." In Heidenreich, *Three Decades*, 143–85. First published in a special issue of *Frontiers: A Journal of Women Studies* 11, no. 1 (1990): 8–20.

————. "The Political Economy of Nineteenth-Century Stereotypes of Californianas." In Heidenreich, *Three Decades*, 37–63. First published in Del Castillo, *Between Borders*, 213–38.

————. "Presidarias y Pobladoras: Spanish-Mexican Women in Frontier Monterey, Alta California, 1770–1821." PhD diss., Stanford University, 1990.

————. "'Que Se Pudieran Defender (So You Could Defend Yourselves).'" In Heidenreich, *Three Decades*, 295–330. First published in *Frontiers* 22, no. 3 (2001): 116–42.

————. "Sexual Violence in the Politics and Policies of Conquest: Amerindian Women and the Spanish Conquest of Alta California." In *Building with Our Hands: New Directions in Chicana Studies*, edited by Adela de la Torre and Beatriz M. Pesquera, 15–33. Berkeley: University of California Press, 1993.

————. "Women of Color and the Rewriting of Western History: The Discourse, Politics, and Decolonization of History." In Heidenreich, *Three Decades*, 103–42. First published in *Pacific Historical Review* 61, no. 4 (1992): 501–33.

Causa Justa. *Development without Displacement: Resisting Gentrification in the Bay Area*. Oakland CA: Causa Justa and Alameda County Public Health Department, 2014. http://cjjc.org/wp-content/uploads/2015/11/development-without-displacement.pdf.

Cedillo, Adela. "Armed Struggle without Revolution: The Organizing Process of the National Liberation Forces (FLN) and the Genesis of Neo-Zapatism (1969–1983)." In Herrera Calderon and Cedillo, *Challenging Authoritarianism in Mexico*, 148–66.

Chakko, Matthai Kuruvila, Yomi S. Wronge, Lisa Fernandez, and Putsata Reang. "Many Knew, None Told Killing Story: Newark Wonders about Silence." *The Channel* 21, no. 11 (November 2002): 18. http://tgsf.org/other-resources/gwen_channel.pdf.

Chan, Sucheng. *Asian Californians*. San Francisco: MTL/Boyd and Fraser, 1991.

Chávez-García, Miroslava. *Negotiating Conquest: Gender and Power in California, 1770s to 1880s*. Tucson: University of Arizona, 2004.

Chiapas Support Committee. "Construction of New Military Base in Chiapas Advances Rapidly." Chiapas Support Committee website. June 23, 2017. https://chiapas-support.org/2017/06/23/construction-of-new-military-base-in-chiapas-advances-rapidly/.

Cho, Sumi K. "Converging Stereotypes in Racialized Sexual Harassment: Where the Model Minority Meets Suzie Wong." In Wing, *Critical Race Feminism*, 349–65.

————. "Multiplicities and Intersectionalities: Exploring LatCrit Diversities; Essential Politics." *Harvard Latino Law Review* 2 (Fall 1997): 433–55.

Cisneros, Jesús. "Working with the Complexity and Refusing to Simplify: Undocuqueer Meaning Making at the Intersection of LGBTQ and Immigrant Rights Discourses." *Journal of Homosexuality* 65, no. 11 (October 2017). https://doi.org/10.1080/00918369.2017.1380988.

Clarke, A. M. *Life of Reverend Mother Mary of St. Euphrasia Pelletier, First Superior General of the Congregation of Our Lady of Charity of the Good Shepherd of Angers.* New York: Benzinger Brothers, 1895.

"Clay Awards." *California Lawyer,* March 17, 2016. http://legacy.callawyer.com /2016/03/immigration/.

"Coalition for Justice in the Maquiladoras." Coalition for Justice in the Maquiladoras Annual Report 2010. Fall 2010, 1–16. http://sdmaquila.org /CJM%20Report%202010.pdf.

Committee for the Development of Subject Access to Chicano Literatures. *Chicano Periodical Index: 1967–1978.* Boston: G. K. Hall, 1981.

Connell, Mikayla. "Fall 2005." *Legal Translations,* Fall 2005, 1.

Contreras, Sheila Marie. *Bloodlines: Myth, Indigenism and Chicana/o Literature.* Austin: University of Texas Press, 2008.

Coonrod Martínez, Elizabeth. "A New Century for Indigenous Writing." *Diálogo* 19, no. 1 (Spring 2016): 1–2.

Cotera, Marta P. *The Chicana Feminist.* Austin: Information Systems Development, 1977.

———. *Diosa y Hembra: The History and Heritage of Chicanas in the U.S.* Austin: Information Systems Development, 1976.

Craig, Richard B. *The Bracero Program: Interest Groups and Foreign Policy.* Austin: University of Texas, 1971.

Crenshaw, Kimberlé. "Demarginalizing the Intersection of Race and Sex: A Black Feminist Critique of Antidiscrimination Doctrine, Feminist Theory, and Antiracist Politics." In Wing, *Critical Race Feminism,* 23–33.

Crenshaw, Kimberlé, Neil Gotanda, Gary Peller, and Kendall Thomas, eds. *Critical Race Theory: Key Writings That Formed the Movement.* New York: New Press, 1995.

Cunningham, Marta, dir. *Valentine Road.* Bunim-Murray Productions, Eddie Schmidt Productions, 2013. DVD.

Curl, John, trans. *Ancient American Poets.* Tempe AZ: Bilingual Press, 2005.

Daley, Chris. "Gwen Araujo Justice for Victims Act Becomes Law!" *San Francisco Bay Area Independent Media Center.* September 28, 2006. http:// www.indybay.org/newsitems/2006/09/28/18315438.php.

———. "Trans Rights Come of Age." Transgender Law Center. Accessed 24 April 2006. http://www.transgenderlawcenter.org/do/trans-rights-2006.html.

Dang, Alain, and Somjen Frazer. *Black Same Sex Households in the United States.* New York: National Gay and Lesbian Task Force Policy Institute and National Black Justice Coalition, 2004.

Davis, Olive. *Stockton: Sunrise Port on the San Joaquin*. Sun Valley CA: American Historical Press, 1998.

Davis, Rachaell. "Polling Results Estimate 94 Percent of Black Women Voters Chose Hillary Clinton." *Essence*, November 9, 2016. https://www.essence .com/news/politics/most-black-women-voted-for-hillary-clinton/.

De Ford, Miriam Allen. *They Were San Franciscans*. Caldwell ID: Caxton Printers, 1947.

Deggs, Mary Bernard. *No Cross, No Crown: Black Nuns in Nineteenth-Century New Orleans*, edited by Virginia Meacham Gould and Charles E. Nolan. Bloomington: Indiana University Press, 2001.

Del Castillo, Adelaida R., ed. *Between Borders: Essays on Mexicana/Chicana History*. Encino CA: Floricanto, 1990.

———. "Malintzín Tenepal: A Preliminary Look into a New Perspective." *Encuentro Feminil* 1, no. 2 (December 1973): 58–78.

De León, Arnoldo. *They Called Them Greasers: Anglo Attitudes toward Mexicans in Texas, 1821–1900*. Austin: University of Texas Press, 1983.

Delgado, Richard. "Liberal McCarthyism and the Origins of Critical Race Theory." *Iowa Law Review* 94 (July 2009): 1509–12.

Delgado, Richard, and Jean Stefancic. *Critical Race Theory: An Introduction*. New York: New York University Press, 2001.

"Demanding True Justice in the Face of Violence." *Community United against Violence Newsletter*. Summer 2007, 1–3. http://www.cuav.org /wp-content/uploads/2012/09/summer-07-web.pdf.

D'Emilio, John. "Gay Politics, Gay Community: San Francisco's Experience." In *Making Trouble: Essays on Gay History, Politics, and the University*, edited by John D'Emilio, 74–95. New York: Routledge, 1992.

de Sá, Karen. "Teen's Sad Tale: Troubled Years Preceded Attack." *The Channel* 21, no. 11 (November 2002): 21–22. http://tgsf.org/other-resources/gwen_channel.pdf.

Desilver, Drew. "For Most Workers, Real Wages Have Barely Budged for Decades." *FacTank, Pew Research Center*. October 9, 2014. http://www .pewresearch.org/fact-tank/2014/10/09/for-most-workers-real-wages -have-barely-budged-for-decades/.

———. "U.S. Income Inequality, on Rise for Decades, Is Now Highest Since 1928." *Pew Research Center*. December 5, 2012. http://www.pewresearch .org/fact-tank/2013/12/05/u-s-income-inequality-on-rise-for-decades-is -now-highest-since-1928/.

Dick-Bissonnette, Linda E. "Gender and Authority among the Yokoch, Mono, and Miwok of Central California." *Journal of Anthropological Research* 54, no. 1 (Spring 1998): 49–72.

Dillingham, A. S. "Indigenismo Occupied: Indigenous Youth and Mexico's Democratic Opening." *Americas* 72, no. 4 (October 2015): 549–82.

Dodds Pennock, Caroline. *Bonds of Blood: Gender, Lifecycle and Sacrifice in Aztec Culture*. New York: Palgrave Macmillan, 2008.

Dougherty, M. Patricia, "Dominican Sisters of San Rafael: Early Years of Hardship and Growth." *Dominican Scholar* 3 (2003): 1–9. https://scholar.dominican.edu/history-faculty-scholarship/3.

Duberman, Martin. *Stonewall*. New York: Plume, 1994.

DuBois, Ellen Carol, and Vicki L. Ruiz, eds. *Unequal Sisters: A Multicultural Reader in U.S. Women's History*. New York: Routledge, 1990.

Einhorn, Jay. "Election 2016: A Psychohistorical, Psychoeconomic Analysis of the 2016 United States Presidential Election." *Journal of Psychohistory* 45, no. 3 (Winter 2018): 192–211.

El/La Para TransLatinas, "Mission and Vision." Accessed December 25, 2019. http://ellaparatranslatinas.yolasite.com/mission.php.

Ellis, Havelock. *My Life: The Autobiography of Havelock Ellis*. Boston: Houghton Mifflin, 1939.

Epstein, Julia, and Kristina Straub, eds. *Body Guards: The Cultural Politics of Gender Ambiguity*. New York: Routledge, 1991.

Esquibel, Catrióna Rueda. *With Her Machete in Her Hand: Reading Chicana Lesbians*. Austin: University of Texas Press, 2006.

Eyler, A. Evan, and Tarynn M. Witten. "Hate Crimes and Violence against the Transgendered." *Peace Review* 11, no. 3 (September 1999): 461–69.

Fajardo, Kale Bantigue. "Queering and Transing the Great Lakes: Filipina/o Tomboy Masculinities and Manhoods across Waters." GLQ 20, nos. 1, 2 (2014): 115–40.

———. "Transportation: Translating Filipino and Filipino American Tomboy Masculinities through Global Migration and Seafaring," GLQ 14, nos. 2, 3 (2008): 403–24.

Farrell, Corey. "Ninth Circuit Grants CAT Protection to Transgender Applicant from Mexico." *Immigration Litigation Bulletin* 19, no. 9 (September 2015): 1, 7. https://www.justice.gov/civil/file/868566/download.

Federici, Silvia. *Caliban and the Witch: Women, the Body, and Primitive Accumulation*. Brooklyn NY: Autonomedia, 2004.

Feinberg, Leslie. *Transgender Warriors: Making History from Joan of Arc to Dennis Rodman*. Boston: Beacon Press, 1996.

———. *Trans Liberation: Beyond Pink or Blue*. Boston: Beacon, 1998.

Feldberg, Roslyn. "Comparable Worth: Toward Theory and Practice in the United States." *Signs* 10, no. 2 (Winter 1984): 311–28.

Ferguson, Michaele L. "Trump Is a Feminist, and Other Cautionary Tales for Our Neoliberal Age." *Theory and Event* 20, no. 1 (January 2017 Supplement): 53–67.

Field, Les, Alan Leventhal, Dolores Sanchez, and Rosemary Cambra. "A Contemporary Ohlone Tribal Revitalization Movement: A Perspective from the Muwekma Costanoan/Ohlone Indians of the San Francisco Bay Area." *California History* 71, no. 3 (Fall 1992): 412–31.

"Figures of Hate." *Community Care*. January 21, 2005, https://www.communitycare.co.uk/2005/01/21/figures-of-hate/.

Finbow, Robert G. *The Limits of Regionalism: NAFTA's Labour Accord*. Aldershot UK: Ashgate Publishing Company, 2006.

Fine, Michelle, Lois Weis, Judi Addelston, and Julia Marusza. "(In)Secure Times: Constructing White Working-Class Masculinities in the Late Twentieth Century." *Gender and Society* 11 (February 1997): 52–68.

"First Declaration of the Lacandón Jungle." *The Struggle Site*. Accessed July 7, 2017, http://www.struggle.ws/mexico/ezln/ezlnwa.html.

Fixico, Donald L. *Indian Resilience and Rebuilding: Indigenous Nations in the Modern American West*. Tucson: University of Arizona Press, 2013.

Flynn, Don, and Elenore Kofman. "Women, Trade, and Migration." *Gender and Development* 12, no. 2 (July 2004): 66–72.

Foner, Philip S. *Women and the American Labor Movement: From Colonial Times to the Eve of World War I*. New York: Free Press, 1979.

Foster, David William. *El Ambiente Nuestro: Chicano/Latino Homoerotic Writing*. Tempe AZ: Bilingual Press, 2005.

Fox, Jonathan. "The Roots of Chiapas." *Economic Political Weekly* 29, no. 19 (May 1994): 1119–22.

"Fray Tomás, Haz que se Vean." Accessed August 13, 2018. http://hazquesevean.org/project/fray-tomas/.

Gabriel, Jesse. "Lessons to Learn from Proyecto ContraSIDA Por Vida," *Latin@ Counterculture*. February 17, 2011. https://latinocountercultures.wordpress.com/2011/02/17/lessons-to-learn-from-proyecto-contrasida-por-vida/.

Galarte, Francisco J. "General Editor's Introduction." *Transgender Studies Quarterly* 6, no. 2 (May 2019): 141–44.

———. "On Trans* Chican@s: Amor, Justicia, y Dignidad." *Aztlán* 39, no. 1 (Spring 2014): 229–36.

———. "Transgender Chican@ Poetics: Contesting, Interrogating, and transforming Chicana/o Studies." *Chicana/Latina Studies* 13, no. 2 (Spring 2014): 118–39.

García, Alma M., ed. *Chicana Feminist Thought: The Basic Historical Writings*. New York: Routledge, 1997.

García, Mario T. *Desert Immigrants: The Mexicans of El Paso, 1880–1920*. New Haven: Yale University, 1981.

Garvey, Jack I. "Trade Law and Quality of Life: Dispute Resolution under the NAFTA Side Accords on Labor and the Environment." *American Journal of International Law* 89, no. 2 (1995): 439–53. https://doi.org/10.2307/2204217.

Gaspar de Alba, Alicia. *Sor Juana's Second Dream*. Albuquerque: University of New Mexico Press, 1999.

——. *[Un]Framing the "Bad Woman": Sor Juana, Malinche, Coyolxauqui, and other Rebels with a Cause*. Austin: University of Texas Press, 2014.

Gaspar de Alba, Alicia, and Georgina Guzmán, eds. *Making a Killing: Femicide, Free Trade, and La Frontera*. Austin: University of Texas Press, 2010.

Gaspar de Alba, Alicia, Maria Herrera-Sobek, and Demetria Martinez. *Three Times a Woman: Chicana Poetry*. Tempe AZ: Bilingual Review Press, 1989.

Gehi, Pooja. "Gendered (In)Security: Migration and Criminalization in the Security State." *Harvard Journal of Law and Gender* 35 (Summer 2012): 357–98.

"Gentrification Focus of West Oakland Tour." *Oakland Post*, December 20, 2006.

Gilly, Adolfo. "Chiapas and the Rebellion of the Enchanted World." In *Rural Revolt in Mexico*, edited by Daniel Nugent. Durham NC: Duke University Press, 1998.

Glenn, Evelyn Nakano. *Unequal Freedom: How Race and Gender Shaped American Citizenship and Labor*. Cambridge: Harvard University Press, 2002.

Godoy, Emilio. "Rural Community Fights a Second Dam and a New Expropriation of Land." *Inter Press Service News Agency*. March 8, 2016. http://www.ipsnews.net/2016/03/rural-community-fights-a-second-dam-and-a-new-expropriation-of-land/.

Goldberg, Isaac. *Havelock Ellis: A Biographical and Critical Study*. New York: Simon and Schuster, 1926.

Gomez, Alma, Cherríe Moraga, and Mariana Romo-Carmona, eds. *Cuentos: Stories by Latinas*. New York: Kitchen Table Press, 1983.

Gómez, Laura E. *Manifest Destinies: The Making of the Mexican American Race*. New York: New York University Press, 2007.

González, Deena. "Gender on the Borderlands: Re-textualizing the Classics." *Frontiers* 24, nos. 2, 3 (2003): 15–29.

——. "The Widowed Women of Santa Fe: Assessments on the Lives of an Unmarried Population, 1850–1880." In DuBois and Ruiz, *Unequal Sisters*, 34–50.

González, Rafael Jesús. "Brief Songs from the Nahuatl." *El Grito* 5, no. 1 (Fall 1971): 13–16.

González, Ray, ed. *Muy Macho: Latino Men Confront Their Manhood*. New York: Anchor Books, 1996.

González Fernández, Luz C. "Immigration Detention in America: Civil Offense, Criminal Detention." *Harvard Journal of Hispanic Policy* 26 (2013–14): 3–12.

Gordon, Tom, and Jeffery R. Webber. "The Overthrow of a Moderate and the Birth of a Radicalizing Resistance: The Coup against Manuel Zelaya and the History of Imperialism and Popular Struggle in Honduras." In *The New Latin American Left: Cracks in the Empire*, edited by Jeffery R. Webber and Barry Carr, 357–82. New York: Rowman and Littlefield, 2012.

Gehi, Pooja. "Struggles from the Margins: Anti-Immigrant Legislation and the Impact on Low-Income Transgender People of Color." *Women's Rights Law Reporter* 30 (Winter 2009): 315–46.

Grandin, Greg. "Waiting for Zelaya." *The Nation*, July 28, 2009. https://www .thenation.com/article/waiting-zelaya/.

Graubart, Jonathan. *Legalizing Transnational Activism: The Struggle to Gain Social Change from NAFTA's Citizen Petitions*. University Park PA: Penn State University, 2008.

Griswold del Castillo, Richard. *La Familia: Chicano Families in the Urban Southwest, 1848 to the Present*. Notre Dame IN: University of Notre Dame Press, 1984.

Grosskurth, Phyllis. *Havelock Ellis: A Biography*. New York: New York University Press, 1985.

Grupo de Mujeres de San Cristóbal de las Casas. "Women's Rights in our Traditions and Customs," translated by María Vinós. In Speed, Hernández Castillo, and Stephen, *Dissident Women*, 5–14.

Gutiérrez, David G. "Migration, Emergent Ethnicity, and the 'Third Space': The Shifting Politics of Nationalism in Greater Mexico." *Journal of American History* 86, no. 2 (September 1999): 481–517.

Gutiérrez, Ramón A. "Community, Patriarchy, and Individualism: The Politics of Chicano History and the Dream of Equality." *American Quarterly* 45, no. 1 (March 1993): 44–72.

———. "Honor Ideology, Marriage Negotiation, and Class-Gender Domination in New Mexico, 1690–1846." *Latin American Perspectives* 44, no. 1 (Winter 1985): 81–104.

Halberstam, Jack. *Female Masculinity*. Durham NC: Duke University Press, 1998.

Haney López, Ian. *White by Law: The Legal Construction of Race*. New York: New York University Press, 2006.

Harvard Law Review Association. "Improving the Carceral Conditions of Federal Immigrant Detainees." *Harvard Law Review* 125, no. 6 (April 2012): 1476–97.

Harvey, Neil. *The Chiapas Rebellion: The Struggle for Land and Democracy*. Durham NC: Duke University, 1998.

———. "Rebellion in Chiapas: Rural Reforms and Popular Struggle." *Third World Quarterly* 16, no. 1 (March 1995): 39–73.

Haskins, Victoria. "Domestic Service and Frontier Feminism: The Call for a Woman Visitor to 'Half-Cast' Girls and Women in Domestic Service, Adelaide, 1925–1928." *Frontiers* 28, nos. 1, 2 (2007): 124–64.

Hayashi, Kris. "Statement from Kris Hayashi on the 2016 Election." Transgender Law Center. November 9, 2016. https://transgenderlawcenter .org/archives/13354.

Healey, Josh. "NAFTA Corn Fuels Immigration." *The Progressive* 77, no. 4 (April 2013): 23.

Heidenreich, Linda. "A Historical Perspective on Christine Jorgensen and the Development of an Identity." In Bullough, Bullough, and Elias, *Gender Blending*, 267–76.

———. *"This Land Was Mexican Once": Histories of Resistance from Northern California*. Austin: University of Texas Press, 2007.

———, ed. *Three Decades of Engendering History: Selected Works of Antonia Castañeda*. Denton: University of North Texas Press, 2014.

Heizer, Robert. *Destruction of the California Indians*. Lincoln: University of Nebraska Press, 1993.

Hennessy, Rosemary. "Duro Bag Workers." *Z Magazine*, November 1, 2002. https://zcomm.org/zmagazine/duro-bag-workers-by-site -administrator/.

Herdt, Gilbert, ed. *Third Sex, Third Gender: Beyond Sexual Dimorphism in Culture and History*. New York: Zone Books, 1994.

Hernández, Monica. "With Heart in Hand/Con Corazón En La Mano." *Colorlines*. October 20, 1999. https://www.colorlines.com/articles/heart -handcon-corazon-en-la-mano.

Hernández, Rafael. "Alliances and Dis-alliances between the United States and Latin America and the Caribbean." *Latin American Perspectives* 178, no. 4 (July 2011): 131–36.

Hernández Castillo, R. Aída. "Between Feminist Ethnocentricity and Ethnic Essentialism: The Zapatista's Demands and the National Indigenous Women's Movement." In Speed, Hernández Castillo, and Stephen, *Dissident Women*, 57–74.

Herrera Calderón, Fernando, and Adela Cedillo, eds. *Challenging Authoritarianism in Mexico: Revolutionary Struggles*. New York: Routledge, 2012.

———. "Introduction." In Herrera Calderón and Cedillo, *Challenging Authoritarianism in Mexico*, 1–18.

Hidalgo-Monroy Wohlgemuth, Neusa. "Alternative to Rural Development: Organic Agriculture and Indigenous Communities in Chiapas, Mexico." *Journal of Latin American Geography* 13, no. 1 (2014): 67–88.

Hillman, Betty Luther. "'The Most Profoundly Revolutionary Act a Homosexual Can Engage In': Drag and the Politics of Gender Presentation in the

San Francisco Gay Liberation Movement, 1964–1972." *Journal of the History of Sexuality* 20, no. 1 (January 2011): 153–81.

Hinojosa, Gilberto Miguel. *A Borderlands Town in Transition: Laredo, 1775–1870.* College Station: Texas A&M University Press, 1983.

Hinton, Leanne. "Advocates for Indigenous California Language Survival: Celebrating 25 Years of Language Revitalization." *News from Native California* 30, no. 7 (Spring 2017): 53–55.

"The History of Newark, California." City of Newark, California. Accessed July 13, 2017. http://www.newark.org/visitors/history/.

Hoover, Kenneth R. "The Rise of Conservative Capitalism: Ideological Tensions within the Reagan and Thatcher Governments." *Comparative Studies in Society and History* 29, no. 2 (1987): 245–68.

Hunter, E. L. "Transcending Pathology, Transforming the Thinkable Transperson: Young Transpeople, the Law, and Gender Self-Determination." Master's thesis, DePaul University, 2014. https://via.library.depaul.edu/cgi/viewcontent.cgi?article=1168&context=etd.

Hurtado, Aída. *The Color of Privilege: Three Blasphemies on Race and Feminism.* Ann Arbor: University of Michigan Press, 1997.

———. "Underground Feminisms: Inocencia's Story." In *Chicana Feminisms: A Critical Reader,* edited by Patricia Zavella, Gabriela F. Arredondo, Aida Hurtado, Norma Klahn, and Olga Najera-Ramirez, 260–90. Durham NC: Duke University Press, 2003.

Hurtado, Albert L. *Intimate Frontiers: Sex, Gender, and Culture in Old California.* Albuquerque: University of New Mexico Press, 1999.

Husselbee, Paul, and Larry Elliot. "Looking beyond Hate: How National and Regional Newspapers Framed Hate Crimes in Jasper, Texas, and Laramie, Wyoming." *Journalism and Mass Communication Quarterly* 79, no. 4 (December 2002): 833–52.

Hutchinson, Darren Lenard. "Ignoring the Sexualization of Race: Heteronormativity, Critical Race Theory, and Anti-Racist Politics." *Buffalo Law Review* 47 (Winter 1999): 1–116.

Iglesias, Elizabeth M. "Structures of Subordination: Women of Color at the Intersection of Title VII and the NLRA. Not!" *Harvard C.R.-C.L. Law Review* 28 (1993): 395–503.

Iglesias, Elizabeth M., and Francisco Valdes. "Religion, Gender, Sexuality, Race, and Class in Coalitional Theory: A Critical and Self-Critical Analysis of LatCrit Social Justice Agendas." *Chicano-Latino Law Review* 19 (Spring 1998): 503–88.

Ikas, Karin Rosa. *Chicana Ways: Conversations with Ten Chicana Writers.* Reno: University of Nevada Press, 2002.

Imperial Court de San Diego. "Empress I José Sarria: The Widow Norton." In *Twenty Five Year of Noble Deeds: A Silver Jubilee History of the Imperial Court de San Diego*. San Diego: Imperial Court de San Diego, 1996.

Johnson, Paula C. "The Social Construction of Identity in Criminal Cases: Cinema Verite and the Pedagogy of Vincent Chin." *Michigan Journal of Race and Law* 1 (Summer 1996): 347–479.

Jones, Robert P., Daniel Cox, E. J. Dionne Jr., William A. Galston, Betsy Cooper, and Rachel Leingesh. *How Immigration and Concerns about Cultural Changes are Shaping the 2016 Election: Findings from the 2016 PRRI/Brookings Immigration Survey*. Washington DC: Public Religion Research Institute, 2016. https://www.prri.org/wp-content/uploads/2016/06/prri-Brookings-2016-Immigration-survey-report.pdf.

Joysmith, Claire. "'Let Us Be the Healing of the Wound': Anzaldúa's Post–September 11, 2001, Testimonial Vision." In *Güeras y Prietas: Celebrating 20 Years of Borderlands/La Frontera*, edited by Norma E. Cantú and Christina L. Gutiérrez. San Antonio: Adelante Project, 2009.

Joysmith, Claire, and Clara Lomas, eds. *One Wound for Another/Una Herida Por Otra: Testimonios de Latin@s in the US through Cyberspace (11 de septiembre de 2001–11 de marzo de 2002)*. Mexico City: Universidad Nacional Autónoma de México, 2005.

———. Prologue in Joysmith and Lomas, *One Wound for Another/Una Herida Por Otra*, 21–25.

Juárez Rose, Vivien. *The Past Is Father of the Present: Family Legends, 1737–1973*. Vallejo CA: Wheeler Printing, 1974.

Kahane, Leo H. "Congressional Voting Patterns on NAFTA: An Empirical Analysis." *American Journal of Economics and Sociology* 55, no. 4 (October 1996): 395–409.

Kampwirth, Karen. *Women and Guerilla Movements: Nicaragua, El Salvador, Chiapas, Cuba*. University Park PA: Penn State University Press, 2002.

Kaplan, Amy. "Manifest Domesticity." *American Literature* 70, no. 3 (September 1998): 581–606.

Katz, Jonathan Ned. *Gay American History: Lesbians and Gay Men in the U.S.A.* New York: Avon, 1976.

———. *The Invention of Heterosexuality*. Chicago: University of Chicago Press, 2007.

Kellogg, Susan. "The Woman's Room: Some Aspects of Gender Relations in Tenochtitlan in the Late Pre-Hispanic Period." *Ethnohistory* 42, no. 4 (Autumn 1995): 563–76.

Kennedy, Glenn A. *It Happened in Stockton, 1900–1925*. Stockton, CA, 1967. Mimeograph copy available at the César Chávez Library, Stockton CA.

Kessler-Harris, Alice. *Women Have Always Worked: A Historical Overview*. Old Westbury NY: Feminist Press, 1981.

Kewanhaptewa-Dixon, Sandy. "Preservation and Sustainability: Barbara Drake, One Elder Making a Difference." *News from Native California* 30, no. 7 (Winter 2016–17): 14–15.

Khasnabish, Alex. "'They Are Our Brothers and Sisters': Why Zapatismo Matters to Independent Labour in Mexico." *Anthropologica* 47, no. 11 (2005): 101–14.

Kitaoka, Hisaya. "The Effect of U.S. Import Tariff Reductions on Expanded Wage Inequality." *Journal of the Indiana Academy of the Social Sciences* 14 (2010–11): 31–46.

Klein, Hilary. *Compañeras: Zapatista Women's Stories*. Oakland CA: Seven Stories Press, 2015.

Kovic, Christine. "Demanding Their Dignity as Daughters of God: Catholic Women and Human Rights." In *Women of Chiapas: Making History in Times of Struggle and Hope*, edited by Christine Eber and Christine Kovic. New York: Routledge, 2003.

Krafft-Ebing, Richard von. *Psychopathia Sexualis*. Stuttgart: Ferdinand Enke, 1886.

Kralik, Joellen. "'Bathroom Bill' Legislative Tracking." National Conference of State Legislatures, April 12, 2017. http://www.ncsl.org/research /education/-bathroom-bill-legislative-tracking635951130.aspx.

Labonté, Ronald, Eric Crosbie, Deborah Gleeson, and Courtney McNamara. "USMCA (NAFTA 2.0): Tightening the Constraints on the Right to Regulate Public Health." *Globalization and Health* 15, no. 1 (May 2019): 1–15.

Lal, Vinaym. "Rebellion in Chiapas: Colonial History of a New World Disorder." *Economic and Political Weekly* 20, no. 25 (June 18, 1994): 1514–16.

Lara, Irene. "Daughter of Coatlicue: An Interview with Gloria Anzaldúa." In *Entre mundos/Among Worlds: New Perspectives on Gloria Anzaldúa*, edited by AnaLouise Keating, 41–56. New York: Palgrave Macmillan, 2005.

———. "The Goddess of the Americas in the Decolonial Imaginary: Beyond the Virtuous Virgin/Pagan Puta Dichotomy." *Feminist Studies* 34, nos. 1, 2 (Spring-Summer 2008): 99–127.

———. "Sensing the Serpent in the Mother, Dando a Luz la Madre Serpiente: Chicana Spirituality, Sexuality, and Mamihood." In *Fleshing the Spirit: Spirituality and Activism in Chicana, Latina, and Indigenous Women's Lives*, edited by Elisa Facio and Irene Lara, 113–36. Tucson: University of Arizona Press, 2014.

León-Portilla, Miguel. *Aztec Thought and Culture*. Translated by Jack Emory Davis. Norman: University of Oklahoma Press, 1963.

Levitz, Eric. "Trump's NAFTA 2.0 Puts Big Pharma First, America Second." *New York Magazine*, March 29, 2019. http://nymag.com/intelligencer/2019/03/trumps-nafta-2–0-usmca-trade-deal-puts-big-pharma-first-america-second.html.

Lewis, Yosenio. "i wish i looked like matthew shepard." *The Laramie Project*. July 15, 2017. https://sites.duke.edu/dukeinlaramie/2011/02/28/queer-history-the-losses-that-bind-us/.

Locke, Michelle. "Defense lawyer: Client 'Not a Bad Guy.'" *Associated Press State and Local Wire*. April 15, 2004. LEXIS.

Lorde, Audre. *Sister Outsider: Essays and Speeches by Audre Lorde*. Berkeley CA: Crossing Press, 1984.

Luibhéid, Eithne, and Lionel Cantú, Jr., eds. *Queer Migrations: Sexuality, U.S. Citizenship, and Border Crossings*. Minneapolis: University of Minnesota Press, 2005.

Luna, Jennie. "Indigenous Knowledge for Resistance, Love, and Land: Lecciones for our Children, for our Future." Plenary address delivered at the National Association for Chicana and Chicano Studies, Albuquerque, New Mexico, April 4, 2019.

Marcos, Subcomandante Insurgente. "Abajo a la Izquierda." *Enlace Zapatista*. February 28, 2005. http://enlacezapatista.ezln.org.mx/2005/02/28/abajo-a-la-izquierda/.

Maffie, James. *Aztec Philosophy: Understanding a World in Motion*. Boulder: University of Colorado, 2014.

Magennis, Ann L., and Michael G. Lacy. "Demography and Social Epidemiology of Admissions to the Colorado Insane Asylum, 1879–1899." *Social Science History* 38, nos. 1, 2 (Spring/Summer 2014): 251–71.

Marat, Jean Paul, and Mark Forrester. "The Touchstone." *Vanguard* 1, no. 1 (1966): 2. https://www.digitaltransgenderarchive.net/catalog?f%5bcollection_name_ssim%5d%5b%5d=Vanguard&f%5binstitution_name_ssim%5d%5b%5d=glbt+Historical+Society&f%5bsubject_geographic_ssim%5d%5b%5d=San+Francisco. Digital archive.

Marcos, Subcomandante, and the Zapatistas. *The Other Campaign*. San Francisco: City Lights, 2006.

Martin, James Kirby, Randy Roberts, James Howard Jones, Linda O McMurry, and Steven Mintz. *A Concise History of America and Its People*. New York: Harper Collins, 1995.

Martín Pérez, Fredy. "EZLN Inicia Actividades para Celebrar el 15 Aniversario de los Caracoles." *El Universal*, July 8, 2018. http://www.eluniversal.com.mx/estados/ezln-inicia-actividades-para-celebrar-el-15-aniversario-de-los-caracoles.

Martínez, Maria Elena. "The Black Blood of New Spain: Limpieza de Sangre, Racial Violence, and Gendered Power in Early Colonia Mexico." *William and Mary Quarterly* 61, no. 3 (July 2004): 479–520.

Martínez-Salazar, Egla. "The 'Poisoning' of Indigenous Migrant Women Workers and Children from Deadly Colonialism to Toxic Globalization." In *Women Working the NAFTA Food Chain: Women, Food and Globalization*, edited by Deborah Barndt, 100–111. Toronto: Sumach Press, 1999.

McLeod, Lisa J. "Transubstantiation of Andrew Johnson: White Epistemic Failure in Du Bois' Black Reconstruction." *Phylon* 51, no. 1 (Fall 2014): 88–101.

Medina, Lara. "Nepantla Spirituality: Negotiating Fluid Identities, Faiths and Practices." In *El Mundo Zurdo: Selected Works from the Meetings of the Society for the Study of Gloria Anzaldúa, 2007 & 2009*, edited by Norma E. Cantú, Christina L. Gutiérrez, Norma Alarcón, and Rita E. Urquijo-Ruiz, 205–14. San Francisco: Aunt Lute, 2010.

Meier, Matt A., and Feliciano Rivera. *The Chicanos: A History of Mexican Americans*. New York: Hill and Wang, 1972.

Mejívar, Cecilia, and Leisy Abrego. "Legal Violence: Immigration Law and the Lives of Central American Immigrants." *American Journal of Sociology* 117, no. 5 (March 2012): 1380–1421.

Melendez, Claudia S. "Globalize This: The Zapatistas Hold a Worldwide Plebiscite to Bring their Struggle back to the International Spotlight." *El Andar* 10, no. 1 (March 1999): 45–47.

Menchaca, Martha. *Recovering History, Constructing Race: The Indian, Black, and White Roots of Mexican Americans*. Austin: University of Texas Press, 2001.

Messinger Cypess, Sandra. *La Malinche in Mexican Literature: From History to Myth*. Austin: University of Texas Press, 1991.

"Mexican Shelter Welcomes LGBTI Refugees." *Impact News Service*, August 28, 2017.

Milanich, Nara. "In the Power Structure of Society: The Politics of Family Law in Twentieth Century Chile and Latin America." *Law and History Review* 33, no. 4 (2015): 767–802.

Millan Moncayo, Márgar. "Indigenous Women and Zapatismo." In Speed, Hernández Castillo, and Stephen, *Dissident Women*, 75–96.

Milliken, Randall. *A Time of Little Choice: The Disintegration of Tribal Culture in the San Francisco Bay Area, 1769–1810*. Menlo Park CA: Ballena Press, 1995.

Minter, Shannon, and Chris Daley. "Creating a Transgender Law Project: Serving the Unique Legal Needs of the Transgender Community." *San Francisco Attorney* 28 (June-July 2002): 46.

Minter, Shannon, and Christopher Daley. *Trans Realities: A Legal Needs Assessment of San Francisco's Transgender Communities*. San Francisco: National Center for Lesbian Rights and Transgender Law Center, 2003. http://www.nclrights.org/wp-content/uploads/2013/07/transrealities0803.pdf.

Mirabal, Nancy Raquel. "Geographies of Displacement: Latina/os, Oral History, and the Politics of Gentrification in San Francisco's Mission District." *Public Historian* 31, no. 2 (Spring 2009): 7–31.

Molina, Natalia. *How Race Is Made in America: Immigration, Citizenship, and the Historical Power of Racial Scripts (American Crossroads)*. Berkeley: University of California Press, 2014.

Moraga, Cherríe. "Entering the Lives of Others." In Moraga and Anzaldúa, *This Bridge Called My Back*, 21.

——. *Loving in the War Years: Lo que nunca pasó por sus labios*. Boston: Southend Press, 1983.

Moraga, Cherríe, and Gloria Anzaldúa. *This Bridge Called My Back: Writings of Radical Women of Color*. 3rd ed. Berkeley CA: Third Woman Press, 2002.

Morgensen, Scott Lauria. "Unsettling Queer Politics: What Can Non-Natives Learn from Two-Spirit Organizing?" In *Queer Indigenous Studies: Critical Interventions in Theory, Politics, and Literature*, edited by Qwo-Li Driskill, Chris Finely, Brian Joseph Gilley, and Scott Lauria Morgensen, 132–52. Tucson: University of Arizona, 2011.

Moya, Paula. "Chicana Feminism and Postmodernist Theory." *Signs* 26, no. 2 (Winter 2001): 441–83.

——. *Learning from Experience: Minority Identities, Multicultural Struggles*. Berkeley: University of California Press, 2002.

Muños, José Esteban. *Disidentifications: Queers of Color and the Performance of Politics*. Minneapolis: University of Minnesota Press, 1999.

Muños Ramírez, Gloria. *The Fire and the Word: A History of the Zapatista Movement*. San Francisco: City Light Books, 2008.

National Center for Transgender Equality. "With Heavy Hearts, Remembering Those Lost and Pressing for Change." National Center for Transgender Equality. November 19, 2015. https://transequality.org/blog/with-heavy-hearts-remembering-those-lost-and-pressing-for-change.

National Coalition of Anti-Violence Programs. "Lesbian, Gay, Bisexual, Transgender, Queer, HIV-Affected Hate Violence in 2012." New York: New York City Gay and Lesbian Anti-Violence Project, 2013. https://avp.org/wp-content/uploads/2017/04/ncavp_2012_hvreport_final.pdf.

National Conference of State Legislatures. "Federal and State Recognized Tribes." NCSL. Accessed January 28, 2020. https://www.ncsl.org/research/state-tribal-institute/list-of-federal-and-state-recognized-tribes.aspx#State.

"Newark Demographics and Community Outlook." City of Newark. Accessed July 13, 2017. http://www.newark.org/images/uploads/comdev/pdfs/calPoly/BackgroundReport_final/Final_3_Demographics%20%26%20community%20outlook_Background_Report_06232012.pdf.

Noyola, Isa. Interview by Amy Goodman. *Democracy Now*, June 14, 2016. http://www.democracynow.org/2016/6/14/activist_latinx_lgbtq _community_its_stories.

———. Interview by Raquel Reichard. "Woman Crush(ing the Patriarchy) Wednesday: Isa Noyola." *Latina Magazine*, January 13, 2016. http://www .latina.com/lifestyle/our-issues/wcw-isa-noyola?page=2.

O'Brien, Susan. "French Nuns in Nineteenth-Century England." *Past & Present* 154, no. 1 (February 1997): 142–80.

Olivera, Mercedes, and Carlos Pérez. "From Integrationist 'Indigenismo' to Neoliberal De-Ethnification in Chiapas: Reminiscences." *Latin American Perspectives* 39, no. 5 (September 2012): 100–110.

Oosterhuis, Harry. "Richard von Krafft-Ebing's 'Step-Children of Nature': Psychiatry and the Making of Homosexual Identity." In Rosario, *Science and Homosexualities*, 67–107.

Oropeza, Lorena, and Dionne Espinosa. *Enriqueta Vasquez and the Chicano Movement: Writings from "El Grito del Norte."* Houston: Arte Público Press, 2006.

Ortiz, Simon J. "Indigenous Continuance." *American Indian Quarterly* 3, no. 35 (Summer 2011): 285–93.

Ott, Brian L., and Eric Aoki. "The Politics of Negotiating Public Tragedy: Media Framing of the Matthew Shepard Murder." *Rhetoric and Public Affairs* 5, no. 3 (Fall 2002): 483–505.

Pagliarini, Marie. "'And the Word Was Made Flesh': Divining the Female Body in Nineteenth-Century American and Catholic Culture." *Religion and American Culture* 17, no. 2 (Summer 2007): 213–45.

Pardo, Mary. *Mexican American Women Activists: Identity and Resistance in Two Los Angeles Communities*. Philadelphia: Temple University Press, 1996.

Paredes, Raymund. "The Origins of Anti-Mexican Sentiment in the United States." *New Scholar* 6 (1977): 139–57.

Partida, Juan Carlos G. "Abordar la Impunidad de la *Guerra Sucia* Ayuda a Analizar la Actualidad." *La Jornada*, March 10, 2012. https://www.jornada .com.mx/2012/03/10/espectaculos/a08n1esp.

Passel, Jeffrey S. "Written Testimony Submitted to the U.S. Senate Committee on Homeland Security and Governmental Affairs Hearing on Securing the Border: Defining the Current Population Living in the Shadows and Addressing Future Flows." Pew Research Center. March 26, 2015, 1–33. https://www .hsgac.senate.gov/imo/media/doc/Testimony-Passel-2015-03-26.pdf.

Passel, Jeffrey S., and D'Vera Cohn. "Unauthorized Immigrant Population Stable for Half a Decade." *FacTank: News in the Numbers, Pew Research Center*. July 22, 2015. http://www.pewresearch.org/fact-tank/2015/07 /22/unauthorized-immigrant-population-stable-for-half-a-decade/.

Passel, Jeffrey S., D'Vera Cohn, and Ana Gonzalez-Barrera. "Net Migration from Mexico Falls to Zero—and Perhaps Less." Pew Research Center. April 23, 2012. http://www.pewhispanic.org/2012/04/23/net-migration-from-mexico-falls-to-zero-and-perhaps-less/.

Patrick, Jordan. "Call Haters to Account: A Case for Bias-Crime Laws." *Commonweal*, November 20, 1998, 6. ProQuest Database.

Peña, Devon G. *The Terror of the Machine: Technology, Work, Gender, and Ecology on the U.S.-Mexico Border*. Austin: Center for Mexican American Studies, 1997.

Pérez, Emma. *Decolonial Imaginary: Writing Chicanas into History*. Bloomington: Indiana University Press, 1999.

———. "Gloria Anzaldúa: La Gran Nueva Mestiza Theorist, Writer, Activist-Scholar." *NWSA Journal* 17, no. 2 (Summer 2005): 1–10.

———. "Queering the Borderlands: The Challenges of Excavating the Invisible and Unheard." *Frontiers* 24, nos. 2, 3 (2003): 122–31.

Pérez, Laura E. "The Performance of Spirituality and Visionary Politics in the Work of Gloria Anzaldúa." In Saldívar-Hull, Alarcón, and Urquijo-Ruiz, *El Mundo Zurdo II*, 13–27.

Perkiss, David Alan. "A New Strategy for Neutralizing the Gay Panic Defense at Trial: Lessons from the Lawrence King Case." *UCLA Law Review* 60, no. 6 (February 2013): 778–824.

Perrin, Karen, and Sharon Bernecki DeJoy. "Abstinence-Only Education: How We Got Here and Where We're Going." *Journal of Public Health Policy* 24, nos. 3, 4 (2003): 445–59.

Pilapil, Vicente R. "Nineteenth-Century Philippines and the Friar-Problem." *Americas* 18, no. 2 (October 1961): 127–48.

Pitt, Leonard. *The Decline of the Californios: A Social History of the Spanish-Speaking Californians, 1846–1890*. Berkeley: University of California Press, 1966.

Pitti, Stephen. *The Devil in the Silicon Valley: Northern California, Race, and Mexican Americans*. Princeton NJ: Princeton University Press, 2003.

Platt, Tony, and Cecelia O'Leary. "Patriot Acts." *Social Justice* 30, no. 1 (2003): 8.

Polanyi, Karl. *The Great Transformation: The Political and Economic Origins of Our Time*. Boston: Beacon, 2001.

Portillo, Suyapa Villeda. "New 'Success' in Post-Coup Honduras: Soccer with Assassins?" *Latino Rebels*, August 31, 2016. http://www.latinorebels.com/2016/08/31/new-success-in-post-coup-honduras-soccer-with-assassins/.

———. "'Outing' Honduras: A Human Rights Catastrophe in the Making." *NACLA Report on the Americas* 45, no. 3 (Fall 2012): 6–7.

Potok, Mark. "Rage on the Right." *Intelligence Report*, Spring Issue, March 2, 2010. https://www.splcenter.org/fighting-hate/intelligence-report/2010/rage-right.

Quince, Charles. *Resistance to the Spanish-American and Philippine Wars: Anti-Imperialism and the Role of the Press, 1895–1902*. Jefferson NC: McFarland and Company, 2017.

Quintana, Victor M. "How NAFTA Unleashed the Violence in Mexico." *Americas Program*, February 7, 2014. http://www.americas.org/archives/11427.

Ramírez, Horacio N. Roque. "Claiming Queer Cultural Citizenship: Gay Latino (Im)Migrant Acts in San Francisco." In Luibhéid and Cantú, *Queer Migrations*, 161–88.

———. "'That's My Place': Negotiating Racial, Sexual, and Gender Politics in San Francisco's Gay Latino Alliance, 1975–1983." *Journal of the History of Sexuality* 12, no. 2 (April 2003): 224–58.

Ramos, Juanita, ed. *Compañeras: Latina Lesbians*. New York: Latina Lesbian History Project, 1987.

Rayas, Lucía. "Subjugating the Nation: Women and the Guerilla Experience." In Herrera Calderon and Cedillo, *Challenging Authoritarianism in Mexico*, 167–81.

Rebolledo, Tey Diana. "The Politics of Poetics: or, What Am I, a Critic, Doing in This Text Anyhow?" In Anzaldúa, *Making Face, Making Soul*, 346–55.

Reis, Beth. "Making Sense of the Senseless: The Murder of Lawrence King." *Teaching Tolerance* 34 (Fall 2008). https://www.tolerance.org/magazine/fall-2008/making-sense-of-the-senseless-the-murder-of-lawrence-king.

Reyes, Bárbara O. *Private Women, Public Lives: Gender and the Missions of the Californias*. Austin: University of Texas Press, 2009.

Rhodan, Maya. "The Facts about Trump's Border Policy." *Time*, July 2, 2018, 31.

Riddell, Adaljiza Sosa. "No Title." *El Grito: Chicanas en la Literatura y el Arte* 7, no. 1 (September 1973): 76.

Robbins, Millie. *Tales of Love and Hate in Old San Francisco*. San Francisco: Chronicle Books, 1971.

Robinson, Paul. *The Modernization of Sex: Havelock Ellis, Alfred Kinsey, William Masters, and Virginia Johnson*. New York: Harper and Row, 1976.

Robinson, William I. *A Theory of Global Capitalism: Production, Class, and State in a Transnational World*. Baltimore: Johns Hopkins University Press, 2004.

Rodriguez, Joe. "See Newark Teen for What He Was: Still Just a Kid." *The Channel* 21, no. 11 (November 2002). http://tgsf.org/other-resources/gwen_channel.pdf.

Rodríguez, Juana María. *Queer Latinidad: Identity Practices, Discursive Spaces*. New York: New York University Press, 2003.

Romo, Ricardo. *East Los Angeles: History of a Barrio*. Austin: University of Texas Press, 1983.

Rosario, Vernon. "Homosexual Bio-Histories: Genetic Nostalgias and the Quest for Paternity." In Rosario, *Science and Homosexualities*, 1–25.

——, ed. *Science and Homosexualities*. New York: Routledge, 1997.

Rowbotham, Sheila, and Jeffrey Weeks. *Socialism and the New Life: The Personal and Sexual Politics of Edward Carpenter and Havelock Ellis*. London: Pluto Press, 1977.

Ruiz, Rita Urquijo. *Wild Tongues: Transnational Mexican Popular Culture*. Austin: University of Texas Press, 2012.

Ruiz, Vicki L. *Cannery Women, Cannery Lives: Mexican Women, Unionization, and the California Food Processing Industry, 1930-1950*. Albuquerque: University of New Mexico Press, 1987.

——. *From Out of the Shadows: Mexican Women in Twentieth-Century America*. New York: Oxford University Press, 1998.

Ruiz-Marrero, Carmelo. "Contras and Drugs, Three Decades Later." *Louisiana Weekly*, November 10, 2014. http://www.louisianaweekly.com/contras-and-drugs-three-decades-later/.

Rumph, Benjamin D. "Avendano-Hernandez v. Lynch: Twenty-First-Century Values and Transgender Communities' Impact of Immigration Policy and Foreign Relations." *Tulane Journal of International and Comparative Law* 24 (Spring 2016): 391–405.

Russell, Malik. "FBI Reports Increase in Hate Crimes against African Americans." *Crisis*, January-February 2005.

Saldívar-Hull, Sonia. "Before Borderlands and Beyond: 'Making the World Luminous and Active.'" In Saldívar-Hull, Alarcón, and Urquijo-Ruiz, *El Mundo Zurdo II*, 7–11.

——. *Feminism on the Border: Chicana Gender Politics and Literature*. Berkeley: University of California Press, 2000.

Saldívar-Hull, Sonia, Norma Alarcón, and Rita Urquijo-Ruiz, eds. *El Mundo Zurdo II: Selected Works from the 2010 Meeting of the Society for the Study of Gloria Anzaldúa*. San Francisco: Aunt Lute, 2012.

Sánchez, George I. *Forgotten People: A Study of New Mexicans*. 1940. Reprint, Albuquerque: University of New Mexico Press, 1996.

Sánchez, George J. "'Go After the Women': Americanization and the Mexican Immigrant Woman, 1915–1929." In DuBois and Ruiz, *Unequal Sisters*, 250–63.

Sánchez, Rosaura. "The Chicana Labor Force." In Sánchez and Martinez Cruz, *Essays on La Mujer*, 3–15.

Sánchez, Rosaura, and Rosa Martínez Cruz. *Essays on La Mujer*. Los Angeles: Chicano Studies Center Publications, 1977.

Sandoval, Chéla. *Methodology of the Oppressed*. Minneapolis: University of Minnesota Press, 2000.

———. "U.S. Third World Feminism: The Theory and Method of Oppositional Consciousness in the Postmodern World." *Genders* 10 (Spring 1991): 1–24.

Sassen, Saskia. *Globalization and Its Discontents: Essays on the New Mobility of People and Money*. New York: New Press, 1998.

Sauer, Stephanie. *The Accidental Archives of the Royal Chicano Air Force*. Austin: University of Texas Press, 2016.

Saxton, Alexander. *The Indispensable Enemy: Labor and the Anti-Chinese Movement in California*. Berkeley: University of California Press, 1971.

Scher, Abby, and Chip Berlet. "The Tea Party Moment." In *Understanding the Tea Party Movement*, edited by Nella Van Dyke and David S. Meyer, 99–123. Burlington VT: Ashgate, 2014.

Schmider, Alex. "Doubly Victimized: Reporting on Transgender Victims of Crimes." Gay and Lesbian Alliance against Defamation. November 9, 2016. https://www.glaad.org/blog/2016-was-deadliest-year-record-transgender-people.

Schoonover, Thomas. *Uncle Sam's War of 1898 and the Origins of Globalization*. Lexington: University of Kentucky Press, 2003.

Sears, Clare. *Arresting Dress: Cross-Dressing, Law, and Fascination in Nineteenth-Century San Francisco*. Durham NC: Duke University Press, 2015.

———. "Electric Brilliancy: Cross-Dressing Law and Freak Show Displays in Nineteenth-Century San Francisco." *WSQ: Women's Studies Quarterly* 36, nos. 3, 4 (Fall–Winter 2008): 177–87.

Serano, Julia. *Whipping Girl: A Transsexual Woman on Sexism and the Scapegoating of Femininity*. Berkeley CA: Seal, 2007.

Sheff-Cahan, Vicki. "Matthew's Legacy." *People Weekly* 52, no. 24 (December 20, 1999), 95–98. http://people.com/archive/matthews-legacy-vol-52-no-24/.

Silverman, Victor, and Susan Stryker. *Screaming Queens: The Riot at Compton's Cafeteria*. San Francisco: Frameline, 2005.

Skidmore, Emily. "Constructing the 'Good Transsexual': Christine Jorgensen, Whiteness, and Heteronormativity in the Mid-Twentieth-Century Press." *Feminist Studies* 37, no. 2 (2011): 270–300.

———. *True Sex: The Lives of Trans Men at the Turn of the 20th Century*. New York: New York University Press, 2017.

Sklar, Holly. *Chaos or Community? Seeking Solutions, Not Scapegoats for Bad Economics*. Boston: Southend, 1995.

Sloop, John M. "Disciplining the Transgendered Body: Brandon Teena, Public Representation, and Normativity." *Western Journal of Communication* 64, no. 2 (Spring 2000): 165–89.

Snorton, C. Riley. *Black on Both Sides: A Racial History of Trans Identity*. Minneapolis: University of Minnesota Press, 2017.

Soldatenko, Michael. *Chicano Studies: The Genesis of a Discipline*. Tucson: University of Arizona Press, 2011.

Solomon, Alisa. "Trans/Migrant: Christina Madrazo's All-American Story." In Luibhéid and Cantú, *Queer Migrations*, 3–29.

"Songs for Matthew Shepard." Queer Music Heritage. Accessed December 25, 2005. http://www.queermusicheritage.com/matthew.html.

Soni, Munmeeth. "A Call to Service: Ensuring Every Gay, Bisexual, Transgender Asylum Seeker Detained at the Santa Ana City Jail Has Access to Justice." *Orange County Lawyer* 57 (October 2015): 32–36.

Soto, Shirlene. "Tres Modelos Culturales: La Virgen de Guadalupe, La Malinche y la Llorona." *Fem* 10 (1986): 13–16.

Southern Poverty Law Center. "*Ebony* Publishes SPLC Report on Violence against Transgender Women of Color." *SPLC News*, May 19, 2015. https://www.splcenter.org/news/2015/05/20/ebony-publishes-splc-report-violence-against-transgender-women-color.

———. "Murders of Trans Women This Year Hits New High." *SPLC Intelligence Report*, October 27, 2015. https://www.splcenter.org/fighting-hate/intelligence-report/2015/murders-trans-women-year-hits-new-high.

Spade, Dean. *Normal Life: Administrative Violence, Critical Trans Politics, and the Limits of Law*. Brooklyn NY: South End Press, 2011.

Spade, Dean, and Craig Willse. "Confronting the Limits of Gay Hate Crimes Activism: A Radical Critique." *Chicano-Latino Law Review* 21 (Spring 2000).

Speed, Shannon, R. Aída Hernández Castillo, and Lynn M. Stephen, eds. *Dissident Women: Gender and Cultural Politics in Chiapas*. Austin: University of Texas Press, 2006.

Starr, Neal L. "Stockton State Hospital: A Century and a Quarter of Service." *San Joaquin Historian* 12, no. 3 (July–September 1976): 115–22.

Staudt, Kathleen, and Zulma Y. Méndez. *Courage and Resistance in Ciudad Juárez: Challenges to Militarization*. Austin: University of Texas Press, 2015.

Stephen, Lynn. *Zapata Lives! Histories and Cultural Politics in Southern Mexico*. Berkeley: University of California Press, 2002.

"Stockton's History." *Stockton, Full of Flavor*. Accessed July 17, 2018. https://www.visitstockton.org/about-us/stockton-history/.

Stone, Sandy. "The Empire Strikes Back: A Posttranssexual Manifesto." In Epstein and Straub, *Body Guards*, 280–304.

Streeby, Shelley. *American Sensations: Class, Empire, and the Production of Popular Culture*. Berkeley: University of California Press, 2001.

Street, Richard Steven. *Beasts of the Field: A Narrative History of the California Farmworkers, 1769–1913*. Stanford CA: Stanford University Press, 2005.

Stryker, Susan. *Transgender History*. Berkeley CA: Seal Press, 2008.

Stryker, Susan, and Stephen Whittle, eds. *The Transgender Studies Reader*. New York: Routledge, 2006.

Sullivan, Louis. "Elvira Mugarrieta alias Jack Bee Garland, or, in Stockton, Babe Bean." *San Joaquin Historian* 3, no. 1 (1987): 1–16.

——. *From Female to Male: The Life of Jack Bee Garland*. Boston: Alyson Publications, 1990.

Taback, Shana, and Rachel Levitan. "LGBTI Migrants in Immigration Detention: A Global Perspective." *Harvard Journal of Law and Gender* 37 (Winter 2014): 1–44.

Takaki, Ronald. *A Different Mirror: A History of Multicultural America*. Boston: Little, Brown, and Company, 1993.

Taracena, Maria Inés. "Displaced LGBT People from Central America, Mexico Head North for Survival." Arizona Public Media News. September 8, 2017. https://news.azpm.org/p/news-topical-border/2017/9/8/116373-displaced -lgbt-people-from-central-america-mexico-head-north-for-survival/.

Terry, Don. "In the Crosshairs." *Southern Poverty Law Center Intelligence Report* (Summer 2015): 27–35.

Theophano, Teresa. "Gender Public Advocacy Coalition." In *GLBTQ Social Sciences: An Encyclopedia of Gay, Lesbian, Bisexual, Transgender, and Queer Culture*. Accessed August 4, 2017. http://www.glbtq.com/social-sciences/ gender_public_advocacy.html.

Townsend, Camilla. "What Have You Done to Me, My Lover? Sex, Servitude, and Politics among the Pre-Conquest Nahuas as Seen in the Cantares Mexicanos." *Americas* 62, no. 3 (January 2006): 349–89.

Transgender Law Center. "Adriana Turcios." *Legal Translations*, Fall 2004, 2.

——. "A Fresh and Evolving Perspective," *Authentic Lives*, 2015, 3.

——. "Honor Trans Immigrant Lives." http://transgenderlawcenter.org/ programs/immigrant-leadership.

——. "Hundreds of LGBT People of Color and Immigrants to Rally at Texas Capitol." Press release, August 1, 2017. https://transgenderlawcenter.org /archives/13974.

——. "Immigration." Accessed January 31, 2020. https://transgenderlawcenter .org/resources/immigration.

——. "Isa Noyla Becomes Transgender Law Center's Director of Programs!" Press release, October 22, 2015. https://transgenderlawcenter .org/archives/12113.

——. "Sylvia Guerrero, Client." *Legal Translations*, Fall 2004, 4.

———. "TLC Challenges Order to Deport Transgender Immigrant Seeking Asylum." Transgender Law Center, August 10, 2017. https://transgenderlawcenter.org/archives/13978.

———. "TLC Welcomes New Program Manager, Isa Noyola." Transgender Law Center, October 20, 2014. https://transgenderlawcenter.org/archives/11172.

———. "TLC Wins BIA (Board of Immigration Appeal) Appeal for remand for trans immigrant to apply for asylum." Transgender Law Center, October 18, 2017. https://transgenderlawcenter.org/archives/14065.

———. "Transgender Law Center Launches Trans Immigrant Defense Effort (TIDE)." Transgender Law Center, January 18, 2017. https://transgenderlawcenter.org/archives/13494.

———. "Victory for #FreeChristina—Transgender Detainee Granted Bond." Transgender Law Center, February 19, 2016. http://transgenderlawcenter.org/archives/12536.

Transgender Law Center and Cornell University Law School LGBT Clinic. *Report on Human Rights Conditions of Transgender Women in Mexico*. May 2016, 1–46. https://transgenderlawcenter.org/wp-content/uploads/2016/05/CountryConditionsReport-final.pdf.

Treviso, Dolores. *Rural Protest and the Making of Democracy in Mexico, 1986–2000*. University Park PA: Penn State University Press, 2011.

Trujillo, Carla, ed. *Chicana Lesbians: The Girls Our Mothers Warned Us About*. Berkeley CA: Third Woman Press, 1991.

Turner, Ilona M. "Pioneering Strategies to Win Trans Rights in California." *University of La Verne Law Review* 34 (November 2012): 5–22.

United Nations High Commissioner for Refugees. *Children on the Run: Unaccompanied Children Leaving Central America and Mexico and the Need for International Protection*. Washington DC: UNHCR, 2014. http://www.unhcrwashington.org/sites/default/files/1_uac_Children%20on%20the%20run_Full%20report.pdf.

———. *Detention Guidelines: Guidelines on the Applicable Criteria and Standards relating to the Detention of Asylum-Seekers and Alternatives to Detention*. UNHCR, 2012. http://www.unhcr.org/505b10ee9.html.

———. "UNHCR Releases New Guidelines on Detention of Asylum-Seekers." UNHCR. Last modified September 21, 2012. Accessed May 4, 2017. http://www.unhcr.org/en-us/news/briefing/2012/9/505c461f9/unhcr-releases-new-guidelines-detention-asylum-seekers.html.

United States. Department of Justice. Bureau of Justice Statistics. *Hate Crime Victimization, 2004–2015*. June 2017. https://www.bjs.gov/content/pub/pdf/hcv0415.pdf.

United States. Department of Labor. Bureau of Labor Statistics. *Highlights of Women's Earnings in 2001.* Report 960, May 2002. https://www.bls.gov/opub/reports/womens-earnings/archive/womensearnings_2001.pdf.

United States. Department of Labor. "Submission under the North American Agreement on Labor Cooperation." Accessed July 9, 2017. http://www.dol.gov/ilab/trade/agreements/naalc.htm.

United States Office of the Press Secretary. "Remarks by President Obama and President Lobo of Honduras before Bilateral Meeting." October 5, 2011. https://obamawhitehouse.archives.gov/the-press-office/2011/10/05/remarks-president-obama-and-president-lobo-honduras-bilateral-meeting.

United We Dream. "LGBTQ Justice." Accessed July 5, 2018. https://unitedwedream.org/our-work/lgbtq-justice/.

Valdes, Francisco. "Queer Margins, Queer Ethics: A Call to Account for Race and Ethnicity in the Law, Theory, and Politics of 'Sexual Orientation.'" *Hastings Law Journal* 48 (August 1997): 1293–1341.

———. "Queers, Sissies, Dykes, and Tomboys: Deconstructing the Conflation of 'Sex,' 'Gender,' and 'Sexual Orientation' in Euro-American Law and Society." *California Law Review* 83 (January 1995): 3–128.

———. "'We Are Now of the View': Backlash Activism, Cultural Cleansing, and the Kulturkampf to Resurrect the Old Deal." *Seton Hall Law Review* 35, no. 4 (2005):1407–63.

Valencia, Sayek. *Gore Capitalism.* Translated by John Pluecker. Pasadena CA: Semiotext(e), 2018.

———. "Necropolitics, Postmortem/Transmortem Politics, and Transfeminisms in the Sexual Economies of Death." Translated by Olga Arnaiz Zhuravleva. *Transgender Studies Quarterly* 6, no. 2 (May 2019): 180–93.

Vásquez, Francisco H. "Aztec Epistemology." *El Grito* 5, no. 4 (Summer 1972): 74–79.

Vega, Patricia. "Nupcias de Liliana y Jesusa: Felices y níveas las contrayentes enlazaron sus vidas." Hemispheric Institute. Accessed February 13, 2020. https://hemisphericinstitute.org/en/hidvl-collections/item/643-habito-nupcias.html.

"The Wage Gap by Education: 2001." National Committee on Pay Equity. Accessed June 2, 2017. http://www.pay-equity.org/info-education.html.

Wallach, Lori. "The Battle over NAFTA 2.0 Has Just Begun." *The Nation*, December 21, 2018. https://www.thenation.com/article/nafta-congress-2019/.

Weber, David. *The Mexican Frontier, 1821–1846: The American Southwest under Mexico.* Albuquerque: University of New Mexico Press, 1982.

Weintraub, Sidney. Foreword to *Negotiating NAFTA: A Mexican Envoy's Account,* by Hermann Von Bertrab. Westport CT: Praeger, 1997.

Weiss, Marley S. "Two Steps Forward, One Step Back—or Vice Versa: Labor Rights under Free Trade Agreements from NAFTA, through Jordan, via Chile, to Latina America, and Beyond." *University of San Francisco Law Review* 37 (Spring 2003): 689–756.

Westermeyer, William H. "Local Tea Party Groups and the Vibrancy of the Movement." *PoLAR: Political and Legal Anthropology Review* 39, no. S1 (September 2016): 121–38.

White, John H. "The Railroad Reaches California: Men, Machines, and Cultural Migration." *California Historical Quarterly* 52, no. 2 (Summer 1973): 131–44.

Wiegers, Gerard. "Managing Disaster: Networks of the Moriscos during the Process of Expulsion from the Iberian Peninsula around 1609." *Journal of Medieval Religious Studies* 26, no. 2 (2010): 141–68.

Wilchins, Riki. *Queer Theory, Gender Theory: An Instant Primer.* Los Angeles: Alyson Books, 2004.

Wilder, Janeen. "Reins, Riggings, and Reatas: The Outfit of the Great Basin Buckaroo." *Oregon Historical Quarterly* 104, no. 3 (Fall 2003): 366–93.

Williams, Patricia J. *The Alchemy of Race and Rights: Diary of a Law Professor.* Cambridge: Harvard University Press, 1991.

———. "Blood, Soil, and Trauma." *The Nation*, July 2018, 10.

Williams, Rhys H. "Immigration and National Identity in Obama's America: The Expansion of Culture-War Politics." *Canadian Review of American Studies* 42, no. 3 (2012): 322–46.

Wing, Adrien Katherine, ed. *Critical Race Feminism: A Reader.* 2nd ed. New York: New York University Press, 2003.

Wiseman, Paul, Linda A. Johnson, and Kevin Freking. "North America Trade Pact Deals Rare Setback to Big Pharma." *Associated Press News*, December 19, 2019. https://apnews.com/fb54abbce60e1fe44926becb84e86edf.

Wood, Charles H., Chris L. Gibson, Ludmila Ribeiro, and Paula Hamsho-Díaz. "Crime Victimization in Latin America and Intentions to Migrate to the United States." *International Migration Review* 44, no. 1 (Spring 2010): 3–24.

Worley, Jennifer. "'Street Power' and the Claiming of Public Space: San Francisco's Vanguard and Pre-Stonewall Queer Radicalism." In *Captive Genders: Trans Embodiment and the Prison Industrial Complex*, 2nd ed., edited by Eric A. Stanley and Nat Smith, 47–62. Oakland CA: AK Press, 2015.

Wronge, Yomi S. "Newark Teen's Family, Activists Differ on Memorials." *The Channel* 21, no. 11: 20. http://tgsf.org/other-resources/gwen_channel.pdf.

Yeoman, Barry. "A Mother Finds Her Voice." *U.S. News*, March 18, 2002, 56.

Index

Page numbers in italics indicate illustrations.

culture, xix, 1, 15, 27, 34, 40, 68, 104, 112, 119, 121; California, 21; dominant, 28; Euro-American, 12; gender and, 68; Indigenous, 12; living between, 109; masculinist, 85; mestiza/o, 12; Mexican, 49; mother, 3; popular, 34, 39; Protestant, 22; railroad, 70; trading/sharing, 69

Daley, Christopher, 86, 87, 101, 104
Declaration on the Rights of Indigenous Peoples, 13
Deferred Action for Childhood Arrivals (DACA), 14
Delgado, Richard, 73
D'Elia, Tina, 86–87
democracy, indigenous, 47–56
deportation, 99, 100, 108, 117, 147n37
detention centers, 97–98, 100, 104, 108
"Different People" (Stefani et al.), 69
Diocese of San Cristóbal, 50, 56
Dirty War, 47–56, 62, 136n8
discrimination, 47, 103, 143n49, 149n56
domesticity, 21, 22, 23, 28
Dominican Republic-Central American Free Trade Agreement (DR-CAFTA), 92, 94, 95
dot-com businesses, 107
Dougherty, Sister Patricia, 28
Douglass, Frederick, 128n65
DR-CAFTA. See Dominican Republic-Central American Free Trade Agreement
drug trafficking, 93, 95
Duro Bag incident, 63, 64, 65
Duro Bag workers, 91, 109, 112–13

economic crisis (2008), 95
economic shift, 32, 67, 97

economic systems, 1, 12, 14, 20, 23, 112
economy, 40, 97; capitalist, 14; global, 15; political, xviii, 21, 113; rural, 92; technology and, 15; women and, 5
education, 8–9, 23, 52, 95, 131n34
Ejército Zapatista de Liberación Nacional (EZLN), xviii, xxvi, 47, 48, 52–53, 55, 56, 60, 91, 114, 121; federal government and, 61; gender roles and, 62; Indigenous peoples and, 66; leadership/infrastructure of, 54; Nepantla massacre and, xxix; offensive against, 61–62; rural communities and, 62
ejido land, 49, 136n20
El Chilar, 48, 137n21
El Grito Del Norte, xxiii, 124n21
Elisa, Comandanta, 53
El/La Para TransLatinas, 105, 106
El Mundo Zurdo, 10, 12, 45, 46, 57
"El Mundo Zurdo" (Anzaldúa), 1, 10
Employment Nondiscrimination Act, 80
Empress I of San Francisco, 148n47
Encuentro Feminíl, xxii–xxiii, 124n21
EPZs. See export processing zones
equality, 98; gender, 54; marriage, 80, 115; natal, 146n21
Equal Justice Works and Public Law Center, 116
Ergestrasse, Louise, 103
Espinosa, Pablo, 87
Esquibel, Catrióna Rueda, xxiii
Esta Noche, 107
Estudiantes y Obreros en Lucha, 51
ethnicity, 20, 33, 34
Euro-Americans, 17, 33, 37, 118; Nueva Nepantla and, 70
evangelicals, 95, 146n22
export processing zones (EPZs), 59, 63, 66, 67, 92

nal property and, 49; Dirty War and, 54; Euro-American invasion and, 111; gender roles and, 72; violence against, 48

Indigenous Revolutionary Clandestine Committee, NAFTA and, 60

industrialization, 30, 36, 53, 70, 107

Inés de la Cruz, Sor Juana, xxvii, 47, 68

INS. *See* Immigration and Naturalization Service

Insane Asylum of the State of California, 29. *See also* Stockton Insane Asylum

insanity, causes of, 30

Interfaith Committee for Corporate Responsibility, 66

International Meeting for Humanity (Ramóna), 117

International Monetary Fund, 53

Izaguire, Raúl, 59

Jesuits, 26, 39, 41, 135n101

Joahana, death of, 93

Joysmith, Claire, 11, 46

justice, xxviii, xxix, 45, 60, 61, 63, 114; racial, 107; struggles for, 108

Kaplan, Amy, 22

Katz, Jonathan Ned, 13

Kerwineo, Ralph, 32, 33, 40, 41, 133n64

Khasnabish, Alex, 55

King, Lawrence, 78, 79, 85, 90

Kitchen Table, 127n44

Klein, Hilary: on EZLN, 52–53

Know Your Rights (Transgender Law Project), 104

Krafft-Ebing, Richard von, 29

La 72, refugees at, 119

Labonte, Ronald, 121

labor: Black, 16; Chicana/Chicano, 16–17, 23; Chinese, 16, 111; gendered, xxviii, 21, 22; Irish, 15, 16, 111; laws, 65; markets, 94; Mexican, 15, 16, 23; monopoly capital and, 12–18; movement, 108; protections, 58; secure, 39; white, 16; women's, 21; working-class, 23

Lacandón jungle, 47, 48, 51, 53, 59, 137n21

Lacy, Michael G., 29

"La Prieta" (Anzaldúa), 10

Lara, Irene, 9, 126n24

The Laramie Project, 72

La Raza Unida, 9

Las Asbejas, 52, 62, 137n27

Latina Magazine, 101

Latinas, 72; transgender, 73, 75, 80

Latinx, 72, 149n82; queer, 73, 107

leadership, 25, 51, 54, 55, 58, 62, 97, 106, 137n32; women's, 138n49

León-Portilla, Miguel, 3, 4

lesbians, xxiii, 91; Third World, 10, 45

Levitan, Rachel, 98

LGBTQ people, 73, 81, 83, 84, 86, 96, 97, 99, 101, 103, 106, 107, 119, 141n14; African American, 82; murder of, 146n25

LGBTQ studies, xxi, xxv

liberation, 50, 54, 104, 137n27

Línea Proletaria, 52

Loaiza, Juana, 14, 128n65

Lobo, Porfirio, 95–96

Lomas, Clara, 11

López, Christina, 43, 108

Los Angeles Times, 83, 144n69

LYRIC, 106

Maffie, James, 2, 4, 5, 45, 125n4

Magennis, Ann L., 29

Magidson, Michael, 74, 77

21; circumstances for, 40–44; ethnicity of, 20; family of, 23; gender of, 20, 44; historical/economic context for, 21; incarceration of, 29, 30, 31, 33–34; legacy of, 43–44; monopoly capitalism and, 40, 41–42; racism and, 41; Spanish-American War and, xxii; transition for, 42–43; youth of, 25–31, 33

Mulhall, Sarah, 27

Muwekma, 69, 70

Nabors, Jaron, 74, 90

NAFTA. *See* North American Free Trade Agreement

Nahuatl, 3, 111

Nakano Glenn, Evelyn, 22

Nation, 96

National Black Justice Coalition, 81

National Council of La Raza, 59

National Gay and Lesbian Task Force Policy Institute, 81

National Latina/o Lesbian, Gay, Bisexual, and Transgender Organization, 77

nation-state, 13, 48, 88, 92, 98, 100, 104

Negotiating NAFTA (Weintraub), 56

neoliberalism, 46, 47–56, 57, 60, 62, 67, 91, 94, 95–96, 97, 114; impact of, 92; policies, 107, 112

Nepantla, 4, 5, 7, 20–21, 45, 51; concept of, xvii, 1; connection to, xviii; macro mappings of, xxvii; mobilization of, 10; nature of, 3; past and, xix; philosophy of, xviii, 2, 4, 6; time/space of, xxviii, 11, 41, 47; using, xx–xxi; violence and, 90

Nepantla (town), massacre in, xxix

nepantlan change, 66; mapping, 10

nepantlan life, 1, 6–12, 56

nepantlan times, 72, 88, 100–101, 103, 120; living in, 67–68

nepantler@s, xxvii, xxix, 72, 106, 109

Newark, 69, 72; Sun Microsystems and, 70

Newark Memorial High School, 72

Nezahualcoyotl, 3

Nimiipuu, xii, xx

Nixon, Richard, 103, 148n56

Normal Life (Spade), xxvii

North American Agreement of Labor Cooperation (NAALC), 65

North American Free Trade Agreement (NAFTA), xxviii, xxix, 46, 47, 112, 120, 138n52; approval of, 57, 59, 67; Duro workers and, 65; immigration and, 93; as inamic destructive force, 56–69; labor side agreement of, 64, 65; semi-skilled/unskilled workers and, 67; small farms and, 66; stability and, 91; U.S.-Mexico border and, 92; Zapatistas and, 60

North American Free Trade Area, creation of, 56

Not1More Deportation, 108

Noyola, Isa, 101, 105, 149n70; El/La and, 105; hiring, 104; motion-change and, 106; TLC and, 107

Nueva Nepantla, 13, 15, 16, 20, 29, 40, 43, 70, 79, 111; examination of, 18; history of, 69

Obama, Barack, 96, 118; DACA and, 114; deportations by, 150n6

Ochoa, Marcia, 105

Ogborn, Anne, 86

Ohlone, 69

Olin, Billie, Sr. 132n39

In the Expanding Frontiers series

Undesirable Practices: Women, Children, and the Politics of the Body in Northern Ghana, 1930–1972
by Jessica Cammaert

Intersectionality: Origins, Contestations, Horizons
by Anna Carastathis

Abuses of the Erotic: Militarizing Sexuality in the Post–Cold War United States
by Josh Cerretti

Queering Kansas City Jazz: Gender, Performance, and the History of a Scene
by Amber R. Clifford-Napoleone

Postcolonial Hauntologies: African Women's Discourses of the Female Body
by Ayo A. Coly

Terrorizing Gender: Transgender Visibility and the Surveillance Practices of the U.S. Security State
by Mia Fischer

Romance with Voluptuousness: Caribbean Women and Thick Bodies in the United States
by Kamille Gentles-Peart

Salvific Manhood: James Baldwin's Novelization of Male Intimacy
by Ernest L. Gibson III

Nepantla Squared: Transgender Mestiz@ Histories in Times of Global Shift
by Linda Heidenreich

Wrapped in the Flag of Israel: Mizraḥi Single Mothers and Bureaucratic Torture
by Smadar Lavie

Queer Embodiment: Monstrosity, Medical Violence, and Intersex Experience
by Hilary Malatino

Staging Family: Domestic Deceptions of Mid-Nineteenth-Century American Actresses
by Nan Mullenneaux

Hybrid Anxieties: Queering the French-Algerian War and Its Postcolonial Legacies
C. L. Quinan

Place and Postcolonial Ecofeminism: Pakistani Women's Literary and Cinematic Fictions
by Shazia Rahman

Gothic Queer Culture: Marginalized Communities and the Ghosts of Insidious Trauma
by Laura Westengard

To order or obtain more information on these or other University of Nebraska Press titles, visit nebraskapress.unl.edu.